WHEN SNOWBIRDS PLAY

GINA GOLDHAMMER

HAY PRESS

HAY PRESS
10 High Town, Hay-on-Wye HR3 5AE

an imprint of

RENARD PRESS LTD
124 City Road, London EC1V 2NX
United Kingdom

info@renardpress.com • 020 8050 2928
www.haypress.co.uk

Where Snowbirds Play first published by Renard Press Ltd in 2025

Text © Gina Goldhammer, 2025

Quotation on p. 7 by Ezra Pound, from *PERSONAE*, copyright ©1926 by
Ezra Pound. Reprinted by permission of NewDirections Publishing Corp
and Faber and Faber Ltd.

Cover design by Will Dady

Printed in the UK by TJ Books

MIX
Paper | Supporting
responsible forestry
FSC
www.fsc.org
FSC® C013056

Limited Hardback Edition ISBN: 978-1-80447-157-9
Paperback ISBN: 978-1-80447-135-7

9 8 7 6 5 4 3 2 1

CLIMATE Renard Press is proud to be a climate positive publisher, removing
POSITIVE more carbon from the air than we emit and planting a small forest.
For more information see renardpress.com/eco.

EU Authorised Representative: Easy Access System Europe – Mustamäe tee 50,
10621 Tallinn, Estonia, gpsr.requests@easproject.com.

CONTENTS

Where Snowbirds Play

PART ONE. THE ISLAND   9

Arrival   11

The Prince   18

On the Nature of Toads   23

The Lost Art of Letter-Writing   28

Friends and Neighbours   37

Gethsemane-on-the-Sea   50

Hatchlings   58

PART TWO: THE MOLTEN LOOKING GLASS   63

Bad Poetry   65

Peacock   76

The Secret Life of Corals   84

The Trouble with Fortune Tellers   91

The Big Three   96

Pearls, Pearls and More Pearls   100

Tempest   105

To the Reef   111

Creature from the Blue Lagoon   116

And the Ceiling Parted…   120
Julietta Rallies the Troops   131
Bridge Lessons   140
Hot Tips and Rumours   144
The Gold-Digger's Tale   150
Battle Scenes   160
State of Grace   172
Pandora's Box   188

PART THREE: THE BELT OF VENUS   201
Bleeding Hearts   203
Mrs Vine Takes Charge   217
Release   227
Open Secrets   232
Sackcloth and Ashes   235
God of the Storm   249

WHERE SNOWBIRDS PLAY

For Bob

S.D.G.

I have sung women in three cities
But it is all one.

I will sing of the white birds
In the blue waters of heaven,
The clouds that are spray to its sea.

PART ONE

The Island

ARRIVAL

Vanessa Vine had just begun dialling the mayor's home number to complain about speedboats coming too close to the beach when she spotted something that made her forget why she was holding the telephone. Lifting her reading glasses up over what remained of her hair – Mrs Vine never wore wigs at home – she tried to see into the distance. But it was no use. Her eyesight, which had been growing more feeble, was beyond repair, and there was only one thing to do.

'Jerzy,' she called, aiming her voice at the far-off kitchen. 'Please hurry. I need you!'

The chef – when he wasn't being the chauffeur, valet and occasional 'walker' at parties – sprinted in the direction of his mistress's voice. Dusting flour from his hands as he dashed towards the tapestried dining room, he was filled with dread that the widow had fallen again. But when Jerzy arrived he found her placed sturdily in one of the high-backed Moorish chairs facing the loggia. The French doors stood open, admitting the breeze and rustling the usual array of morning papers lying open on the table. Positioning himself protectively behind the elderly woman, Jerzy fixed his eyes on the stretch of sun-speckled sand to which she was pointing.

'Be a dear and fetch my opera glasses,' she sighed. 'I'm afraid I can't see that far.'

The valet lifted the small mother-of-pearl field glasses that were buried beneath the newspaper and handed them to her. 'It's the English lad you hired for the marine life institute, madam. And Mrs Caulfield.'

'Surely not Louisa!' Mrs Vine exclaimed peevishly. She held the magnifiers to her eyes but, still not seeing clearly, tossed them back on the table.

'I meant the young Mrs Caulfield,' Jerzy clarified, in a sharp-edged accent the widow had no will to explore. The last thing a woman her age needed was to discover that her beloved Man Friday was in the country illegally.

Having completed his valet's duty, the now chef sped back to the kitchen, from which a mouth-watering smell was emanating. Mrs Vine sniffed the air and smiled contentedly. Losing interest in the mayor, she replaced the phone in its cradle and tried looking once more through the field glasses. This time she had better luck, confirming her long-held belief that the secret to the fountain of youth was never to stop being astonished by life. Moving the magnifiers this way and that, she concluded that Jerzy had been right after all; and that the young Oxford graduate she had hired to run the institute was already making friends. Not just any friends, but poor Hannah Caulfield, who was surely as much in need of saving as the Florida sea life.

But what *were* they doing? Mrs Vine pondered. They might almost be dancing, she thought, her heart leaping at the orb of shared Englishness she imagined hovering over the unsuspecting pair. Giving the focus dial another turn, the longer Vanessa Vine considered the possibilities the more it seemed to her that the unusually hot January of 1991 had just turned a few degrees hotter.

* * *

Shielding her eyes from the sun with the back of her hand, Hannah Caulfield crossed the hard-packed morning sand towards the young man. The waves nipped at her ankles, darkening the beach with a trail of air bubbles and crushed seashells. Squinting in the glare that bounced off the water, she studied the peculiar scene taking place a few yards ahead of her. At first glance a young man Hannah had never seen before seemed to be wrestling a giant sea turtle. But as she drew nearer she noticed that the hawksbill lay motionless on the sand and the youth, splashing sea water over its mottled carapace, was bent anxiously over it.

'Do you need help?' she called.

Philip looked up at the sound of her voice. Straightening to his full six feet, two inches, he wiped the sweat from his brow and waited for the woman to come nearer.

She was a little older than him, fair and of small build, with fine sandy hair that caped her bare shoulders and turned more gold than brown as the sun combed through it. In a different setting she might have been considered plain. But in the early morning sun everything about the woman navigating the shore, her small footprints disappearing in the wet sand behind her, struck him as beautiful. There was, Philip thought, something oddly familiar in the way she suddenly stopped and extended her arm.

'What happened here?' she asked, in what sounded like a British accent. Falling to her knees next to the turtle she guided her hand over its barnacled shell.

Philip said that he wished he knew. 'I came out here at first light and found it lying on the sand. It's breathing fine but I need to find a way to move it to the lab.'

'The poor thing must weigh three hundred pounds,' Hannah reflected. A diamond-speckled gold wedding band glinted on her left hand as she moved it gently back and forth to comfort the reptile.

Lying on the sand next to Philip was a long piece of sailcloth he hoped might serve as a raft. 'Once the turtle is secured to it I can drag the load through shallow water, and there is a pulley system at the institute. I just can't seem to get the tarp wrapped round it.'

Hannah suggested that she help him. 'After all, we Brits must stick together. You *are* British, I take it?'

Philip nodded, trying to think of a polite way to say that he didn't want help – even from a fellow countryman. It wouldn't do for word to get out – and it would definitely get out – that the new head of the marine life institute had required assistance on his first day on the job. The woman surprised him, however, by suggesting something Philip hadn't considered: wedging the sailcloth beneath the turtle's flippers and nudging the hawksbill on to it by increments.

They set to, pushing, prodding and heaving, with Philip on one side of the sailcloth and Hannah on the other. For a long time they seemed to be struggling in vain, while the turtle, lying inert, studied its rescuers through half-drawn lids. Then, all at once, the advancing tide lifted the heavy weight on to the tarp.

'Well done you!' cried Philip.

'And you.'

Their eyes met and the feeling that he had seen her before returned. Philip had begun growing a beard that partially concealed a small cleft in his chin, and he noticed the woman looking at it.

Brushing the hair away from her face she half-turned and lifted her sun-tanned arms in the air. 'My son,' she explained, waving to a pink stucco house peeking through the palm fronds, 'has been watching us through his new telescope. He was the one who first spotted you out here and sent me to investigate.'

Philip followed her gaze. His new lodgings were in the guest annexe of one of the homes behind the row of coconut palms, and he tried to work out the distance between it and the pink house. But before he could get very far, his calculations were interrupted by a flock of pelicans swooping through the air just above them. Flying in formation, they unfurled like a wide, flat ribbon against the cobalt blue sky in a trajectory shadowed on the sand.

Philip watched them abruptly change direction and fly out to sea. 'Warm temperatures in winter cause snowbirds to think about migrating north,' he said. 'Is it always this hot in January?'

The pelicans had been making too much noise, and the woman didn't hear him. Turning, she offered him her hand and said: 'By the way, I'm Hannah Caulfield.'

The colour drained from his face, leaving only the sunburn. In none of Philip's imaginings had he pictured Hannah as the confident, prosperous-looking woman standing before him. Forcing a smile, he introduced himself as: 'the new hireling at your marine life institute.'

'Ah, so it is you! I wonder what you make of our little island.'

Philip, who had arrived less than a week ago, rattled off the usual platitudes about the weather, offshore reef and world's largest population of sea turtles. 'Sadly, these ancient creatures have become one of the most endangered species on our planet.'

'Well,' she said doubtfully, 'one hears all sorts of things…'

'Our friend here might disagree. If I had to guess, this hawksbill was dazed by a boat propeller, and no one did anything to help. I won't know how seriously it's hurt until I examine it, but from what I've seen there is far too much activity along this shore – boating, fishing, ballooning. Even something as innocent as building sandcastles can interfere with sea-turtle nesting patterns.'

'But my son adores sandcastles!' Hannah protested. 'Funnily enough,' she added, with a touch of irony, 'until today I never did see a turtle stranded on our beach.'

Philip bristled at the suggestion – even in jest – that he'd had something to do with it. 'At any rate,' she said more mildly, 'and whatever the facts, everyone on the Island is thrilled about the new institute. Mrs Vine, bless her, donated a portion of her estate to house it and gave a huge fundraising ball at The Breakers. Our table raised fifteen thousand.'

Philip assumed that she meant dollars. 'And now you're stuck with me for the next three months!'

'Is that how long you're staying?'

'It's when my visa expires.'

'Ah yes. The all-important visa.'

A speedboat careening close to shore caused the waves to rise above their knees and the raft wobbled. Philip struggled to keep it steady and turned to leave.

'Wait!' Hannah waded after him. 'You haven't told me your name.'

His back was to her and he mumbled something.

'Sorry?' she said, trying to get him to turn around.

'My name's Philip,' he called over his shoulder. 'Philip Godolphin.'

'And the turtle? My son will want to call it something.'

He spun round so quickly that he almost let go of the raft. 'Must everything have a name?' he said.

'I'm afraid so,' she smiled.

Philip thought for a moment. 'Princess,' he said, sprinkling a fistful of water over the hawksbill. 'I christen thee Princess, from a kingdom beneath the sea.'

'Jesse will like that.'

'Your son?'

She nodded.

Another wave rolled to shore and the raft wobbled again. 'I really must go now,' he said.

'Of course you must. But won't you join us for lunch? I mean, once Princess has settled.'

'She may never settle.'

'Oh, but she will! And you shall have something to eat. Our house is just the other side of that white picket fence, and you can freshen up inside the beach cottage. Please come,' she entreated. 'Jesse will be ever so thrilled to meet you.'

Philip didn't reply, and they parted quickly, the young man hauling the coracle behind him through the shallow water while Hannah, moving in the opposite direction, ascended the sand ridge back to shore. He stole a look at her small figure growing smaller: the hollow of her spine in the backless halter top and the sway of her hips inside a pair of high-waisted linen shorts. Was it pure chance that he had run into her so quickly? Or was there more at play – something that neither he nor his deceased father could have divined? Philip had never believed in destiny, and his father had believed in nothing but his own genius. And yet...

Glancing back one more time, he saw Hannah slip through a gate in the white picket fence, the twinkle of an azure-blue swimming pool showing through gaps in the sea grape.

THE PRINCE

During his two-mile trek to the institute Philip regretted not having shown more enthusiasm for Hannah's invitation. Fortunately, she had left it sufficiently open so that, if he hurried, it might still be possible to make Princess comfortable and jog back along the beach in time for lunch.

The lab glistened with newness, smelling of varnish, fresh paint and ammonia as Philip experimented with the pulley mechanism for transporting giant reptiles from the beach. Compared to what he had been through that morning the state-of-the-art machinery made the task seem almost effortless, and Philip was able to place the turtle inside a special recovery berth without difficulty. He measured its vital signs and scraped the fetid barnacles from its shell, then administered an IV drip to replenish its fluids. The drip would take two hours – time enough, Philip reckoned, to get a quick bite with Hannah and the boy.

He was sweating, and his shirt was soaked by the time he reached the white picket fence. He undid the latch and followed a sandy footpath to the beach cottage, the moist and warm air scented with flowering jasmine and some tropical bloom he couldn't identify. *Anglo Bubbly* popped into his head, because the scent reminded him of a popular gum he had chewed as a boy. Thinking back to his childhood in Highgate he remembered an incident that made him think that might have been where he had seen Hannah: not the Hannah he had met on the beach that morning, but a pale slip of a girl with something of the same quality, standing beneath a lamp post on the rain-splattered pavement outside his home.

The image didn't last, vaporising in the midday light and depositing in its place a tiny cottage overgrown with blue and white flowering clematis, resembling a scene from some fairy tale. Philip climbed on to the veranda and peered through its slatted double doors, the pink stucco walls on either side dotted with lizards.

'Mrs Caulfield?' he said under his breath, not sure what to call her. Getting no answer, he opened the door and went inside.

Sunlight seeping through the lowered plantation shutters filled the one-room cottage with the liquid radiance of swimming underwater. The walls were of whitewashed plaster and the floor bamboo: a daybed tucked inside a niche between two tall windows and a small wicker writing desk and chair the only furniture. Having spent the year since his father's death going through desks and filing cabinets, Philip instinctively went over to the desk and pulled open the drawer.

It didn't occur to him until later that he ought not to do this. Leafing through sheets of paper inside the drawer, his pulse quickened when he recognised Hannah's neat, squat, nearly block lettering. Glancing furtively at the door, he scanned the first few stanzas of a poem lying on top. The writing, which was in free verse, described with painful precision a type of loneliness Philip knew well – the kind that always seems worse in a roomful of people. He grew dreamy amid the perfect stillness, purr of the ceiling fan and drone of a motorboat in the distance. Somewhat reluctantly he replaced the poem in the drawer, feeling a pang of regret that once he'd met Hannah and her son his main purpose in coming to the Island would be accomplished. Philip had imagined offering to help them with the small legacy he had inherited, but now even that seemed no longer necessary since their new life appeared to lack nothing. Trying to decide whether it really changed things, he went to the bathroom to wash.

Hannah had told him to 'freshen up' if he liked, and Philip hoped that she hadn't meant for him to dress up as well. It was in any case too late to do anything about it since he had only the T-shirt and bathing trunks he had put on that morning. Despite the casual atmosphere the Island seemed very much a place in which appearances mattered. The bathroom reflected this attitude, with towels stacked neatly by colour and matching terry robes hanging from brass hooks, as in a resort. The only time Philip had been to such a resort was the year before, with his now ex-girlfriend: a holiday that had effectively ended the relationship, with Philip holding on to the bitter end. He never found out why exactly the girl had left him until it was over, when he learned almost by accident that she had been seeing someone else the entire time. Then, after ditching them both, she landed a position with a large investment bank in the City, where Philip imagined her now: gazing into her Quotron with the winter damp misting the windows and the mid-January dusk already gathering. Replacing the mental image with his own sunburned reflection in the mirror above the sink he ran his fingers through his hair, smiling appreciatively at the scraggly beard that made him finally feel like the rugged undersea explorer he dreamed of becoming.

'You ought to beware of that looking glass,' came a small voice from the door. 'The last prince who was here fell right through it and into the sea.'

A little boy had been watching him from the doorway. Pigeon-toed and holding one hand to the wall the child advanced with halting steps amid a harness of tube socks, braces and rubber-soled shoes. He was neatly dressed in khakis and a mint green polo shirt, the upper portion of his face swallowed by a pair of rimless goggles that brought a strange reflective quality to his grey-blue eyes. Philip noticed the indentation in his chin, elfin smile and tufts of sandy hair he had seen in his own childhood photos.

'I shouldn't like to fall through a mirror,' he said, 'since I've only just arrived.' Philip grasped the tiny hand stretching towards him and the boy let go of the wall. A ray of light fell through the window, illuminating an elastic bandage over his forearm that only partially concealed a purplish bruise.

'Is it true that you're an English prince?' the boy asked shyly.

Philip didn't want to disappoint him. But neither did he want to mislead a child pleading with him to be someone he wasn't. Well, he thought, I am that already. 'In England being a prince isn't all that unusual. Some think we have too many.'

'Pleased to meet you, prince,' said the boy as they shook hands. 'I'm Jesse James.'

A shadow appeared in the door behind him and a broad-chested woman in a print housedress, open-toe slippers and a madras turban stepped into the bathroom.

'This is my new friend, Marta,' Jesse cried. 'A prince from England who came to meet the outlaw Jesse James!'

'And I'm the Mexican Spitfire!' the woman laughed. 'Now how's about Jesse James and me has a little catnap before lunch. And you, Mr English prince,' she chaffed as she scooped the boy into her arms and carried him to the daybed, 'had best go on ahead to the pool. Miss Hannah be waiting lunch for you there.'

'Please don't go, turtle prince,' Jesse murmured, laying his head on her shoulder.

Philip's heart melted. 'I'm not going very far,' he said. 'I promise.'

Responding to another sign from Marta he tiptoed to the veranda, passing a small metal walking frame by the door. The sound of the woman humming, mingling with the rise and fall of cicada song in the sea grapes, made Philip think of his childhood again: of getting up on winter mornings while it was still dark, his mother babbling Velvet Underground lyrics as she struggled to get him ready for school; the smell of tea, cigarettes and last night's wine on her breath and the touch of her fingers like icicles as she fumbled with the buttons on his uniform.

A shiver passed through him, triggering another memory: of boys at St Michael's teasing each other that when you shiver it means the ghosts in Highgate Cemetery are walking over your grave. Inhaling the sweet smell of orange blossoms, Philip found it hard to imagine ghosts on the Island. Blocking everything from his mind except the future, he shut the door to his past and went to find Hannah.

ON THE NATURE OF TOADS

Sheltering inside the jasmine pergola he watched her put finishing touches on the outdoor lunch table. Hannah had changed into a creaseless white linen sundress, ballerina flats and a wide-brimmed straw hat, stylish cat's eye sunglasses shading her eyes. Bougainvillea petals floated like confetti on the kidney-shaped swimming pool behind her. A strange sort of pool, Philip thought; sloping gently and without steps, a fibreglass Adirondack chair sitting in the shallowest portion with a wide sun umbrella attached to its high back. From the other end of the pool rose a spacious two-storey pink stucco house with a barrel-tile roof and purple bougainvillea vines climbing the stone pillars of the loggia. Shutting his eyes, Philip tried to imagine the first world of salt marshes, palmettos and cabbage palms that had been displaced by all this opulence. When he opened his eyes again he realised that Hannah had spotted him, politely making no attempt to interrupt his reverie.

Philip waved as he prepared to make his entrance. But it all fell apart the instant his bare feet came in contact with the pool deck. The tiled surround had been baking in the sun and, hot as a live wire, sent him, limping and cursing, straight into the pool. Shambling through the shallow water to cool his burning soles, worse than the pain was the sound of Hannah's stifled laughter.

'A bit of advice for my fellow Englishman,' she said, 'is never to leave home without sun cream and a pair of flip-flops.'

'Right,' Philip muttered, humiliated by his performance.

'But how lovely that you've come after all. Jesse was over the moon when he heard that you might join us for lunch and insisted on going to meet you.'

'If you mean the outlaw Jesse James, I was just with him in the cottage. Marta put him down for a catnap.'

Hannah sighed. 'They'll be along soon, I expect.' Bending over a wicker basket full of beach balls, she tossed Philip a pair of rubber flip-flops. He caught one in the air, but the other flew over his head. 'Can I pour you a glass of lemonade?' she asked. 'The lemons are from our own trees.'

'I'd love some.'

He drank thirstily, studying Hannah's movements over the rim of the glass, the way she inclined her head a little as she refilled it. Yes, he thought, it must have been her all those years ago in Highgate. But what was she doing there? Lifting his eyes to the sky, searching for the answer, Philip nearly choked on his lemonade when he recognised, partially concealed by palm fronds, the small wooden balcony outside his lodgings.

'That's my room, up there,' he blurted, pointing to it with his glass.

Hannah raised an eyebrow but said nothing.

'Free room and board at the home of one of the institute's trustees was part of my contract.' Philip raced through how he had learned about the position and the terms of his appointment; justifying what needed no explaining and nearly forgetting that he was telling the truth.

Hannah nodded. 'Very sensible.'

But it was hard to tell what she was thinking behind the blue-black lenses of her Dior sunglasses. There was in any case no time to reflect on it, Marta and Jesse having already emerged from the pergola. The boy looked refreshed after his nap, one side of his face pink from lying on it as he advanced slowly towards the table on his little walking frame. Hannah waited patiently for him to complete his journey, then lifted him on to her lap.

'Did you have a good rest, poppet?' she asked as he nestled against her, stealing looks at Philip sitting beside them. 'I understand that you two gentlemen have met,' she said. 'And will see a good deal more of each other since Philip is living next door.'

'What? Living with Julietta?' Jesse cocked his head impishly.

'With all the Alonsos,' Hannah corrected. 'They're a big family – much too big!'

Jesse said that he liked Julietta best. Turning to the guest he said: 'She's the one who told us that you're a prince – from a kingdom across the sea.'

Philip smiled. 'The last bit is accurate, but I'm not sure how princely I am.'

'Oh, but you are. You're the prince of turtles. I saw you on the beach with one of your subjects this morning.'

'And you're an outlaw.'

'I am. James is my middle name. What's yours?'

Philip hesitated. 'Actually it's James – like yours. My family name is Godolphin.'

Jesse's eyes rounded. 'Are you descended from dolphins?'

'Not that I'm aware of.'

'I'm sure there's one or two in the family. We all came from the sea, you know.'

'I do know. I'm an oceanographer.'

'Whatever you are,' said Jesse. 'I shall call you Dolphin.'

'Speaking of dolphins,' Maria chuckled. 'My old man's been waiting these twenty years for the Miami Dolphins to win another Super Bowl.'

'They're a football team,' Hannah clarified. 'But, more importantly, how is Princess?'

'Doing rather better than I expected,' Philip said, describing the institute's pulley system for transporting large amphibians to the lab. 'She's resting comfortably in a recovery berth and is hooked up to an IV.'

'I had an IV yesterday!' Jesse swaggered, showing off the bandage on his forearm.

A chirping sound that had been coming from the lilyturf suddenly ceased; and was followed a moment later by a large toad hopping towards the table.

'Get away, you!' Marta shrieked as the toad took a giant leap closer.

'It's Sylvester,' Jesse called to the housekeeper, who was already escaping to the house.

Philip moved to the edge of his seat. 'Bufo toads can emit a poisonous spray,' he warned.

Jesse, his face shining, shook his head. 'Sylvester would never do a thing like that. He is a prince after all – the Prince of Bufos – and only attacks in self-defence.'

Hannah explained that the toad had resided on the property since before their home was built. 'He wasn't at all pleased when the construction began, and sprayed the workers in protest. But once we moved in and Sylvester got to know Jesse,' Hannah added with a smile, 'he has been a changed toad ever since. Only Marta is still afraid of him.'

A telephone rang from somewhere inside the loggia, and Hannah, checking her watch, quickly rose from the table. Jesse giggled as he watched his mother frisk through bougainvillea pots and beneath seat cushions, searching for a cordless phone that finally materialised inside a beach towel. She stood with the handset cradled against her shoulder, her expression turning solemn as she listened to what was being said at the other end of the line. Looking out over the pool, her gaze came to rest on Jesse and Philip sitting together at one end of the table.

'Your father's flight has landed early,' she said when the call ended. 'And now it seems that we're to have lunch at Louisa's.'

'Can Dolphin come with us?'

'I'm afraid not, poppet.' Lifting Jesse on her hip, she apologised to Philip. 'We have to go now. But there's plenty of chicken salad and crisps in the kitchen – or, if you'd rather, Marta can make you a packed lunch to take back to the lab.'

And with that she was off.

Philip stared after them. What had brought this on? he wondered. Was it something to do with Hannah's husband coming home early, or something to do with him? Perhaps he shouldn't have mentioned that James was his middle name. He had sensed a change in her when she learned that he would be living next door, and became distant after the phone call.

Chilled by the thought that Hannah had picked up on some likeness between him and Jesse, Philip stood up from the table and kicked the chair. Sylvester, his belly splayed in front like a seated Buddha, glowered meditatively on the ground beside him. From the other side of the sea grapes the ocean – serene and watchful – returned their melancholy gaze.

THE LOST ART
OF LETTER-WRITING

That evening, sitting cross-legged on his bed, Philip reviewed the evidence in his possession. The letters, in the same handwriting as the poems inside the beach cottage, had been addressed to his father – some to the poet's office at Durham University and the rest to his home in Highgate. Nothing about the plain brown business envelopes gave any hint of the distressing nature of their content. Or that a teenage girl's desperate one-sided correspondence with the award-winning modernist poet James Muir had ended in a final, and to Philip's knowledge unanswered, appeal for help.

None of the letters had been opened by their intended recipient. That task had fallen to Philip in the months following Sir James's untimely death (*Sir* being his father's preferred title since his knighthood). Philip, who didn't believe in titles, had dropped Muir from his name upon entering Oxford and adopted Godolphin – a family name on his mother's side and one of two middle names that appeared on his birth certificate – effectively severing any link between him and the then newly appointed poet laureate to the British nation.

When Muir died – in never entirely clear circumstances at a seedy resort in Ibiza – Philip, who had just turned twenty-one, learned that he had been named executor of his father's literary estate. The copyright to the great man's poems provided a small but steady stream of royalties for Philip and his mother – Lady Muir, as she was now, the title being her principal legacy from a man Philip assumed she must have cared for as little as he did. In his role as executor he was obliged to wade through the poet's papers, an undertaking that raised a long-lingering distrust of his father to a new level. The most damning evidence – from the betrayal and backstabbing of friends and colleagues to the systematic corruption of minors, bordering on paedophilia – had been kept in a padlocked drawer of Muir's desk. Philip had to hire a locksmith to force it open and discovered Hannah's letters near the bottom, tied with a rubber band so dry that it snapped with a bite in his hand.

He kept his mother away from these and other lurid discoveries. She had spent too many years drinking alone in a draughty Edwardian house backing on to Highgate Cemetery to be told any more than she already guessed. Yet it was to this house that Muir had returned every weekend without fail from his teaching post in Durham and travels to poetry readings around the country and abroad. Why he bothered to come back at all was another of the great man's enigmas: as if calling a place home and holding his family hostage in it every Friday to Sunday somehow vindicated his offences during the week.

Reading Hannah's letters had a profound effect on Philip. From those near the top of the pile he learned that she had become pregnant with Muir's child and of her struggle to keep the baby: from the last few, that the child had been diagnosed soon after birth with a rare congenital disorder and had only a few months to live. The need to find out what had become of the pair – Jesse, after all, was Philip's half-brother – turned into a mission. By then Philip had completed his studies at Oxford and was looking for work. When he discovered that his search for Hannah and Jesse was leading to the same seven-mile-long barrier island off the south Florida coast as his search for employment, he leaped at the opportunity. Overlooking the meagre salary, Philip applied for the position and was given a three-month placement starting immediately.

He may have been the only applicant. It would explain why an offer reached him so soon after sending his CV and list of references. There was not even the usual request for an interview and, so far as Philip was aware, none of his references were checked. The offer came handwritten in an unusual purple ink that smelled faintly of gardenias, with a gilt-edged palazzo on the letterhead and capital letters pirouetting across the creamy vellum.

A smile came to Philip's face as he reread it:

My dear Philip (if I may),

It is with the greatest pleasure that, on behalf of the Trustees of the Palm Beach Marine Life Institute, I offer you the position of Intern for a trial period of Three Months commencing in January. We are happy to arrange for your Green Card, food and lodging at the home of one of the Trustees, together with a bi-weekly stipend of $50 towards living expenses!

We hope very much that you will accept our humble offer and unique experience to engage with the <u>unprecedented</u> environmental initiative being launched by our community.

Awaiting your response, I remain

Faithfully yours,

Mrs Sanford Vine (Vanessa)
Chairwoman and Trustee

Hearing a sound, Philip's eyes leaped to the door. But it was too late and Julietta, his hosts' teenage daughter, was already halfway across the room. She had a maddening habit of prowling about barefoot, confirming Philip's hunch that she might have been lurking outside his door for some time.

'I saw your light and came to say goodnight,' she said, approaching the bed.

Julietta Alonso had the prominent family nose, deep-set charcoal eyes and thick black wavy hair. Unlike her family, she was long-limbed with a narrow waist and small breasts that showed like tight fists through her cotton tank top. Philip had the impression that she was dropping by his room in the annexe rather too often, using one excuse after another. Being a guest in the house and unsure of American customs he was at pains to find a polite way of discouraging her.

'Just checking that you've got enough filtered water for the night. Make sure you never drink from the tap, Phil.'

He cringed and counted to ten. There were few things he disliked more than people calling him Phil. It reminded him of his father coming through the door every Friday afternoon on the dot and crying out: 'It's no use hiding, Phil: Daddy's home.'

More calmly than he felt, he explained that where he came from people tended to use full names. 'For example, James instead of Jim, Philip rather than Phil, Andrew, John and so on.'

'Do they do that with all names or just with the names of the Apostles?'

Philip, who had hoped to distract Julietta long enough to slip the letters beneath one of the cushions, found himself distracted instead. 'Apostles?'

'Well, all the examples you just gave are the names of Apostles in the New Testament. Yours too. Actually,' Julietta pursued, taking a seat primly at the edge of the bed, 'Grandmalita thinks we should call you *Sir* Philip to show respect for – what did she call it? – ah yes, for the Prince Consort.'

Philip had no idea what the girl was going on about. Americans, it seemed to him, had a peculiar obsession with names – and knew nothing about British royalty. Now, moving aside a little, it seemed to him that Julietta was also making faces.

If only Philip knew how many hours she had spent practicing the new 'bedroom eyes' technique that was all the rage among girls at her school. Launched in the sold-out January issue of *Cosmopolitan* magazine, it involved the gradual lowering of one's lids to show off the lashes and bring a dreamy expression to the face. 'Count to ten,' the magazine instructed its readers. 'Then, very, *very* slowly, open them again.'

Try as she might, Julietta couldn't tell whether her exertions were having the desired effect. She would in any case have been devastated to learn that the look they produced reminded Philip of the heavy-lidded turtle he and Hannah had rescued on the beach. Failing to get a reaction Julietta tried to remember what the magazine had said to do next. But, as usual, she had spent far more time looking at pictures than reading, and had got only halfway through the article.

It was just one of the items on Julietta's private list of imperfections. Growing up in the Island's hothouse atmosphere, girls of a certain age were perilously aware of their slightest defects; with the predictable result that two of Julietta's classmates at the Day Academy were being treated for anorexia and three more were at a popular rehab centre on the West Coast. Another group had been dispatched to 'fat farms' in New England by mothers eager to see them slim down to the acceptable norm; and the rest evacuated to boarding schools 'up north' to prepare for entry into an Ivy League university. And there were always the one or two that flared like rockets, outshining everyone at slumber parties and teen fashion shows before their lights extinguished and they were never mentioned again.

In Julietta's case none of these exit strategies were possible. Grandmalita would never risk being parted from her only granddaughter – and prize jewel of the Alonso family virtue – by permitting her to leave home under any circumstance. Even less would she allow her to date whomever she pleased. Julietta objected, of course: it was the prerogative of youth to object. And yet, given a truth serum, she would have to admit in the hidden depths of her Latin soul that Grandmalita was right about most things: and that even in the final decade of the twentieth century a wise and clever girl could still expect to make the same sort of match, and live the same wonderful life, as her forebears.

The arrival of the English houseguest had brought a new sense of urgency to Julietta's mission. Blushing for no reason in his presence, she longed only to be alone with him. But when she was, it seemed that she could do nothing right – apparently not even address Philip by his proper name. Perhaps, Julietta thought, the most she could hope for at this juncture was simply to protect him – that is, to protect him from her family.

They were the formidable Alonso clan that had fled Communist Cuba by boat (actually, it was in the family's forty-foot yacht), bringing with them what some on the Island described as the fiercest set of values since the Pilgrims had landed on Plymouth Rock. Once safely ensconced in Florida, Julietta's grandfather Ernesto set out to resurrect the family's sugar empire in the New World. He built vast plantations in the fertile wetlands and a grand house in Palm Beach that was a replica of the family's home in the Pinar del Rio. Using philanthropy as an entrée into society the Alonsos funded charitable balls from one season to the next, rubbing shoulders with European nobility and American presidents until it began to seem that no season could begin without them. (To grandfather Ernesto's eternal credit he established and gave half of what he earned to a refugee relief fund for the boatloads of less fortunate Cubans who were also fleeing to America.)

Julietta's parents were Patsy and Eduardo, dutiful offspring of the two most prominent Cuban émigré families in Florida. There was never any question that they would marry, bringing together in a splendid wedding at St Christopher's the state's tobacco and sugar empires. The couple cheerfully assented to their arranged union, as Patsy did to living under the same roof with Carlotta, Eduardo's rambunctious, recently widowed mother. For the next three decades they hosted lavish parties, raised money for charity and played tennis and polo – and of course golf – at the Mangrove, Bath & Racquet and Shore Clubs. Eduardo proved as fierce a competitor on the polo grounds as he was in business; while the Alonso women played bridge and backgammon and attended fashion-show luncheons at their private clubs, membership to which was obligatory for anyone hoping to matter on the Island. True, the peculiarities of the clan's traditions occasionally gave their friends and neighbours pause, but these were deemed to have more to do with them being devoutly religious than being foreign. In reality, the Alonsos' Catholicism was in name only, it being more expedient to perpetuate the myth than constantly have to justify values they could neither explain nor do without.

Julietta and her four older brothers were the first generation born on American soil. Three of the boys were presently away at boarding school or university, and the eldest, Armando – who detested books – was being schooled in the family trade. Unlike the rest of his family he preferred to live in a modest rental on the mainland with a group of surfing buddies and disapproved loudly of the way the sugar business was run. Philip had so far met none of these Alonso heirs-in-waiting, whose dashing features and picture-perfect lifestyles appeared in portraits and inside gaudy picture frames showcased on the walls, top of the grand piano and fireplace mantle of the hacienda. They were shown dancing, sailing, playing polo and eating – to Philip it seemed they were always eating – in a grand depiction of a way of life that seemed to assume the twentieth century was only just beginning instead of ending.

On Philip's uninitiated face Julietta saw starkly mirrored how astonishing her family's domestic arrangements must appear to the outside world. For instance, the way they said grace before meals, attended Mass as often as they played croquet and the staff wore white gloves and uniforms and used a separate entrance. They hung an Olympic-size American flag outside their home and, like many recent émigrés, were utterly devoted to their adopted country: worshipping the new-world system of values so long as it didn't encroach on their old-world attitudes.

'I'm so excited about the barbeque,' Julietta announced, hoping to inject some life into the conversation. 'Grandmalita has been baking non-stop.'

'Yes, I know,' Philip said. The guest annexe stood directly above the kitchen and for the past two days Carlotta Alonso's culinary endeavours had emitted powerful gusts of garlic, fried onions and molasses through the floorboards and windows of his room.

'You'll get to meet some of my friends from school,' Julietta coaxed. She spoke in a sing-song voice that turned up at the end of sentences and made her seem always to be asking for permission.

Hoping it would get her to leave, Philip said he didn't think that he was invited to the barbeque.

'Oh, but you are! At any rate, I'm inviting you now.' Julietta's eyes slid surreptitiously over the letters Philip had been at pains to conceal. 'It was meant to be my quinceañera but we're doing a barbeque instead.'

'Your *quincea* what?'

'Oh, it's one of those Cuban things,' she sighed. 'A silly party Latino families give when a daughter turns fifteen.'

'Is that what you are – fifteen?'

The question made Julietta briefly lose her train of thought. Trying to weigh the benefits of Philip thinking her either older or younger than she was, the girl, picking at her cuticles, admitted that she had turned fifteen at Christmas. 'But there was too much on the social calendar to throw another party. Besides which, I don't go in for arcane customs.' With a cunning look she said: 'Let's see what you've got there, Phil–ip,' and slid her hand towards the cushion.

He thrust it aside, but that only made Julietta laugh. He suspected her of going through his things when he was out, and now she had seen the letters. The room might almost be made of glass for all the privacy he had, with the housemaid coming in and out and Julietta snooping about. Not for the first time, Philip considered renting a safe deposit box at the bank where he could store the letters and his personal effects. Hearing the familiar click of the air conditioner, he braced himself for the blast of cold air from the grid in the ceiling that was about to slide like an ice cube down his back.

'They're just some letters from my mum,' he said. 'Same old stuff, you know.'

Brightening, Julietta felt that she and the English houseguest were finally on common ground. She longed for the day when she would have a home of her own and could exchange letters and phone calls with her family instead of having to submit to their demands. 'Mothers can be such a nuisance,' she said. 'All the girls at the Day Academy feel the same.'

Philip wondered. 'Never mind,' he suggested tactfully. 'You'll get through it, and then, all at once, you'll be free as a bird.'

'Free? To do what exactly?'

'Spread your wings and fly!'

Julietta considered this advice. 'Does that mean you're coming to the party?' she asked.

FRIENDS AND NEIGHBOURS

A dozen high tables draped in red, white and blue were spread evenly across the loggia and pool deck, a single beeswax candle inside a tall Mason jar burning in the middle of each table. Fairy lights silhouetted the mission-style roof and climbed the palm trees at the rear of the Alonsos' mock hacienda, the poolside tiki bar glinting with a rainbow of bottles and fiesta bowls filled with Meyer lemons, Key limes and three types of Spanish olives. The smoky smell of roasting pork, beef and onions misted the air above the rustic summer kitchen while, far in the distance, like an inky blue extension of the infinity pool, the ocean absorbed the last light of day.

It being a buffet, the guests were expected to serve themselves and eat while standing at the tables – or, space permitting, seated on lounge chairs surrounding the pool. They began arriving as early as six o'clock, many coming straight from golf and tennis courts and games of bridge, canasta and backgammon. Friends and neighbours streamed through the circular foyer paved with smooth brightly coloured Spanish tiles leading into a living room the size of a small concert hall. (Carlota Alonso loved the way the English houseguest referred to it as the *drawing room* – 'as if anyone in this house ever learned to draw!') As in most homes on the Island the flow of movement was towards the rear of the house, swimming pool and ocean, so that every window, at some point of the day, would be filled with nothing but sea and sky.

Upstairs in the guest annexe Philip was struggling to pull buttons through the stiff eyelets of his new Turnbull & Asser shirt. He wasn't looking forward to the party and would much rather have spent the evening quietly in his room – if it were possible for any part of the house to remain quiet for very long. He checked the new diving watch his mother had given him as a graduation present, surprised that so many people had already arrived. At home it had been drilled into him never to go to a party at the appointed time. Yet, judging from the commotion below his balcony, the multitude turning up at the ridiculously early stroke of six appeared to be unaware of any such rule.

Philip went out on his terrace and looked up at the night. Jupiter, winking like a spaceship, replaced the North Star as the most prominent planet, bringing the firmament nearer than it had appeared in the misty skies of London. At the sound of Nat King Cole crooning '*Quizás, Quizás, Quizás*' – 'Perhaps, Perhaps, Perhaps' – from outdoor speakers on the loggia, Philip unconsciously began humming to the music. As he tucked a silk square inside the breast pocket of his blazer it occurred to him that Hannah would very likely be at the party; putting a spring in his step as he skipped down the outdoor stairs.

Every light in the house had been lit and the sliding glass doors facing the pool were wide open. Looking in from outside, the drawing room reminded Philip of the stage set in a Chekhov play he had seen at the Hampstead Playhouse, with Carlotta Alonso in the role of the ageing matriarch. As in the play, those familiar with Carlotta – seated plumply among the cushions of her tufted sofa – would be aware that, beneath her squat figure, swathed in foamy taffeta and rows of pearls, lurked the primal instincts of a tigress guarding her lair.

The widow's pearls were always the first thing that caught the eye, cascading like a shimmery waterfall from round her neck to just below where her waist used to be. These days Carlotta was on far better terms with her pearls than most people she knew. They grew friendlier and more luminous in the evening, with the short-est strand (though it was hardly short) of the irregularly shaped South Sea variety. These were accompanied by rose-tinted Tahi-tians and – rarest of all – a triple strand of natural diver pearls. In widowhood Carlotta was now wedded only to her pearls and never ventured into the world – or even downstairs – without them. When challenged about her pearl habit she responded by borrow-ing a quote from one of the Island's legendary hostesses, who had famously replied, in response to the same question, that she too used to feel that way: 'But that was before I had these.'

For tonight's party, and despite the casual setting, Carlotta had gone all out in the pearl department. After all, she was the hostess – never mind that it was her son and daughter-in-law's house and that they had issued the invitations. Guests fluttered like moths round the matriarch, attracted to the flame but afraid of approaching too close. Flirting with their drinks, canapés and, whenever possible, with each other, anyone lingering near the tufted sofa for longer than was strictly necessary faced the risk of becoming impaled on one of Carlotta's helpful observations. Now, having spotted her English houseguest – tall, polite and exquisitely unknown – the tigress lost interest in everyone else.

'Sir Philip,' she cried, gesturing him to the sofa.

The widow hadn't been able to resist giving him a title. She had done it to be amusing but also in part due to her ignorance of English forms of address. Philip acknowledged the greeting with a polite nod as he waded shoulder-deep through the all-male crowd at the tiki bar. To his untrained eyes they all appeared to be wearing, with minor variations in style and colour, the same crisp, pale blue or pink shirt with linen trousers and velvet loafers without socks. This was in contrast to their often much younger wives and girlfriends who, congregating separately in tight groups, dressed as differently from each other as they could invent.

Carlotta stood out from most women her age – and there was a surprising number of them at the barbeque – in having made no attempt to look younger. The mesh of fine lines cobwebbing a face that had for decades been exposed to the sun, droopy chin and prominent family nose all conveyed the message that Carlotta Alonso had more important things to think about than her age. Chief among these were her progeny – specifically Armando and Julietta, the eldest and youngest of her grandchildren who showed the greatest promise. This was in sharp contrast to the dowager's three intermediate grandsons, whom she suspected of harbouring some of the unwholesome tendencies that lurked in the family gene pool. And now, out of the blue, Sir Philip had landed on her doorstep; as tantalisingly unexpected as the opportunity he presented for expanding the Alonso bloodline in an entirely new direction.

Her face glowed when he arrived at the sofa, bowing deeply as he lifted her crooked fingers to his lips. Carlotta adored the young man's curious turns of phrase as much as his enunciation, so crystal clear that she never had to ask him to repeat a word. After decades of not being entirely sure what Americans were saying – let alone what they meant – Carlotta felt as if she were getting her hearing back.

'No one has seen fit to offer me a drink,' she complained, denouncing her daughter-in-law who was busy greeting guests at the door. 'As usual, Patsy is too busy chit-chatting.'

Philip offered to fetch her something from the bar. 'And perhaps a canapé or two?'

'Well, I do quite like the look of the stone crabs. But what a long line there is. You had better elbow your way through and tell Eduardo I want my usual. Threaten him if you must!' she said with a throaty laugh.

A moment later Carlotta was bubbling with happiness when she saw her favourite grandson come through the door. She had been fretting over reports that morning of another violent scene between Armando and his father at the head office of Consolidated Sugar. According to the widow's informants among the staff Armando had stormed out, pale and unapologetic, vowing never to return. Although she was careful not to say so, in Carlotta's estimation

Armando's outbursts were a credit to the family, together with the fact that he never accepted money he hadn't earned. Less to her grandson's credit, she thought, was that he had recently moved in with a busty waitress from the Dune Dog Dive Bar – whatever *that* was.

Philip, in the mean time, was struggling to catch his host's eye over the heads of men who seemed to be permanently posted to the bar. Squeezing through them sideways, he overheard some of their hushed asides: about the uptick in the stock market since the start of another war in the Middle East and of tensions brewing in the Balkans. The most amusing was one man's suggestion – accompanied by a wink – that Eduardo was looking ever more like the Cuban-Hollywood heart-throb Cesar Romero, who had been a friend of the Alonsos. Taking a closer look at his host, Philip discerned an astonishing resemblance: the same broad shoulders, pencil-thin moustache, silvered mane of wavy hair and sideburns. Surely not, Philip thought, glancing at pudgy Carlotta, seated like Queen Victoria on the sofa, eyes flashing at her subjects as if she were daring them either to fall at her feet or get out of her house.

Eduardo, whoever his real father, was definitely cut from Carlotta's cloth. Wearing the top of his shirt open with sleeves rolled up over his hairy arms, jaw protruding and a wet cigar end clamped between his large, evenly spaced front teeth, the Alonso scion grinned at the purple-tinted sky and thumped a Bakelite cocktail shaker to the tune of a rhumba playing over the outdoor speakers. Dispensing luscious-looking cocktails into his guests' outstretched glasses, he emitted great plumes of cigar smoke from his nostrils while dabbling in conversations it seemed unlikely he was able to hear over the general din.

'I'm afraid, gentlemen,' he announced upon receiving Carlotta's message, 'that there will be no more drinks served until Mamita gets her Tootsie Roll.'

Philip gave a polite smile, assuming that this was an inside joke. But his grin was arrested by the intense silence that gripped the entire group, a sober expression on every face but his own.

41

The Tootsie Roll, as Philip learned from the man standing next to him, was a popular cocktail launched at the bar of The Breakers hotel in 1925. When the Alonsos arrived on the Island and Carlotta had her first taste of the iconic Tootsie Roll she took to imbibing the drink as a kind of daily health tonic. It came to be said that in Eduardo's skilful hands the classic mix of vanilla vodka, Kahlua, Cointreau, orange juice and a handful of crushed ice cubes tasted even better than the original, causing people to flock to his parties. But none flocked more than his Mamita, whose scrupulous gaze was at this moment following every rattle and roll of the cocktail shaker, a performance Eduardo ended with a pirouette. As he poured the Tootsie Roll into a tall glass filled to the rim he spotted his son Armando among the guests. Having drunk two daiquiris and a mojito in quick succession, Eduardo's resolve to bring his eldest son to heel surged and surged.

Trying not to spill a drop of the precious concoction, Philip headed back to the sofa. His eyes travelled from the glass he was holding to the foyer, wondering if Hannah and her husband were among the latest arrivals. But so far it seemed that nearly everyone in the neighbourhood had arrived except the Caulfields.

'Come meet my grandson,' Carlotta said, snatching greedily at the cocktail. 'You boys have a lot in common.'

It wasn't readily apparent if they did: the Englishman tall and impeccably dressed, Armando paunchy and no higher than Philip's shoulders, wearing cut-off jeans and a tie-dyed T-shirt.

'What I meant,' Carlotta clarified, 'is that you are both passionate about the environment.'

'Unlike Papi,' Armando snorted, with a toss of his wavy, pitch-black hair that was nearly as long as Julietta's. 'I was after him again today to stop burning the sugar canes, but he won't do a damn thing about it. Don't you find it ironic, Grandmalita,' Armando said, looking accusingly at Philip, 'that our family should donate money to the new marine life institute while our own business spews tons of toxic ash into the atmosphere? There's a lot more to the planet than the ocean.'

'Everything affecting the planet begins in the ocean,' Philip suggested.

'Maybe. But at the moment I am a great deal more worried about our wetlands. The Everglades regulate Florida's entire ecosystem and no one – at least, no one in this room – seems to care.'

'But I thought all kinds of new laws were being proposed to protect the wetlands,' said Carlotta.

'They're being proposed, but aren't enacted because no politician dares to oppose Consolidated Sugar. We're the biggest offenders *and* employ the most people in the state.' Armando glared at the patio where Eduardo, shouting louder than his son, announced that the buffet was open, and the bar would never close.

'You mustn't let it upset you so,' Carlotta protested cheerfully, patting the back of her stiff new permanent wave. 'Your father revamped the entire business after Grandpapi died, and he's sure to think of a solution.'

'He had better think fast – for the sake of all our children and not just his own.'

'Oh dear, I hope you're not thinking of having any with that…' Carlotta struggled to keep from saying more.

His curiosity aroused, Philip showered Armando with questions. 'How does growing sugar lead to toxicity in the environment?'

'It has to do with the way the cane is harvested. The fields are set on fire to expose the sugar-laden stalks, releasing tons of pollution. The fires must then be put out, depleting freshwater supplies and creating clouds of smoke and ash. In the old days it was much better done by hand.'

'In the old days,' Carlotta said, 'they used slaves.'

'Actually, now that you mention it,' Philip said, 'I *have* noticed a dark residue over the outdoor furniture and water tank at the institute – like soot from the old coal fires in London. But surely there is some other way to harvest the cane?'

'Not as efficiently,' Armando said. 'And they'll never find a way unless Consolidated Sugar invests in research.'

A commotion erupted in the foyer as several groups of guests arrived at the same time. With only a few minutes left until the start of the buffet, this was, Philip thought, the Caulfields' last chance to make an appearance. He was curious to see what sort of man Hannah had married – presumably the same Dr Caulfield who, according to Philip's research, had saved Jesse's life and brought mother and son to America. Instead, a gaggle of teenagers, accompanied by Julietta and several sets of parents, charged noisily indoors. The girls, some of whom were still in their tennis outfits, prattled in the same question-mark tone of voice as Julietta.

Carlotta, who took every pause in conversation as a token of agreement, assured Philip that the situation wasn't nearly as dire as Armando had portrayed it. Smiling affectionately, she added: 'I have a feeling we'll survive the burning sugar canes in the same way we survive the hurricanes, year in and year out, and live to tell all about it.'

'That's because you always leave the Island ahead of hurricane season!' Armando laughed. 'Now, if you must know, the real reason I came tonight was to gorge myself on Grandmalita's award-winning plantains.'

The widow's milky eyes lit up; and were positively beaming when she spotted her granddaughter smiling fetchingly at Sir Philip from the other end of the salon. Was it too soon to hope that something might come of it? Carlotta had been acquainted with a succession of British royals wintering on the Island – for instance, Edward VII, an avid polo player and cigar afficionado who had from time to time accompanied Ernesto home from the polo grounds to smoke and drink and watch the sun go down. But it was the new Prince and Princess of Wales that had captivated Carlotta's heart. She adored the splendid Diana, who had been seated next to her at a charity ball, gazing at Carlotta with those impossibly blue eyes and wearing a slim-fitting silk dress that had launched an immediate fashion craze on the Island. The embers of those few hours the widow had spent in the company of the fairy-tale perfect prince and princess were now suddenly and tantalisingly fanned back to life by Sir Philip's unexpected appearance in her home.

As the last arrivals drifted towards the buffet a bony, feral-looking blonde was left alone in the foyer. She stood in front of the hall mirror, teetering on a pair of stilettos and holding a hand to her forehead as she tried to make out her reflection in the glass. Philip, who had been watching her, was about to go over and offer his assistance when his wrist was handcuffed by Carlotta's powerful grip.

'She'll follow you over here if you're not careful,' the widow whispered.

Holding on to the furniture, the blonde was in fact making her way towards them. It took all the strength she had to finally reach the sofa. Carlotta, forcing a smile, introduced her to Philip.

The woman, whose name was Sunny Sloan, stared past him. Tugging at a strand of the coarse peroxide-tinted hair that kept falling into her eyes, she murmured: 'You must be that new turtle man my mother's going on about.'

'Your mother?' Philip couldn't imagine who the blonde was referring to. A moment later his face broke into a smile when he learned that it was Vanessa Vine, who had hired him to work at the institute.

Bleary-eyed after the ten-hour flight from London, during which he had been squeezed into one of the middle seats of Economy class, Philip had landed at Miami airport feeling like a stray cat. Grilled by a pair of surly Latino border agents about his reasons for entering the country he had finally been released into a sprawling arrivals area that provided no information about how he was to reach his final destination. Apparently only freight trains travelled with any regularity to Palm Beach, and one or two buses a day that no one knew very much about. Wheeling his sole piece of luggage through the biggest revolving door he had ever seen, Philip was brusquely apprehended by a thin man wearing a white Nehru jacket and what looked like a fez. Philip, assuming he was a porter, tried to shoo him away. But the man, who introduced himself as Jerzy, stood absolutely firm.

'Come with me,' he said, marching with Philip's suitcase under his arm to an outdoor car park the size of a cricket field. Philip hurried after him, terrified that the man would make off with his only piece of luggage. Instead, Jerzy stopped next to a glistening vintage Rolls-Royce and, bowing, opened the door. With an apologetic smile, he explained that Mrs Vine had sent him.

Philip tumbled gratefully into the passenger seat and they set off together in the 1980 Silver Shadow. A few minutes into the journey the chauffeur announced that Mrs Vine wished to speak to him. Philip glanced incredulously over his shoulder at the back seat, wondering if she had somehow managed to be in the car with them. The chauffeur, smiling patiently, handed him a car phone attached to the armrest while steering the Rolls into four lanes of seventy-mile-an-hour traffic on Interstate 95. Philip had seen car phones advertised, but they were hugely expensive, and he had never actually used one. Now, at the press of a button, he was connected to his benefactress who, for the next hour, regaled him with her plans 'to save our little island'. In a high-pitched and occasionally theatrical voice she boasted with girlish bravado that she had converted a portion of her land ('one of the choicest properties on the Island!') into a state-of-the-art marine life institute.

'And now, my boy,' she concluded grandly, 'it's all yours.'

The phone call had left Philip excited about his new commission. His impression of Mrs Vine had been of a breathy, slightly eccentric and expansively built woman who, it seemed to him, couldn't possibly have any family connection to the waif-like creature swaying like a reed in the Alonsos' drawing room.

'You don't believe me,' said the blonde. 'No one does. That's because I am not – I repeat *not* – her daughter.'

'What Sunny means is that she was adopted,' Carlotta said quietly.

Her breath smelling of alcohol, Sunny Sloan, who Philip guessed was somewhere in her thirties or early forties, had the downcast, faintly preoccupied look of a convalescent. Suffering visibly as she stared at Carlotta's cocktail she mumbled something about going to pay her respects to Eduardo. But instead of heading to the bar she remained rooted to the spot.

There was a time Carlotta would never have permitted someone in that condition to enter her home. With Ernesto staunchly beside her to enforce the rules they had reigned together as a team of equals. In the mean time, Carlotta had steadily gathered force, like a tropical depression so far out to sea that no one is aware of it until it's too late. When Ernesto died prematurely and Eduardo took over at Consolidated Sugar, Carlotta ceded control of the family business in exchange for near total control over their lives. Now, fingering the pearls round her neck with the same reverence she bestowed on her rosary, the widow Alonso permitted herself a measured smile when she noticed her son and grandson standing together in the buffet line.

So, she thought to herself, watching them pretend to patch things up for her sake. In her many years of experience in such matters, even just pretending had a delightful way of turning real: leaving no doubt in Carlotta's mind that, with sufficient time and coercion, every last dissident in the family would come to see things her way.

'Sir Philip,' she said, tugging at his sleeve. 'If it isn't asking too much, I wonder if you might—'

But before she could finish the sentence, Sunny Sloan tumbled over the side of the sofa and practically into the dowager's lap. With lightning reactions honed during the Communist siege of the Pinar del Rio, Carlotta grasped her pearls and jumped to her feet. Philip looked on, not sure whether, or even how, to intervene. For a few terrifying seconds all they could see of Sunny Sloan was her back-combed bouffant and mannequin-like limbs lying half-buried among the cushions.

No one came over. But someone did notice – a large dapper-looking, middle-aged man with russet-red hair. 'Looks like it's time for the Sloans to head home,' he said, and with one hand lifted the blonde to her feet. 'Sorry about this, Carlotta. Lovely party, really,' he added, half-carrying Sunny under his arm to the door.

Carlotta relaxed her hold of the pearls and straightened the cushions. Assuming once again her pose on the sofa she requested Philip to bring her a plate of food from the buffet. 'And tell Eduardo,' she instructed imperiously, 'to fetch me a cigar from the humidor.'

Grumbling silently about how he was expected to manage two plates simultaneously – and not a little surprised that the widow smoked cigars – Philip went to stand in the buffet line. There he was intercepted by Julietta who darted into the line ahead of him, so quickly and seamlessly that Philip wondered whether her appearance might have been more orchestrated than it appeared.

'I see you met Sunny,' she said. 'It's all too sad really.'

'What's the matter with her?'

'By this time, pretty much everything. We're not supposed to talk about it.'

'Who was the man she left with?'

'Her husband. Everyone thinks he's a saint. Some say,' Julietta lowered her voice to a conspiratorial aside that piqued more interest among those standing near her than if she had been shouting, 'that only a top-notch lawyer like Addison Sloan would put up with a wife like Sunny.'

'I fail to see the logic…'

'The thing is,' Julietta interjected, shovelling as much food as she could fit on her plate. 'Lawyers, unlike normal people, know exactly what it costs to get a divorce in this town.'

The party ended as punctually as it had begun, with guests thinning out as soon as the antique Emperor clock in the foyer struck nine. Philip was among them, leaving half a dozen of the Alonsos' closest friends still milling about the infinity pool: the men on one end, puffing contraband cigars from Eduardo's private stock, and the women sprawled on deckchairs, loud and gossipy after a few drinks.

Philip, feeling stuffed, climbed with heavy steps back up to his room in the guest annexe. He spent a few minutes on his balcony, listening to sounds of merriment from below that made him feel more than ever like an outsider. Even the night sky felt different, with the moon and Venus paired so closely that they outshone all the other planets: stars hovering round them like fireflies. Thinking about Hannah and Jesse and his reasons for coming here, Philip's eyes drifted to the house next door. Through the dense foliage he noticed a bluish light in one of the upstairs windows and climbed on the balcony railing to see better. Peering past the branches he was able to make out the back of three heads facing a large-screen television, Jesse's unmistakable mop of hair showing above the rim of the sofa, his head resting on Hannah's shoulder.

It nearly cost Philip his footing when he realised that the strangely familiar, red-haired and husky man sitting on the sofa with them was the lawyer from the party. Turning his leonine head to profile he and Hannah kissed slowly, neither of them paying attention to the TV programme. Philip looked away in disgust, wondering how Addison Sloan had managed to dispose of his pathetically drunk wife before making his way to Hannah's house – and with Jesse on the sofa beside them.

But where was Dr Caulfield? Philip wondered in confusion. Was this what his father had turned the young girl who wrote those letters into? Or had Muir merely tapped into something already present in Hannah's nature?

I was a fool to come here, Philip thought miserably, as he returned to his room and undressed in the dark. Throwing his clothes on the floor he flung himself across the bed, the pinwheel-shaped wings of the ceiling fan twirling overhead; while, from below the terrace Nat King Cole crooned 'Perhaps, Perhaps, Perhaps' as the outdoor audiotape rewound to the tracks that had played at the start of the evening.

GETHSEMANE-ON-THE-SEA

When Philip awoke his room was ice-cold and his neck was stiff. The air conditioning had been running on high the entire night, leaving him as chilled to the bone as he had been on those long-ago winter mornings in Highgate. Throwing a blanket over his shoulders he went out on the terrace to warm himself. The sun stood higher in the sky than the past few mornings when, victim to jetlag, Philip had risen before first light. Putting aside his negative impressions from the night before he tried to feel excited about the coming day. In the afternoon a local veterinary surgeon was coming by the institute to remove the obstruction from the injured turtle's gullet, and Philip was keen to observe him so that he could soon begin doing extractions on his own.

Hearing noises from the kitchen below he remembered that the Alonsos would be getting ready for church. He had observed with a sense of wonder their over-the-top preparations on the previous Sunday, Carlotta regal in her widow's black and the family of women driven to St Christopher's by Eduardo. Philip had narrowly escaped having to accompany them thanks to Julietta, who had asked, point-blank in front of the whole family, whether Philip was a practicing Catholic. Up until then the question seemed not to have occurred to anyone, and Philip's reply that he was not resulted in an abrupt change of plans.

'In that case we're going to have to leave you at home,' Carlotta had informed him, explaining with polite restraint that only members of the 'true faith' were allowed to receive Communion at St Christopher's – or, apparently, allowed through the door.

'Allied Patriot missiles downed two more Iraqi Scuds overnight...' Philip heard from a twelve-inch, black-and-white Sony television as he entered the kitchen. The TV sat permanently on top of the counter and was always on, V-shaped antennae sticking up from it like a pair of ears. V for victory, thought Philip when he learned that Allied forces had just won a decisive air battle in the Middle East war. Carlotta, standing by herself in a corner of the kitchen and paying no attention to the news broadcast, was shouting over the announcer's voice into a pink Trimline phone mounted on the wall.

'Oh, here he comes now,' she exclaimed when Philip entered. 'Yes, I'll be sure to tell him.'

With her daytime pearls swinging, Carlotta paraded through the sun-drenched kitchen like a pudgy Amazon in haute couture (Galanos, who had famously dressed Nancy Reagan at the White House, was her favourite designer).

'I've just spoken to Dr Caulfield,' she announced, her face radiant with the news she was about to deliver. 'And he says the family would be delighted to have you accompany them to Gethsemane.'

Philip clenched his fingers over the handle of the tea kettle. 'Gethsemane?'

'Gethsemane-on-the-Sea is the name of the Protestant church. I personally never go there except for funerals and baptisms, but Hannah – who, by the way, is also British – tells me that it's about as high Church of England as you're likely to find this side of the pond.'

Mistaking the look on Philip's face for one of joy instead of alarm, Carlotta finished tidying up the remains of breakfast. The help had Sundays off, and she delighted in having full charge of the kitchen. Cooking a big sabbath meal for the family was one of the last great pleasures of her life, and she was thinking about the menu as she gazed dreamily at a small inflatable globe her granddaughter had given her for Christmas – to help Grandmalita keep track of geography since the glorious collapse of Communism.

Her reverie was cut short by a litany of instructions spewing from her lips: about how Philip must wear a tie to church and the time at which he had been promised to arrive at the Caulfields'; finally, that there was a 'small problem' with their son that was better not discussed. Emptying the breadcrumbs she had swept from the table into the sink, and with her spiritual duty to the English houseguest accomplished, Carlotta blew Philip a kiss and sailed from the kitchen with a grand rustle of her Galanos pleats.

Waiting for the kettle to boil, he tried to collect his thoughts. It seemed like the height of hypocrisy for Hannah to attend church with her husband the morning after Philip had seen her kissing Addison Sloan. How can I face her, he asked himself; or her husband and son? Pouring more milk than he intended into his tea, Philip carried it up to his room.

He washed and carefully trimmed his beard with a small pair of scissors, checking and rechecking the seconds dial on his watch. Then, at exactly half-past ten he changed into the same shirt and navy blazer he had worn to the party, adding to the ensemble the only tie hanging in his closet – a last-minute, duty-free purchase from a Tie Rack kiosk at Heathrow airport. Half expecting the phone to ring and Hannah to ditch him again, he almost wished that she would, saving him the extreme embarrassment of sitting through a church service with the betrayed husband.

The street outside gave the first impression of a ghost town, the homes in Hibiscus Way screened off from each other by tall viburnum hedges to make them feel hidden, forbidden and apart. As Philip approached the pink house with Corinthian columns he noticed a spotless white BMW convertible with the top down standing by the door. He paused to admire the dials and tan interior, then rang the bell. He waited, but there was no answer and Philip, checking his watch, grew anxious that his hosts might not hear the doorbell and think he was late. Trying the handle, he stepped inside.

For a moment or two he was blinded by the intensity of light. It cascaded like a slow-motion waterfall from twenty-foot-high French doors and windows into the living room and foyer, gilding the walls and travertine floor that connected the foyer, open living-cum-family room and kitchen. Jesse's little metal walking frame stood by the front door, and there was another like it at the entrance to the family room.

'Race you downstairs!' he heard Hannah's voice saying from the floor above.

Looking up, Philip saw her skip down a flight of winding stairs in a lime-coloured, ankle-length dress with buttons down one side. She slowed her steps as she neared the bottom, timing her descent so that it would come a few seconds after the elevator door in the foyer slid open. Unaware that he had been standing in front of it, Philip found himself face to face with the large russet-haired man he had seen kissing Hannah the night before, Jesse straddling his shoulders. Only he wasn't the lawyer.

'Good morning.' The man smiled and held out his hand. 'I'm Dr Caulfield.'

Philip almost didn't believe him, so astonishing was his resemblance to the lawyer he had met at the party. Soon, however, he discerned that the doctor was younger and not nearly so well put together as his counterpart. Philip had met his share of dishevelled doctors at Oxford (mainly of philosophy), but none that had seemed quite so out of place in their surroundings.

'I couldn't have managed without your wife,' Philip said when Dr Caulfield began to question him about the sea turtle rescue.

'Princess,' Jesse squealed. 'The turtle's name is Princess.'

Hannah went over to the full-length mirror and lifted one of many hats from a tall stand by the door. She positioned it carefully over her hair, which she had pinned up, smiling at her husband and son in the mirror. Lifting the blue-black sunglasses to her face, she asked the doctor what he thought of them. 'Jesse picked them out.'

'I love them.'

And you, Philip imagined him saying, had they been alone. The image of the pair kissing on the sofa rose before him again, as it had done at various times during the night.

'We had better leave or we'll be late,' said the doctor, looking at his watch.

'Like Aunt Sunny every week!' Jesse tittered as they filed through the door and into the convertible.

There was only just enough room for everyone, with Philip in the narrow back seat. He would have offered to walk had he known the church was so close. It took them only five minutes to arrive at a Spanish-style mission with two open bell towers on either side of a plain wooden cross. Jesse asked to ride on Philip's shoulders when they got out of the car, his parents strolling arm-in-arm a few paces ahead of them, greeting a parade of gaily dressed people heading in the same direction.

'Gethsemane has a lovely garden in back,' Jesse said through the peal of church bells. 'And there's a Tree of Jesse inside one of the stained-glass windows. Ma says they named it for me.'

A breeze rolled in from the ocean, rippling the hem of Hannah's dress and nearly taking her hat. The doctor caught it in mid-air and clumsily replaced it, which brought her hair down. She chided him and laughed, adjusting the hat without breaking their stride, while the church bells pealed and pealed. Hannah looked over her shoulder to make sure that Jesse and Philip weren't far behind, and he noticed her jewellery – a tri-colour gold bangle bracelet, emerald drop earrings and solitaire diamond ring hugging her wedding band. The women they passed were even more richly adorned, wearing designer outfits, high heels and hats, the likes of which Philip had only ever seen at Ascot.

The inside of the church was air-conditioned, sunlight filtering through midnight-blue stained-glass windows above the high altar that turned the bright winter morning to dusk.

'That's my tree up there,' Jesse said, pointing to the central window.

'Ssssh.' Hannah raised a finger to her lips as they entered their pew.

Philip had never been a regular churchgoer. Still, like many children in the UK, his parents had sent him to a Church of England primary school because it nearer than the local state-run school. Philip's father warned him to beware of the clergy, and to take with a grain of salt any 'rubbish dogma' they might try to force on him. But as it turned out they had forced nothing on Philip except, possibly, an appreciation for choral music. And the Mass at Gethsemane-by-the-Sea was all about music. The hymns and order of service adhered closely to what Philip had been used to at St Michael's, making him feel instantly at home. The Caulfields remained seated during Communion and Philip followed their example. He stole a look at Hannah's profile, the sun warming half her face and her head bowed, lips moving in silent prayer and her features animated by the rose-coloured tint of the stained-glass window.

'May the Lord bless you and keep you and shine His light upon you.'

Startled, Philip looked up and saw one of the priests making the sign of the cross over him. The priest moved to Hannah next and placed a small round wafer on her tongue. 'The body of Christ,' he said in a rich Southern voice, lifting the chalice to her lips.

As he progressed through the aisle, giving Communion or a blessing to the elderly and infirm who had also remained seated, Philip noticed that the priest was having difficulty walking. He was young and otherwise robust, with a swarthy complexion and broad shoulders beneath his ceremonial robes.

The congregation charged for the exit as soon as the closing hymn ended. Looking about the church during the postlude Philip recognised Sunny Sloan's flat face and vacant, wide-set eyes among those who had arrived late and were seated nearest the door. The redhead lawyer he had mistaken for Dr Caulfield towered over her like a sentry, and Sunny's peroxide bouffant, flattened where she had slept on it, was clumsily back-combed slightly higher than it had been the previous evening. Dragging her husband by the arm, she came running over to embrace Hannah.

'I see that the Brits have found each other!' she gushed, apparently unaware that she was shouting. A few people turned around, and quickly turned away. 'Say, I've got a swell idea. Why don't we do something different for a change and bring Philip with us to brunch?'

The lawyer shook his head. 'I don't think that's such a good idea, hon. You know how Louisa is about seating at her table. Nothing to do with you,' he added with a friendly nod at Philip.

'But just think of the fun we could have spoiling Louisa's plans,' cried Sunny, blinking furiously in the natural light streaming through the door.

Trapped as they were in a slow line of people waiting to shake hands with the clergy, nothing further was said about brunch. The head vicar, a round-faced man with a shaved head and a diamond ring on his little finger, shook every hand that was offered. Some, Philip noticed, avoided taking his hand – or even looking at him – pretending to be deep in conversations of their own. Philip would have liked to shake hands with the young priest who had blessed him, but he was missing from the assemblage of clerics. At last Philip spotted him, limping painfully across the lawn towards a wisteria-capped courtyard in which a group of disabled children in wheelchairs, some with oxygen tanks, had listened to the Mass through outdoor speakers. He watched as the priest and children from the Sunday School distributed trays of cookies to the handicapped. Feeling a small pressure on his arm Philip became aware of Sunny Sloan leaning against him. They were standing alone to one side and he had no idea what she wanted. But Sunny wanted nothing, her blank stare fixed on the children. Then, suddenly, her expression changed.

'See how they avoid me?' she whispered, glaring at people parting on either side of them. 'They're terrified, every last one of them.'

'Terrified of you?'

'Of what I have.'

'What – what *do* you have?'

Sunny shrugged, her skin the colour of granite. 'Some disease of the heart.' Swaying, she seized Philip to keep from falling. 'I think they may be right,' she muttered.

Their faces were so near that he could smell alcohol – or some mixture of alcohol and breath freshener. And there was no question that people were keeping their distance. 'Come along now, I'll see you to your car,' Philip offered in response to another impatient gesture from the lawyer.

'Too bad they won't have you to brunch. It's all on account of Louisa.'

'Your mother-in-law?'

'Mine and Hannah's Our husbands are half-brothers – Addison the lawyer in the family and Thaddeus the doctor. The bitch wouldn't have produced them any other way.'

HATCHLINGS

Philip draped a moist towel over the turtle and removed the oxygen mask from its beak. Doc Preston, the vet from Delray Beach who had volunteered for the procedure, had just finished sterilising the endoscopy implements and began to insert forceps inside the turtle's throat. Philip, who had dissected frogs in Biology, held his breath as he watched the vet guide the instruments deeper, twisting the forceps this way and that. After what seemed an eternity Doc Preston pulled out a long plastic syringe.

'Heaven only knows what else is in there,' he sighed. 'The last extraction I did was on a manatee up in Jupiter Inlet, and you'll never guess what I found.'

Philip loved manatees, the bovine, sweet-natured water mammals that reminded him of the walrus in Lewis Carroll's poem — and were also on the list of the most endangered species.

'Hospital waste, with the manufacturer's label still on it. I felt like calling the eight hundred number printed on it and giving them hell.'

'Or calling the hospital,' Philip suggested.

'But which one? Where do we begin? At least there are no plastic straws in this poor critter. Straws are the absolute worst, because they rupture the intestines.'

They did the cleaning up in a cheerless silence. When they finished Philip placed a clean towel over Princess's carapace and reattached the oxygen mask. 'What do you suppose are its chances?' he asked.

'About fifty-fifty. And that's pretty good, overall. I'm afraid you're gonna have one hell of a time convincing Islanders that their paradise is a graveyard.'

'Yet everyone I meet tells me how excited they are about the marine life initiative.'

'What they really mean is that they're excited about the next big fundraising party *for* the initiative. There's a difference, you know.'

'Yes, I know,' Philip said gloomily. 'Where did you learn to do extractions?'

'I apprenticed with an old-timer over by Lake Okeechobee and got my training on the job. Most of my business these days is handling gators for the Florida Department of Wildlife. Not so very long ago, up in Vero, I found twenty-four dog collars in the belly of one of 'em.'

'Why are they so vicious?'

'Less vicious than just plain hungry. I should think a learned fellow like you would be familiar with their preferred method of consumption.'

Philip confessed that he knew very little about alligators, having taken up marine biology in his final year at university.

'A gator's likely to snap up any tasty-lookin' specimen that comes along. He'll break its back, then drag it down to the bottom of its lair inside the bog. They're a patient lot, these gators, and they'll keep the body hid till it's nice and decomposed. And that,' Doc Preston said, smacking his lips, 'is when the banquet begins.'

That evening, while thinking about the extraction and what he had learned from it, Philip tried to blot out the vet's grizzly commentary. Turtle nesting season was due to begin in the morning, and Philip planned to get up at dawn to check the beach for signs of overnight activity. He was about to turn off the light when the extension phone next to his bed started to beep, the button on a panel labelled *Guest Annexe* blinking red. Only vaguely aware that he even had a phone, he lifted the receiver.

It was, Philip thought, a measure of Dr Caulfield's dignity that he called to apologise for his sister-in-law's performance. 'You must have thought us very rude not to ask you to brunch. But you would understand better if you knew my mother.'

The line went quiet as he waited for Philip to say something. When he didn't, the doctor said: 'I leave for New York in the morning – my usual run – and I'd be much indebted if you would take a small interest in my boy. He's fascinated with anything to do with the sea and, well, with me away during the week, Jesse has only his mother to keep him company. He's got health issues, to be sure, but he's spry and the fresh air and sunshine are so good for his health…'

'Of course. I'd love to help.'

Philip rose at first light and packed his rucksack with everything the textbooks had said he might need. Then he slipped quietly down to the kitchen, grabbed a carton of Gatorade and jogged to the beach. The sun rose molten from the rim of the ocean, spilling over its glassy surface, the air moist and very still except for the cry of seagulls. Philip's heartbeat quickened when he spied flipper tracks covering a wide area, as if a tank had criss-crossed an entire stretch of beach during the night. He would have to act swiftly, choosing which of the newly laid mounds seemed most vulnerable to predators and move them to a safer location. The procedure would have to be accomplished in the first twelve hours of incubation, when the eggs were least susceptible to injury, and Philip set to it at once. He had just finished relocating the second mound when he saw Hannah come through the picket fence.

She waved, carrying Jesse on her hip and a canvas beach bag slung over her shoulder. Hannah wore a one-piece, bright red swimsuit and Jesse a pair of Hawaiian-print bathing trunks. Smiling as she lowered her son to the ground next to Philip, Hannah removed a beach towel from the canvas bag and spread it on the sand.

'We didn't think you had had breakfast,' she said, handing Philip a Thermos filled with English Breakfast tea. 'And here's some cornbread, fresh from the oven I'm afraid it's from a mix,' she said. 'But very good.'

Philip drank thirstily from the Thermos, stuffing chunks of cornbread into his mouth while he continued to dig. Jesse followed his movements, asking detailed questions at each stage of the procedure.

'Using a spade to retrieve the eggs risks damaging them,' Philip explained. 'So we always use our hands, digging straight down in a scooping fashion to make a narrow cylindrical hole. The sand between your fingers will begin to feel looser as you approach the clutch, but still well packed. Here, you try it.'

Philip guided the boy's hand down the hole until they felt the sand near the top of the egg chamber begin to give way. 'Feel the eggs with your fingers if you can,' he said. 'It won't hurt them if you're gentle.'

Jesse's eyes shone from behind the immense goggles as he helped Philip transfer the remaining eggs to their new home. 'Now comes the hard bit – how to camouflage the relocated nest in a way that keeps out animal predators and alerts beachgoers to keep their distance.'

Philip reached inside his rucksack and removed a roll of wire mesh and the implements he had brought to build the cage.

'Like a chicken coop,' Jesse laughed.

Hannah insisted on helping and they laboured without pause for nearly an hour. From time to time she paused to look up and down what appeared to be an empty beach. But as everyone on the Island knew, the windows and terraces of the houses peering through the palm trees and over the tops of hedges had eyes – and a few powerful telescopes. Islanders had a knack for latching on to any whiff of intrigue, and the handsome English oceanographer had begun to attract their attention. Hannah, who had never entirely got used to the heat, felt as if she were suffocating.

Brushing the sand from her legs, she jumped to her feet. 'It's getting awfully close out here, poppet,' she said. 'Let's cool off with a swim.'

Jesse didn't want to leave, and clung to his mother as she lifted him on to her back, wrapping his scrawny legs round her waist and his arms round her neck as she trotted with him across the hot sand. Watching them plunge into an oncoming wave Philip marvelled at Hannah's courage to venture into a stretch of ocean known for rip currents. Yet she showed no fear, pressing further and further into the deep, while the water around her turned from a transparent blue to slate green.

Philip followed their progress, Jesse's head bobbing on the waves as he clung to his mother's back. Blinded by the reflecting light, for a few moments Philip lost sight of them. Throwing down his hammer and posts he dived into the water; the ocean was welcoming and deliciously cool, its sandy bottom dotted with seashells and blue crabs darting beneath his fast-moving shadow. Advancing with powerful strokes he swam underwater nearly the entire way until, Jesse screaming with delight, Philip caught up with the pair.

PART TWO

The Molten Looking Glass

BAD POETRY

Hannah was hardly unfamiliar with water, having grown up on the North Sea. But she didn't learn to swim until she came to Palm Beach.

For one thing, it had rained a good deal in Northumbria. For another, and no matter what the season, the wind had an edge to it and the sky above Hannah's tiny village was the same gunpowder grey as the sea. There was always dampness in the air due to the amount of rainfall, making the grass grow greener and flowers more abundant. Stitchwort, pansies, red campion and roses overflowed the window boxes and kitchen gardens, with the predictable result that the village florist did hardly any business between May and October.

Hannah grew up in a narrow Victorian terraced house with a monkey-puzzle tree in the front yard. Instead of leaves the tree had razor-sharp triangular scales that endowed its silhouette, particularly at dusk, with a dragon-like appearance. As a child Hannah lived in fear of the tree coming indoors, especially during the stretch of time after school when neither of her parents were home. Once a week Gran came over on the bus from Bamburgh, bringing a Jemima bag filled with packets of biscuits or Welsh cakes from the bakery, and they would watch the afternoon matinee on the telly. When the films ended Gran would put the kettle on for tea, leafing through *Woman's Weekly* while Hannah did her homework.

'Never mind,' and a pat on the shoulder were Gran Burleigh's remedy for any sort of ailment. Hannah believed her, repeating those two magic words like a mantra on the afternoons when she was home by herself. Her mum often worked till seven as a manicurist at a hotel spa in Berwick-on-Tweed and sometimes didn't come home until the following day. Mr Burleigh travelled the country selling wholesale kitchen appliances and returned on weekends. Every few months or so the parents would pack up the Vauxhall and go somewhere, and then Gran would come to stay.

'Children aren't allowed,' Mum would say when Hannah was old enough to ask if she could go with them.

'Never mind,' Gran consoled as they watched the door shut behind them. 'You don't want nothing to do with the bunch they're going to be with.'

Hannah loved being with Gran. They watched television and baked and never tired of playing Sorry! The time passed much too quickly before the motor sounded in the drive again and the parents were heard arguing even before they had properly come through the door.

In a part of England where the armies of Lancaster and York had once clashed up and down the Northumbrian coast, the only sound of discord in Hannah's day was of her parents' endless bickering. Her chance to escape came at the end of secondary school, when she won a national poetry competition, followed by a scholarship to study at Durham University. The triumph, however, proved as short-lived as Hannah's education; for by the time she returned home at the end of her first year she was four months pregnant and felt ten years older.

Hannah discussed it with her mum straight away. They sat down in the kitchen, where the house always retained less of the damp. Mrs Burleigh had just come from work and was still in her hotel uniform. She was tired, and despite her make-up, or perhaps because of it, looked nearly the same age as Gran as she studied with tightly compressed lips the gingham-patterned oilcloth covering the table. 'It's so working class,' she sighed and sighed.

'But, Mum, we *are* working class.'

'I'd hoped you'd want for more.'

Hannah did want more. Well, more than this, she thought, following her mum's gaze to the Asda crockery drying in the sink and sound of the washing machine churning out the daily load. Her eyes rested a long time on the clothes drying on the airer next to the Aga, considering perhaps the volumes of soiled fabric a baby would produce. Feeling as if she were about to be sick again, Hannah rose from the table and hurried from the kitchen.

Mr Burleigh received the news when he came home the next day. His fleshy neck above the stiff shirt collar turned more pink as he ripped off his tie, but in the end he said nothing. This was hardly what he wanted to hear after slaving all week to put the girl through school. They spoke little during dinner and, as was the family's custom when the dishes were cleared, carried their tea and Victoria sponge to the lounge to watch *Potter*. But as soon as the programme ended the parents began to bicker. Almost anything triggered it, as if the pair didn't know any other way to communicate. The sound of their exchanges trailed behind them like an odour, from the lounge up to their bedroom. That night, as Hannah lay in bed with hands clasped over her ears, reliving a childhood of similar late-night rows, she made a shattering discovery through the paper-thin walls of the narrow house. For it turned out that Hannah too had been the result of an unwanted pregnancy and was the primary cause of her parents' unhappiness. And so on and so forth, even later than usual into the night.

Silence returned at breakfast. In the tenuous light showing through the kitchen curtains Hannah began to see that what had happened to her parents seventeen years ago, and had now also happened to her, was either an unfortunate coincidence or a family curse – in the absence of which she would not exist.

As on every Saturday that Hannah could remember Mrs Burleigh was busy scribbling her weekly grocery list as she drank her morning tea, impatient to finish shopping at Morrison's before it grew busy. But before leaving the table she took the time to place a small pamphlet next to Hannah's bowl of Weetabix. Still saying nothing, she patted her daughter on the shoulder and walked with hurrying steps from the kitchen.

Hannah opened the leaflet, which contained a brief description of a clinic in Newcastle-on-Tyne where unwanted pregnancies could be legally terminated. She wondered how her mother had obtained this information so quickly. Perhaps Mum had been to the clinic or knew someone who had. Glancing anxiously at her father, Hannah was unable to detect any sign of life behind the pages of *The Racing Post*, in which he had kept his face buried all through breakfast.

She went to the sink to do the washing up, rooks shrieking in the yard and the washer droning beneath the counter. Half turning to the table Hannah caught her father's bloodshot eyes peering over the rim of the newsprint to see whether she had taken the leaflet. It filled her with pity to see red-faced, middle-aged Harry Burleigh like this; who, like her mum, had for too long put happiness on hold for her sake. To show her gratitude Hannah went back to the table and took the brochure. Holding it visibly in her hand, she wished her dad success at the races. 'Maybe this time your horse will win,' she said hopefully.

'I wish,' he replied.

Back up in her room Hannah sat on the unmade bed, hugging her knees as she waited for her father to leave for the racetrack. The room hadn't been tidied for her arrival and there was dust on the furniture and oak floorboards. Never mind, Hannah thought as she repacked the soft leather Jemima bag with which she had arrived. At length she heard her father's footsteps in the hall and the front door close behind him. Shouldering the bag that was all she had left of Gran, Hannah took a last look at her childhood. At Little Miss No Name and Mrs Beasley nodding goodbye from their perch at the child's dressing table edged with ruffles: the lustre of the pink Yardley cosmetic jars and Lucite mirror, brush and comb set that had shone so brightly when Hannah was thirteen, grown as dull as the indifferent gaze of the North Sea in the window.

Mrs Burleigh was a fast shopper and Hannah didn't want to still be here when she returned. Walking stealthily down the narrow stairs, she lifted her old Barbour waterproof from the coat rack in the hall, threw it over her shoulder and opened the door a crack. The street outside looked just as it always did, with a car parked in front of each narrow, grey-brick terraced house and not a soul in sight: the air misty, and the sky thickly overlaid with clouds. Walking bravely past the monkey-puzzle tree, Hannah shut the gate in its face and hurried to meet the train.

She was sick twice on the journey back to Durham. Gazing at the fields and pastures through the sooty window of her compartment she felt again the anticipation of the first time she had boarded the same train bound for Durham. Thinking back on her year at university she remembered the wonder of it, the highlight of which had been James Muir's lectures on Romantic English poetry. But by the time the train trundled into Durham station Hannah's thoughts took a darker turn, moving forward in time to the afternoon, not so very long ago, when she had informed the poet that she was expecting his child.

She had gone to see him at his office in Hallgarth House. The door was closed with a 'Tutorial in Progress' sign pinned above Muir's nameplate, and Hannah took a seat on a bench by the window. On just the other side of the glass, buds were sprouting inside the wet branches of a tall birch tree. Watching them, Hannah likened the budding branches to the little fist of life growing inside her and composed a small haiku poem about the shoots. Gazing dreamily through the window pane, she noticed that it was still smudged with traces of rain from the previous winter: the same period in which, behind the now closed door of Muir's office, Hannah and the poet had become lovers.

She remembered every detail: their first outing to Lindisfarne, where, trapped by the tide, they had spent the night at a guesthouse on Holy Island. Muir had asked for a large double room with a view of the sea, and that evening treated Hannah to her first gourmet meal. A fire had simmered in an immense Tudor fireplace near their table, filling the dining room with a smell of pine needles and smoke. Hannah, who had been shivering in the car, felt the warmth from the grate spill through her as she took her first sips of wine. She talked and Muir listened – about her life so far and dream of becoming a poet. Muir nodded attentively, refilling her glass and, so it seemed, drinking in every nuance of her narrative. Then, almost as if he hadn't heard anything she had said, he spread open her hands and kissed her palms.

'You are beautiful,' he whispered.

Hannah knew that she wasn't, but she liked hearing the poet say it. Later, as she followed him dutifully up to their room, she even began believing it.

'I have something for you,' he said as he bolted the door. It was a new edition of his collected poems, which he had inscribed: 'For Hannah Burleigh, who turns my teaching into poetry.' Leading her over to the bed he asked her to read to him.

She began reciting the lines slowly, then with more abandon, the poet's eyes caressing her. Once or twice he seemed to want to correct her but didn't. Then, all at once, like a siren song or dirge, they heard a mournful wail from below their window.

'I can hear the mermaids singing…' Hannah began.

Muir acknowledged the quote. 'But the sound you hear is coming from seals, not mermaids.' Lifting the book from her hand, he placed it on the nightstand. 'There are hundreds of such creatures among the rocks – slippery and black as the night, they only come out after dark.'

Hannah, trembling, watched him turn off the light: afraid less of what he might do to her than of disappointing him.

There were other outings, including one to Edinburgh where Muir was feted at a poetry reading. Hannah, seated among the audience, pretending they didn't know each other, felt as if she mattered for the first time in her life.

When at length the door to Muir's office swung inwards Hannah recognised a shy girl from Iona who lived on her floor at the dormitory. For a moment or two the girl stood in the doorway, unaware that Hannah was watching her. Her normally pale cheeks flushed, and her thin, bluish lips curled up into a smile.

Hannah rose from the bench and, nodding hello, took the girl's place in the door. She entered Muir's office without knocking, fully aware of the gravity of what she was about to tell him. She hadn't come expecting an offer of marriage. Muir, after all, was already married. He had never hidden that from her, as he hadn't hidden his London wife – whom he described as 'not altogether right in the head,' but to whom he remained married for the sake of their son. Rather than feel jealous, Hannah had admired Muir's sense of duty towards his slightly mad wife and their son, giving her hope that once their baby was born he would display the same fidelity to his new family. She imagined them sharing a bohemian life in some cottage by the sea, with Muir coming and going while she raised the child. Hannah pictured herself wearing a long peasant dress, picking sea heather among the dunes with her baby in a sling on her back: the nights, seals singing in the distance, filled with poetry and love. Eventually, she thought, they might have more children, and by then Muir would be free.

These and other images flipped like index cards through her mind as she stood in the door of Muir's office. The poet was sitting at his desk, gazing meditatively out the window and smoking his pipe. Hannah felt a surge of intimacy with this man, her eyes passing lovingly over the slope of his back, the leather wing chair in the corner, books of poems on the shelf and crumpled papers in the waste basket: the wonderful inky smell of Muir's blotter.

She cleared her throat and he gave a start, swivelling his seat round with a look of annoyance. Seeing that it was Hannah he gestured with the stem of his pipe that she take her usual place in the wing chair. She did as he directed, the leather still warm from the girl who had just vacated the seat.

Hannah began to speak, and Muir listened. He let her talk, as he had done on their first night together at Lindisfarne. At some point she realised that she was beginning to repeat herself, and still he listened, or seemed to, without comment. When at length the poet rose from his chair it was to open the window and let out some of the cigar smoke. The sound of bells from Durham Cathedral broke the silence, and when they stopped ringing he said: 'I trust that none of this has upset you.'

Hannah assured him that it hadn't.

But she was aware of the difficulties.

'Well, yes.'

What she heard next seemed to come from someone else in the room. Even the poet's voice changed, becoming deeper and more like it sounded when he was teaching class. The foetus – Hannah was quite sure that was the word he used – would have to be terminated – immediately if possible. 'Waiting only makes this sort of thing harder.'

'This sort of thing?'

Muir was a short, solidly built man. He was scrupulous about his appearance and always wore a waistcoat and bow tie, his straight, longish hair parted down the middle. His pipes were made of briar and his collection of leather notebooks were embossed with his initials. There was a touch of Swinging Sixties flamboyance in his manner that was appealing even when, at times, it felt artificial. One was always aware of his presence even when he was silent – as Muir was now. Thumbing through a small black moleskin notebook he removed from his waistcoat he jotted on a piece of paper the name and address of what he described as 'a first-rate private clinic,' adding: 'I shall of course take care of the expenses.'

Then, leaning to one side of his seat, he pulled out his wallet and removed a wad of twenty-pound notes. He didn't count the notes, but added to them the scrap of paper with the name of the clinic and placed the lot inside a brown business envelope from inside his desk. His movements were practiced, like a man paying one bill among many. Giving Hannah a look that left no room for discussion, Muir leaned across his desk and held out the envelope.

It took Hannah somewhat longer than it should have to understand that he wasn't going to get up. She looked searchingly at the envelope that contained more notes than she had ever seen outside a bank, trying to think of something to say. But every word that came to mind froze on her tongue. Finally she took it, weighing the bundle briefly in her hand before quietly retracing her steps to the wing chair. Picking the rucksack with her schoolbooks up off the floor she tucked the envelope next to the haiku poem she had meant to read to him and went to the door.

Since then, Hannah had somehow passed her exams and returned home. There, the verdict had been the same: a slip of paper with the name of a clinic, followed by another full stop. Now, as she climbed the footbridge over the River Wear towards the city centre she wondered why she had come back to Durham. What did I expect to find that hadn't been here before? she thought, gazing up at the immense tower of the Norman cathedral. Feeling another wave of nausea, she hurried inside to look for a seat.

The pews, however, had been cleared to make room for visitors to the tomb of St Cuthbert, for whom the twelfth-century cathedral had been built as a shrine, and there was nowhere to sit. Choral evensong had begun, and the smell of incense and hot beeswax made Hannah feel a touch lightheaded. 'O God, make speed to save us, O Lord, make haste to help us,' the choristers chanted antiphonally. Afraid that she might lose her balance and fall, she placed her hand on the saint's tomb.

Several minutes passed. Feeling somewhat better, Hannah was about to leave when she discovered that she couldn't lift her hand – as if it were fastened to the shrine. She tried again and again, and finally gave up. Feeling drowsy from her uphill hike from the station, she rested her cheek against the cold grey stones of the tomb. Suddenly, hearing a voice that seemed to come from the tomb, Hannah jumped and her hand came free.

Perhaps, she thought afterwards, it had something to do with the angelic voice of the choristers and quality of light falling through the stained-glass windows. Yet what happened next was in some respects even more astonishing: a sensation that felt like tiny air bubbles popping against the walls of her abdomen. In the days, weeks and months ahead the sensation would become more familiar. But at that instant, the first time Jesse kicked inside Hannah's womb, it felt like an omen.

Using some of the money Muir had given her she checked into one of the rooms of her old dormitory that were let out to tourists in the summer. Sitting on the narrow cot before daybreak Hannah composed the first of her letters to the poet, ending it with: 'I've returned to Durham and must see you.'

She posted the letter to Muir's home in Highgate, north London. It was where his fan mail was addressed – the place to which Hannah knew he returned every weekend without fail. And yet, as much as he had admired her poems, Hannah's prose seemed not to affect him at all, for she received no response to her letter, or to the next three she posted.

It occurred to her that Muir might not be receiving them. Could his wife be intercepting his mail? Had the family gone away for the summer? Time was passing and Hannah had to do something. Even Durham seemed no longer the same, its once familiar streets, curio and book shops somehow more remembered than real. Hannah felt isolated, as she had increasingly become during her affair with Muir. All the same, she dreaded running into someone she knew. The superintendent of the dormitory had remembered her as a student and was beginning to ask questions. When he asked why she hadn't gone home yet, Hannah knew that her time was up.

Trying to decide what to do, she wandered over to Hallgarth House. A cleaning crew was busy mopping the corridors and had left the doors open. Hannah slipped inside the building and climbed the stairs to Muir's cubicle on the second floor. She found the door ajar and the window open, the morning light slanting over the wing chair and knots in the oak floor. She went over to the leather seat and curled her feet beneath her, leaning her head against its high back. She closed her eyes, remembering how the radiators had clanged and the wind howled in the window the first time Muir crossed the forbidden boundary of his desk and, leaning over the wing chair, had kissed her.

Silencing her sobs, she reached inside the Jemima bag, rummaging past the envelope with the money and slips of paper with the addresses of private clinics. Near the bottom of the bag she found the old notebook with the haiku poem she had written for Muir and ripped the page out. Crushing it in her hand she aimed it perfectly across the room and tossed it in the bin.

'Never mind,' she whispered to the little life inside her as she went over to the poet's desk. Sitting in his seat she selected a biro from his pencil holder, removed a clean page from the notebook and began a new letter. This one was to her parents. Brief and to the point, it said only what needed to be said: asking for nothing and offering nothing in return.

PEACOCK

She arrived at King's Cross station by the overnight train on a clear midsummer morning. The chimneyed rooftops and red-brick buildings of Bloomsbury shone with the brightness of a landscape that seemed filled with promise. Not far from the station Hannah noticed a 'To Let' sign for a furnished bedsit on the fifth floor of a Victorian terraced house in Regent Square. The landlady, who lived on the ground floor, opened the door, took one look at Hannah and asked when the baby was due. Hannah flushed. It was the first time anyone had guessed that she was pregnant – and the first time anyone had smiled about it.

The bedsit had a window overlooking St George's Gardens at the back, and Hannah paid the first month's rent with what remained of Muir's money. It was still dark when she rose the next morning, and with a cup of tea in one hand and a biro in the other she pored through the classifieds columns of the *Sunday Express*. Hannah didn't hold out much hope for a single-mother-to-be at a time when Britain was tottering on the verge of bankruptcy and the Chancellor of the Exchequer had just announced (on page two of the *Express*) that the rate of inflation was fourteen per cent. She circled every opening the paper listed for a sales clerk, office receptionist, childminder or cleaning woman, and at the start of business hours set out for Oxford Street.

Every seat in the windowless waiting room was full. Looking around her, Hannah hoped that they hadn't all come seeking the same sales clerk position in the Books & Stationery department of Debenham's. They might, for instance, be applying for janitorial, secretarial or bookkeeping jobs, for none of which Hannah was qualified but was willing to try.

She rose as soon as she heard her name called. A pencil-thin woman stood waiting in one of the doorways that had until now been shut. The woman stood aside to let Hannah pass and told her to sit. Holding an application form with what Hannah recognised as her own distinctive handwriting – more square than slanted in a running hand that made it look acceptably cursive – the woman, who did not introduce herself, took the seat opposite her at a table not much bigger than a school desk. She read out Hannah's name and address from the application and reminded her that the country was in a severe recession and people were not in any mood to shop.

'We have ten applicants for every sales position.'

Hannah indicated that she understood this.

'How long have you resided at No. 5 Regent Square?'

'Since yesterday. I've only just arrived in London.'

'Where did you arrive from?'

'From the North, ma'am.'

'How old are you?'

'Eighteen, ma'am,' Hannah lied.

'Do you live alone?'

Hannah nodded.

'I see you spent a year at university. Why have you left school?'

Hannah explained that it was to do with money. 'I need a job, ma'am.'

'To finish school?'

Hannah remained silent.

At last the woman looked up from the papers on her desk. 'Do you understand the question?'

'I understand it perfectly. But I'm not sure how to answer. In case it makes you not want to give me a job.'

'And why would I do that?'

'Because I'm going to have a baby in November, ma'am, and that does rather complicate things.'

A week into her new position a leather-bound journal was returned due to a defect in the binding and Hannah asked the floor manager if she could keep it. During her lunch and tea breaks in the employee canteen, sitting by herself at one of the laminated tables, she began writing poetry again.

By autumn Hannah had a proper baby bump and was fitted for a larger work uniform. Motherhood became more real as more people, even strangers, began congratulating her. Each week she diligently set aside a portion of her pay cheque for baby items that she purchased in-store with her employee discount. The tiny, poorly lit bedsit in Regent Square grew more cheerful the more it came to resemble a nursery. On the day Hannah's former classmates at Durham were registering for the fall term she splurged on a charming Beatrix Potter-themed bassinet. She almost had enough money saved up for a stroller when, two weeks before her due date she began to bleed and was rushed for an emergency delivery at University College Hospital.

She named her son Jesse James Muir. On the line of the birth certificate asking for the father's name, she wrote 'James Muir', wondering if any of the staff would recognise it. No one mentioned it if they did, and after spending a week in an overcrowded maternity ward Hannah brought her baby home to Regent Square. She wrote Muir another letter, the shortest yet, full of motherly pride at the arrival of their son, and enclosed a poem she had written to mark the occasion. She closed the letter with just her first name and address: No. 5 Regent Square, three miles from the poet's home in Highgate.

Having looked older than she was during her pregnancy, once Hannah had given birth she looked suddenly younger – to the point that people assumed she and Jesse were brother and sister when she took him with her to the shops in the new Brunswick Centre. From their top-floor bedsit, ever present through the window facing the St George's Gardens, loomed the weather-beaten, red-brick fortress of London's oldest Foundling Hospital. For three centuries before it closed its doors the hospital had served as a place of refuge for any child left on its doorstep. Pacing in its shadow at night with her restless infant, Hannah began to comprehend the magnitude of what she had let herself in for.

The landlady took a keen interest in the young single mother and her child. A colossal figure who went by the name Peacock – no one in Regent Square could remember the landlady being called anything else – she offered to watch the baby on the days Hannah was at work. The young mother was delighted and refused to be bothered by Peacock's somewhat odd appearance: her carpetbag robes, spiked silver hair that rose like a corona round her head and tapestried slippers that she wore both indoors and out. It never occurred to Hannah to doubt Peacock's occasionally unreasonable assertions about her past, or question the late-night visits from suspicious-looking men, some hauling suitcases – visitations that were typically followed a day or two later by a knock on the door from the local authorities.

The five slender floors of the landlady's townhouse were connected by a corkscrew staircase that allowed limited privacy for tenants. Poking about her home at all hours – Peacock had a key to every bedsit – she insisted that, whether they liked it or not, her lodgers were 'part of the family'. Bumping into her late at night in the narrows of the stairwell was not for the faint of heart, causing about half of all new tenants to leave after a month or two. Those who stayed never left.

Toiling up the corkscrew stairs at night, knees popping and steps creaking beneath her, Peacock would climb to the summit to see whether she might, with her vast experience of childrearing − 'and child-beating', she laughed − do something to quiet Hannah's infant. As a last resort, and to give her lodgers respite, the landlady, wearing her slippers and a shawl thrown over the carpetbag tunic, would escort the young mother and her noisy bundle into St George's Gardens at the rear of the house. She knew a secret way in that bypassed the locked gates at night, and there the two women would pace the gravel paths until Jesse's lungs gave out and he fell into an exhausted sleep. Peacock, who loved to talk, would entertain Hannah with titbits of local lore. For instance, that in the previous century No. 5 Regent Square had served as one of a chain of charity shelters for homeless women waiting to give birth; so that as soon as the babies arrived they could be dispatched to the Foundling Hospital and the mothers sent to work.

'Most went back on the streets − till they showed up 'ere agin.'

Finally, during one of their nocturnal tours of the gardens, the landlady offered some practical advice. 'Your little one, luv, seems to me − 'ow shall I put it? − not altogether right. 'Ave you thought of 'avin' 'im checked?'

Hannah nodded weakly. Yes, of course she had thought of it. But it was finally on Peacock's advice that she brought Jesse to the nearby Great Ormond Street Children's Hospital for observation. Tests soon showed that he had been born with a hole in his heart, cataracts in his eyes and progressive renal dysfunction.

'It makes me love him more,' Hannah wept quietly to herself each time she was told of something else that was wrong with her son.

They soldiered on, with Peacock watching him while Hannah sold books and stationery at Debenham's and the neighbours complained about the noise. It took several more weeks for Jesse to be admitted to the Great Ormond Street Hospital, and worse news followed. Tumours had developed on his kidneys and were spreading quickly to other organs. It was now only a matter of time, sighed every attending physician on the ward.

Hannah penned a final letter to Muir. She no longer pleaded for affection, or even kindness, but for his assistance with the mounting cost of their son's treatment. Having received no reply to any of her petitions and hanging from the cliff edge of despair, she decided to pay the poet a house call.

She went on a Friday afternoon, hoping to intercept him on his way home for the weekend. Hannah walked the entire three miles from Jesse's hospital room in Portland Street to Highgate Hill. It was her first outing since she had given birth and she gazed with childlike wonder at the bric-a-brac shops in Camden, longing to stop and look at their wares and have a hot Cornish pasty from one of the outdoor food stalls. But she was afraid of missing Muir's arrival, and dreaded ringing the doorbell in case she came face to face with his wife. So she marched on, the November sky lowering like a pewter lid that turned the afternoon to dusk. Schoolchildren, raucous at the start of the weekend, jostled each other on the pavement as Hannah pushed past them.

She quickened her pace through hilly Hampstead and continued up Highgate Hill. The sky above the Heath grew muddied with the smoke of chimney fires, and it was nearly dark by the time Hannah reached an address she knew by heart. She posted herself on the pavement outside Muir's home and inspected the windows, some of which were already lit: wondering which was his study and which the bedroom in which he slept with his wife. It had been a rainy autumn, and the iron-grey bricks of the house were patch-worked with damp. Looking round one side to the back of the building, Hannah caught her breath when she saw the tombstones and statues of Highgate Cemetery showing through the leafless trees, rooks shrieking in the branches of a tall cedar of Lebanon.

It began to rain, falling softly and stealing what remained of the light. A moment or two later the streetlamps came on, lifting Hannah's shield of darkness at the very instant that she heard footsteps on the pavement opposite. A boy of about eleven or twelve came splashing through the puddles in a forest-green mackintosh, kicking the water ahead of him like a football. When he reached the poet's house he stopped and placed his hand on the gate. Turning slowly, as if he had just remembered something, the boy looked over his shoulder and saw Hannah.

It's Muir's son, she thought, noticing tufts of sandy hair beneath his rain bonnet. They studied each other with guarded curiosity, Hannah's thoughts darting from the boy at the gate to the poet's other son, confined to a hospital bed and with only a few months to live. Her eyes pooled with tears, and she was seized with a sudden longing to take this boy, a stranger, into her arms and hold him. No longer able to see clearly, she extended her arm towards him and stepped into the road.

The boy charged through the iron gate, letting it clang shut behind him, and ran towards the house. The door opened and a woman in a dowdy housecoat and shearling slippers appeared in the rectangle of light. Something in Hannah snapped when she saw the woman's lined face and the naked fear with which she herded the boy protectively indoors. Hannah fled, running to the corner of Swain's Lane just as the No. 174 double-decker came through the roundabout. So intense was her need to get away that she jumped aboard the bus while it was still moving and, her heart pounding, clambered to the open top. Shivering beneath a steady rain she sobbed all the way back to Bloomsbury.

It was the patients' dinner hour when she reached the hospital. A dozen trays stood stacked on trolleys in Jesse's ward – causing Hannah to suppose that the heavy-set, red-haired man in a white frock coat standing next to her son's bed was one of the kitchen staff. The man looked up at the sound of her footsteps crossing the linoleum floor. Smiling, he held out his hand and introduced himself as head oncologist at Memorial Hospital in New York.

The cancers, he told Hannah, had spread to her son's liver. Infants born with oculocerebrorenal syndrome (how easily he pronounced it) typically developed tumours on their eyes and kidneys, but Jesse had a more virulent form of cancer that was spreading quickly to his other organs.

Hannah, who had heard much of this before, if not in such precise terms, her eyes red from crying, burst into tears again.

The doctor placed his hand on her shoulder. 'I came to London to present my research at an international conference at the Royal Marsden. One of the oncologists I met there has been treating your son and asked me to examine him.' The doctor spoke in a soft American dialect Hannah had never heard before. 'Having analysed lab samples of every type of tumour growing in your son's body, I have an idea that might interest you.'

Afterwards, what she remembered most about this encounter was the passion with which Thaddeus had described his research. 'I recently began using monoclonal antibodies to slow, and in some cases reverse, the spread of tumours in mice and human tissue. The type of cancer the treatment has been shown to be most effective against is the same as the one your son has. The serum I am developing has never been tried on humans but, with your permission, I'm willing to give it a shot.'

The doctor paused.

'But I can't promise anything.'

But to Hannah's ears, everything about the appearance of this rumpled-looking man at Jesse's bedside, on a bleak November evening when she had lost all hope, felt promising. It was a chance she knew she would be mad not to take.

THE SECRET LIFE OF CORALS

Ten years and four thousand miles from Bloomsbury, Muir's other son had an idea for how to save the coral reefs. With Julietta as his helper – whom he had put in charge of Princess – Philip was finally able to turn his attention to research on bioluminescent dinoflagellates. It had been the subject of his Oxford thesis, winning him first-class honours, and Philip hoped to spend a part of each day gathering live samples from the Island's offshore reef. Beyond the thrill of exploring the undersea world he saw it as an opportunity to begin a whole new line of research: one he hoped would prove beyond doubt that the chemical balance between glowing marine algae, crustaceans and corals could predict the health of oceans.

'Uh-oh.' Julietta brought her face to the window. 'I think we have a visitor.'

Looking up from his microscope Philip recognised the Silver Shadow that had met him in Miami, crawling like a tank across the pebbled drive. Jerzy, the chauffeur who had rescued him at the airport, jumped out and held the rear door open for a substantially built woman who seemed well into her eighties. He held his arm out to assist her and she leaned against him as she lumbered with some difficulty from the back seat. Standing up at last, the woman, attired in a loose-fitting kaftan and a raffia hat swathed in cream-coloured tulle, gave her helper an endearing smile. Dangling what looked like a knitting bag with a designer label from her other arm, picking at the pebbles on the path with the ivory tip of her folded parasol, she proceeded with heavy steps to the door of the institute.

'Looks like Mrs Vine is paying you a call,' Julietta tittered.

Philip scrambled to put away his slides, trying to remember the beginning of the speech he had prepared for the all-important first meeting with his benefactress.

'Well, well,' she exclaimed when he held open the door. 'No one can say I haven't got a knack for picking handsome men!' Winking at Julietta: 'And I can even do it sight unseen.'

The jewels on the old lady's plump fingers and around her wrists shed a rainbow of colours over the tulle as she lifted the veil from her face to inspect the candidate. A scent of gardenias and pressed powder escaped briefly into the air, mingling strangely with the odour of canker from the turtle's carapace. 'I've brought you dears something to brighten the day,' she said, signalling to the chauffeur. 'But first you must tell me what you've been up to here – your plans, dreams – in short, everything!'

Philip glanced at Julietta for guidance, but for once the girl seemed to have gone mute. 'Well, as I mentioned to you when we spoke on the phone...' He launched into a lengthy discourse on his research with bioluminescent dinoflagellates, not sure how much the old woman understood. 'These are the samples I've been gathering from the reef and hope to begin seeding in the lab,' he said, showing her the slides.

'Seeding?'

Mrs Vine, who had understood everything, bombarded Philip with one razor-sharp question after another. He rose to the challenge, addressing her queries, and concluded with: 'The implications for the Island's residents couldn't be more serious. Given the present health of the reef I would predict that, possibly much sooner than anyone here thinks possible, this whole place will be underwater.'

'With dolphins and sea creatures swimming through the rooms of my house?' Mrs Vine's violet-green eyes shimmered. 'What a charming notion.'

'It's been underwater before,' said Julietta. 'According to my earth science textbook half of Florida was once a lagoon.'

Mrs Vine raised an eyebrow. 'I think that must have been before I arrived, dear.'

'A good hundred thousand years before anyone arrived!'

'Well, we won't let that happen, will we? After all, it's the reason I hired *you*.' Mrs Vine tapped Philip on the nose. 'Love that beard, by the way – so Jacques Cousteau.'

But she was moved to tears when Philip showed her a tray containing the syringe, fishing hooks and shards of plastic Doc Preston had extracted from Princess's gullet. 'As you can see, people and sea turtles don't mix very well.'

Mrs Vine's ruddy cheeks turned ashen. Grabbing Philip's log of marine algae samples from the counter, she fanned her face with it. 'I'm afraid I feel a bit faint,' she announced, exhibiting a shortness of breath that alarmed the young people.

They tried to assist her into the fresh air but, listing starboard, she nearly brought them down with her. Jerzy sprang into action, and with the ease of a professional weightlifter transported Mrs Vine to a bench at the picnic table. He then dashed back to the car and returned with a delicious-smelling baking tin that brought the little round apples back to her cheeks. Philip, hoping to retrieve his data log from the old lady's grip, straddled the bench and sat down beside her.

'I can see that it's going to take a great deal more than another fund raiser to turn things around.' Mrs Vine sighed. 'What we need are foot soldiers to march in the frontlines – young people like you and Julietta and...' She paused, peeling a corner of aluminium foil from the cake tin to sniff the aroma. 'Mmm... Where was I? Oh yes, foot soldiers like you and Julietta and, for instance, Hannah Caulfield. Didn't I see you two together on the beach the other day?'

It was never what Mrs Vine said, but the way she said it.

'Hannah is just the sort of person to help you, and Jesse too, bless him, despite his condition.'

'I've become rather fond of the boy,' Philip said. 'I wish he were better.'

'We all wish he were better. It's terribly hard on poor Hannah.'

Philip knew from Hannah's final letter to his father that Jesse had been diagnosed with terminal cancer. Pretending to be a relative − they shared the same surname after all − he had obtained access to medical records that showed Jesse had been released from the Great Ormond Street Hospital into the care of an American oncologist. The doctor had apparently taken Jesse to New York for an experimental treatment that eventually saved his life. From old newspaper accounts that Philip researched in the Reading Room of the British Library he learned that a novel monoclonal antibody therapy had produced the equivalent of a small miracle, and that Jesse had been released − cancer free − from Memorial Hospital less than two years after his treatment began. A 1983 follow-up human interest story in *People* magazine had shown a picture of Hannah − now Mrs Thaddeus Caulfield − and her son enjoying the Florida sunshine. But there was still a great deal Philip didn't know, and it occurred to him that chatty Mrs Vine might be just the person to shed light on it.

'Did I mention that I've had a new hip installed?' she rambled. 'I'm afraid it's still not fully up and running − not that I plan to go running like those fools I see jogging on the beach. Young people should be out dancing, not jogging! It is certainly the case, so far as my poor hip is concerned, that I did a tad too much dancing over the years. Have I told you,' she asked with a coquettish smile, 'that I was a Rockette in the chorus line at Radio City?'

Jerzy, who knew all about it, quietly withdrew to the car.

'But what's this?' She pulled a face, having noticed that the kimono-style sleeves of her Gucci kaftan were stained with what appeared to be soot.

'That'll be the ash from Papi's sugar canes,' Julietta said through a mouthful of strudel dripping in powdered sugar. 'It's everywhere.'

'Your Papi ought to know better,' Mrs Vine rebuked, using Philip's marine log to wipe the table. 'I'm surprised that Carlotta permits it.'

Philip, giving up on ever retrieving his log, asked Mrs Vine about Jesse. 'You still haven't told me what is actually wrong with him.'

The old lady, who had been about to lift a slice of strudel from the baking tray, withdrew her hand. 'The poor child,' she said, shaking her head, 'was diagnosed with stage four renal cancer and would certainly have died if Thaddeus hadn't come along. Mind you, I've known both Thaddeus and Addison since they were born, and neither of them had seemed very promising. Their fathers, who I also knew, died young and Louisa was widowed twice. Living in the same house with a woman like that was akin to death row and the brothers, who were born a decade apart, grew up close. No one in those days imagined that Addison would become a top Palm Beach lawyer or that Thaddeus would win the Nobel Prize in medicine.' Mrs Vine reflected. 'Well, he hasn't won it yet, but I fully expect that quite soon he will.'

Philip felt a twinge of envy. His father had been famous, and now it seemed that so was Dr Caulfield. In just the short time he had known Hannah he found it hard to believe that she could be attracted to either man.

'Thaddeus's father died of cancer,' Mrs Vine continued. 'And from the time he was a boy his one ambition in life was to find a cure. For years Thad struggled to develop a new line of research using monoclonal antibodies that was largely ignored by the medical community. Louisa coerced people on the Island to invest in his research, and we were of course happy to oblige. Then, after nearly ten years of one setback after another, Thaddeus hit on a way to starve cancer cells by depriving them of nutrients from the blood. His big breakthrough came with Jesse.'

'He experimented on his own son?'

'Jesse isn't his son. Not that it matters whose child anyone is. My own daughter is adopted.' Mrs Vine lowered her eyes. 'I believe you've met her.'

Without her veil, the anguish of any reference to Sunny showed clearly on the old woman's face. Becoming aware that her hat was slipping and about to take the wig with it, Mrs Vine readjusted the concoction on her head and lowered the tulle over her eyes. Leaning on her parasol, they heard it creak as she rose stiffly from the bench and announced that she must be off.

'Jerzy and I drive round the Island every day at this time to feed the cats. The poor dears have come to expect us, and I don't like to keep them waiting.'

Philip walked her to the car. The widow moved slowly, giving him time to ask one more question about Jesse. 'How was he cured in the end?'

Mrs Vine stopped to rest. 'I'm a bit fuzzy on the medical jargon. What I do know is that he had a very short time to live when Thad brought him from London. Time was so short and his condition was so dire that permission was granted on compassionate grounds to launch the first-ever experiment testing monoclonal antibodies on humans. By the time Jesse turned two, his cancers had shrivelled to the point where they could be surgically removed, and Thad's work became an overnight sensation. The Food and Drug Administration, which had for years been sceptical about his research, finally took notice. Soon, eligible end-of-life patients were allowed to enrol in clinical trials across the country. At one point the waiting list was so long that they had to institute a lottery.'

'It sounds – unbelievable,' Philip said.

'So unbelievable that the ever-enterprising Addison suggested they form a company to raise public monies and eventually mass-market the serum. The brothers named it Pandorex and, so far, the serum has made it through every stage of clinical trials. It is on course to receive full approval from the FDA, and those of us who invested in the early days are all going to be rich!'

'But aren't you rich already?' Philip asked as he helped Mrs Vine into the car.

'Well, richer, then.' The widow's violet-green eyes blazed. 'I shall in any case donate every penny to my animal charities.'

Having got settled in the back of the Rolls, she held out her hand. 'If you come over to my place some time, I'll teach you a little dance step I used to do on stage in which you get to throw me into the air.'

It must have been a very old line from the coquette's repertoire. Realising perhaps how difficult it would be to lift her now, she added: 'I mean, when my hip is better.'

Philip made no reply. Bowing deeply, he brought her hand to his lips. It was plumper and had more liver spots than Carlotta's, her palm soft as a pincushion. 'I'm becoming rather good at this,' he thought.

THE TROUBLE
WITH FORTUNE TELLERS

Hannah rose from the faux-leather sofa and went over to the window that separated the waiting room from the dialysis chamber. Bringing her face to it, her breath misting the glass in the air-conditioned room, she blew her son a kiss.

'I love you,' Jesse mouthed back from the grown-up recliner. His head lolled against the high-backed seat, the too-big hospital garment sagging and his misshapen feet protruding from it like a pair of matchsticks. Hannah smiled bravely, averting her eyes from the intravenous tube in her son's forearm. She tried not to think about the future: or that, despite Thaddeus's best efforts on the cancer front, Jesse's illness had continued to progress, and his kidneys could no longer function without dialysis. With her husband away in New York during the week, the initial treatment at St Mary's the previous autumn had felt like a bad dream repeating. Then, almost as if she had summoned him, the Revd Dr Leopold Harris entered her life.

'Feeling blessed matters more than feeling happy,' he told Hannah the first time she had gone to see him. Fr Leo had just been appointed associate curate for pastoral outreach at Gethsemane-on-the-Sea and Hannah was among the first to go and pay her respects. She was instantly drawn to the soft-spoken Southern gentleman whose childhood polio had left him with a painful limp.

Part Creole, Fr Leo hailed from a long line of Baptist ministers with the benefit of a degree in theology from an Ivy League seminary. The priest's initially reserved manner dissolved as soon as Hannah confided in him about her son's condition.

'My dear lady, a day doesn't pass that I am not made aware of my own infirmity. Sometimes, especially when the humidity is high, the pain in my hip is almost unbearable. Doctors tell me that a post-polio syndrome will set in as I grow older, and will very likely confine me to a wheelchair.'

'How do you endure it?'

'By the only means we are given, which is to trust and obey God. His wisdom far transcends what we are able to perceive, and while we may not like it at the time, it eventually leads us exactly to where we need to be.'

'I haven't had much time to meditate on God's wisdom,' Hannah said tactfully. 'My every waking moment is devoted to caring for my son.'

'There is only one way – one truth, one life.' The priest spoke softly, but his convictions were rock solid. 'Speculating about the future is in any case futile. I for one make it a point never to look beyond the next step I am taking – out of necessity, I might add,' he said with a small downward smile at his bad leg. 'For fear of falling.'

Hannah explained that Jesse's kidneys were failing, and dialysis had become their only option. Fighting tears, she said: 'They implanted a fistula into his little arm.'

'Fistula?'

'Plastic tubing inserted beneath the skin to enlarge a vessel and flush out impurities during dialysis. They told me…' Hannah could barely get the words out, 'that the fistula will never be removed from his arm. No one wants to say so – least of all my husband, who is an excellent doctor…' Hannah swallowed. 'Yet I cannot help feeling that we are taking the last few steps to death's door.'

'And heaven's gate,' Fr Leo said quietly.

They had been talking in the priest's small office at the rear of the church with a door open to the garden, the scent of ylang-ylang wafting indoors. Hannah stifled another sob, her head lowered over her chest and the cotton bodice of her dress catching the tears. Heaving, she told Fr Leo about her experience at the saint's tomb in Durham Cathedral.

'Was it a religious experience?'

'No – well, not exactly. But I felt... an unseen presence.'

'Unseen in what way?'

'I felt...' Hannah searched for the right words. 'That St Cuthbert had done as I asked.'

'And what did you ask?'

'I asked him to bless my unborn child.'

Fr Leo's tawny cheeks flushed a deeper colour. 'I am sure that he did. This is what I have been trying to tell you!'

'Jesse's life has hardly been a blessing. And yet the Bible is full of miracles. All I'm asking for is one.'

'Have you considered the usual time frame for such miracles?'

Hannah confessed that she didn't read the Bible.

'Then how do you know it is full of miracles?'

'Everyone knows it is.'

'I won't bore you with details, but it frequently takes several generations for biblical miracles to become fully manifest.'

Hannah shook her head. 'My son's condition is fatal, and we're running out of sand in the hourglass.' Her eyes, swollen red, pleaded for assurance.

Fr Leo leaned back into his chair and, cupping his fingers in his lap, began a curious little tale about a fortune teller and a man who had gone to consult her about his future. Gazing into her crystal ball, for the first time in her career the fortune teller drew a blank. With a look of horror she informed the man that she could see nothing of his life beyond the next three months and advised him to put his affairs in order.

The man took the fortune teller's advice. He left his job, sold his home and wrote his will. He said goodbye to his family and friends and went off by himself to wait for death to come for him. Three months passed, then six, and he was still alive and well. Unable to stand it any longer he decided to go back and consult the fortune teller. When he arrived at her lodgings he found the place boarded up and a *For Sale* sign on the door. Enquiring about the fortune teller's whereabouts he learned that she had died three months after he first went to see her.

The story, it seemed to Hannah, could hardly be true. More likely it had been a parable of the priest's own composition, or a fragment from one he had heard. Yet she had understood its meaning, and that the man who would soon become her spiritual advisor was offering her an entirely new kind of hope.

With a few minutes still remaining in the dialysis session, Hannah lifted today's copy of *The Shiny Sheet* from a pile of newspapers and magazines strewn on the coffee table. The Island's oldest daily wasn't really a newspaper but a kind of pictorial montage depicting the social lives of the locals. It was the first thing Islanders consulted each morning to check their standing in the community, even before they checked the weather or the state of the world. For ten years, Hannah had managed never to be mentioned in the glossy pages that gave *The Shiny Sheet* its name, regarding with a mixture of amusement and pity her neighbours' sculpted faces, sham marriages and designer-decorated homes. Yet halfway down the front page her attention was arrested by a startling photo. Looking more closely at the picture, Hannah was astonished to see, of all people, Julietta Alonso and Philip Godolphin beneath the caption: 'New Head of Marine life Institute and Faithful Helper Feed the Rescued Turtle.'

In the photo Julietta gazed reverentially at Philip, while the turtle they had named Princess lay recuperating on a cot between them. Anyone can see, Hannah thought, that Julietta is head over ears in love with Philip. Hannah had no idea how old Philip was – only that he was too old for Julietta. It made her feel inexplicably vexed, and also somehow responsible. Julietta after all had grown up alongside Jesse, and was the only person other than Marta that Hannah had ever entrusted with his care. But if what people said was true and the camera reveals more than one can see with the naked eye? Then Julietta was blossoming into womanhood and the English oceanographer was anything but disinterested, judging by the way he returned her smile. Hannah shuddered at the thought that they were living in the same house together. For a horrifying moment she was transported back in time to Durham: only a little older than Julietta and wearing the same worshipful look on her face while she had waited for James Muir to notice and love her. I must do something, she thought. Or at the very least have a word with Carlotta.

'Five minutes left, Mrs Caulfield,' called the nurse, peeking round the door of the waiting room. 'Shall I give valet parking the heads-up?'

Hannah remained quiet and the question was repeated.

'Yes, please,' she replied, tossing *The Shiny Sheet* furiously back on the coffee table.

THE BIG THREE

'Who were they, exactly? And where had they come from?' was the question people new to the Island frequently asked. To everyone else it seemed that the Big Three had always been there, like the giant fig tree in front of the Royal Poinciana Hotel that had catapulted them to prominence. Hurricanes came and went, vast estates were razed and rebuilt and people got richer. But the Big Three remained timeless; and seemed to remain exactly the same age.

Only a handful of Islanders still remembered that, long before the Big Three, there had been the Porch Club. Founded in 1918 by a group of business moguls too old to fight in the First World War but not too old to build its armaments, the secretive Porch Club had invisibly ruled the Island for nearly ten years before the women wrested power away from it. In that blissful decade of male dominance, members of the Porch Club enjoyed mornings of golf and tennis and lounged every afternoon on the porch of the Royal Poinciana Hotel – so named after an indigenous variety of flame tree known for its vibrant orange-red blooms – in which they were spending the winter. They drank bourbon, smoked Cuban cigars and exchanged stock tips. Talking politics and baseball with their heads resting on high-backed wooden rocking chairs on which their names – and, of course, nicknames – had been carved, the men played high-stakes games of poker, backgammon and gin rummy while subtly regulating all civic activity on the Island.

Palm Beach in those days was still a jungle, sprinkled with pineapple and vegetable farms, and the locals, who lived in cottages along the Lake Worth Lagoon, enjoyed alligator wrestling, fishing and bear hunting. But each winter more and more wealthy people from 'up north' migrated south for the season, taking rooms at the Royal Poinciana Hotel. It was said to be the world's biggest hotel at the time, boasting one thousand rooms, formal afternoon tea dances and fairy-tale gardens. As the mangroves and salt marshes were cleared and luxury residences rose in their place – enormous Moorish-inspired estates that sprawled from lakefront to beachfront – the snowbirds' social life moved from the hotels to private homes. Practically overnight, women seized the reins, ruling the Island through a succession of widow meritocracies that culminated in a small female version of the Porch Club that became known as the Big Three.

Of all the changes that took place over the course of the twentieth century the giant fig tree that had shaded the Royal Poinciana Hotel since the 1890s wasn't destined to be one of them. With serpentine above-ground roots and fruit that changed from green to purple with the seasons, the giant fig survived multiple fires and hurricanes and became a much-loved local icon. When a Miami developer bought the hotel in the 1970s and announced plans to raze the tree, Carlota Alonso, Louisa Caulfield and Vanessa Vine sprang into action. Backed by Eduardo, who was serving as pro bono mayor at the time, the women, still vigorous in their sixties, joined forces with the venerable Garden Club to spearhead an Island-wide effort to defeat the developer. Children from the Day Academy were brought in after school to join them for sit-ins beneath the 150-foot branch spread of the giant fig and – as reported in *The Shiny Sheet* – they were prepared to fight, 'even if it comes to ladies in white gloves chaining themselves to the tree.'

It marked the Big Three's debut as a force to be reckoned with. At weekly games of bridge the widows asserted their iron grip over local affairs while they gossiped, outlined plans to support worthwhile causes and meted out punishment when necessary. They assisted the homeless, endowed scholarships and from time to time helped out friends who had fallen on hard times. Regulating the Island's moral compass, and to make sure that they kept a sharp eye on the effectiveness of their policies, dressing up and attending parties was part of the job – and a delicious pretext for the widows to dress up and go out instead of having to stay home. Peacock would have made an ideal fourth in this curious sisterhood of rivals, had she been fantastically wealthy or married rich and moved from Bloomsbury to Palm Beach. Unaware of their loss, the Big Three carried fearlessly on, throwing their combined weight – which, it must be said, was considerable – into keeping unsuspecting Islanders in line.

'I do hope you've got something besides that blue blazer to wear to the pearl collection,' said Julietta as she slid her vinyl-and-chrome bar stool nearer to Philip's.

He ignored the comment, feeling sure that he hadn't heard her correctly. Glancing at Malachi, the family's beloved butler and only other person at breakfast with them, Philip got no response, his attention razor focused on preparing beans on toast 'the English way'.

'Why would I wear my blue blazer to go diving for pearls?'

Julietta suppressed a smile, emptying a bowl of blueberries over her cereal. 'Mrs Caulfield is hosting a garden party for poor Sarah Silvers, to collect money for a new set of pearls, and we all have to go and show our support. I'm afraid that includes you.'

'I don't recall that garden parties were included in my job description.'

'That was before you became a celebrity,' Julietta said, pointing to the morning edition of *The Shiny Sheet* lying on the table.

The limits of Philip's incredulity were stretched to the limit when he saw his picture on the front page. He somewhat vaguely recalled a reporter from the paper coming to interview him and take pictures of the turtle infirmary, never imagining that it would be featured in a tabloid that seemed to be devoted mainly to people dancing, air-kissing and partying.

Suddenly a new thought occurred to him. 'Did you say that Hannah Caulfield is giving the garden party?'

'Hannah never gives parties. It's Louisa Caulfield that's hosting the pearl collection, though I'm willing to bet it was Mrs Vine's idea. She's always eager to help when it's to do with animals or the down and out.'

'I didn't think anyone in this town was down and out.'

'I'm afraid poor Mrs Silvers is. Her husband was accused of embezzling from his company last year and had to declare bankruptcy. The children can no longer attend boarding school and they've moved from their beachfront home to a boat in the marina. Imagine!'

Philip, who rather liked the idea of living on a boat, said nothing.

'The ladies want to get poor Mrs Silvers a string of pearls and one or two matching earrings to help make up for the jewels she had to pawn. This way at least she can still attend a few parties during the season and see some of her old friends.'

'While Mr Silvers goes to jail?'

'Heavens, no,' Julietta said, aiming her eviscerated grapefruit at the metal bin. 'He'll appeal his case all the way to the state supreme court, and that could take years. By then he will have found some other way to get rich.'

Philip protested that he didn't know Mrs Silvers and saw no reason why he should give her money.

'No one expects *you* to give money,' Julietta laughed, hopping off the bar stool and throwing the satchel with her schoolbooks over her shoulder.

'Then why am I going?'

Julietta hesitated. Exchanging a furtive look with Malachi, she said: 'Grandmalita is dying to show you off. Everyone at the garden party will have seen our photo in *The Shiny Sheet*, and they'll want to hear about Princess – and, of course, about the institute. I should think you'd be thrilled.'

PEARLS, PEARLS
AND MORE PEARLS

It took no small effort on Philip's part to keep to the right-hand side of the road. He had very little experience driving cars, and none driving a Bentley. In London he had relied on public transport and used a bicycle to get around Oxford. Yet here he was, chauffeuring a group of women he barely knew to a social event so bizarre in nature than no one back home would have believed him. Malachi, who was normally recruited for such occasions, had gone to Miami to visit a sick relative and Carlotta, looking strangely lost without him, insisted that Philip take his place: all of which, as Philip realised after the fact, had been known to everyone except him well in advance.

On the way to the garden party they stopped at the Day Academy to pick Julietta up from school. She was still in her uniform, her thick hair braided, as she sat squeezed between her mother and grandmother in the back seat, trying to do her homework.

'I bet you know all about sine, cosine and tangent,' Julietta said, sidling up behind Philip in the hope of getting a quick answer to one of the Geometry problems in her assignment.

'*Déjalo conducir!*' Carlotta rebuked her granddaughter in Spanish, pulling Julietta roughly back to her seat. '*O se estrellará!*'

The women switched back to English as soon as the Bentley passed through the scallop-shell bronze gates of Villa des

Coquilles. Rows of Florida stranglers – so called due to the trees' immense trunks and gangly roots that dangled from their branches like rope – lined both sides of a long driveway composed entirely of crushed seashells. Philip pulled up behind Hannah's white convertible and, mimicking Jerzy, jumped from the Bentley and held the rear door open.

'Here we are, ladies,' he announced, feeling more cheerful now that Hannah had arrived at the party. Looking up, he saw the words *Villa des Coquilles* painted in the style of Della Robbia on a blue and white terracotta tile above the front door.

No name described better the house they were about to enter. Erected on a sea wall facing the Lake Worth Lagoon, its doors and windows stood open and the sound of water, lapping beneath tall windows framed by balconies and trickling fountains, was ever-present. The seashell motif appeared in much more than the villa's name. It was in the silk wallpaper, embossed with real cockle and scallop shells, coquina-patterned damask curtains and trompe l'oeil ceilings that seemed to float from the Lagoon into the drawing room or the back of the clouds. But the pride and glory of the old estate was the Shell House, an octagonal cottage with a conical roof resembling a dovecot and constructed entirely of seashells. It had been perfectly placed at the end of a mossed path leading from the courtyard to the same landing strip on the Lagoon where flappers with bobbed hair and gentlemen in bowler hats had once disembarked from their boats to attend tea dances and garden parties exactly like the one Louisa Caulfield had organised today.

A maid in uniform received Philip and the women at the door, serving cool drinks from a sliver tray. Another maid could be seen moving unobtrusively from window to terrace, repositioning the drapery to keep sunlight away from the antique furniture, oil paintings and carpets without spoiling the view. Lowering his eyes from the painted ceiling to the drawing room below, Philip became suddenly and painfully aware that he was the only man among more than two dozen women – a squadron of mannequins with surgically altered body parts and faces that were, without exception, all looking at him.

Louisa Caulfield was the squadron leader, with the opaque eyes of a statue and silver hair pulled back in a curt little bun at the nape of her thin neck. The chatelaine of Villa des Coquilles had been taught the rules of being a hostess at a very early age. Among them was always to greet guests with an anaemic smile and one arm held out in front like a dagger – a gesture meant to make them feel more at her mercy than at home. And right at this moment all of Louisa's daggers were pointing at Philip, as she studied with cool deliberation the rubber flip-flops he had forgotten were still on his feet.

Looking down, he blushed crimson. All conversation gradually subsided as the group crowded nearer to inspect the handsome marine biologist. But what impressed these women far more than Philip's looks was his youth.

'Oh, how I wish I could claw that shine off him and wear it tonight,' exclaimed one of them.

Louisa, overhearing the comment, and wanting none of that sort of talk in her house, called for silence. 'Cake and punch are being served in the courtyard!' she rallied the troops, leading her guests through a series of double doors to an outdoor colonnade canopied with clematis blooms.

The pack swarmed behind her in columns of two and three. Carlotta, leaving Philip by himself, hurried over to the fireplace to break up a row that was brewing between Vanessa Vine and her daughter. At the other end of the drawing room Philip spotted Hannah conversing quietly with Julietta in one of the bays overlooking the Lagoon, the stainless blue sky behind them giving no hint of a colossal blizzard said to be forming in the mid-Atlantic. Julietta, listening to Hannah without interest, perked up as soon as she saw Philip, and they waved to each other across the room. Hannah, who had been in the middle of a sentence, followed Julietta's gaze. Seeing Philip coming over to join them she marched Julietta by the elbow across the room to where Carlotta stood talking with the others.

'Would you mind accompanying me?' An elderly gentleman in a baggy poplin suit and boater hat appeared next to Philip. 'I seem to have misplaced my cane and fear I may need assistance to the table.'

He was the only other man at the party, and his name was Dixon Wainwright – or Dixie, as he was known. The former head of the oldest bank in Boston and Louisa Caulfield's companion for the past fifteen years, Dixie's stature had diminished from running corporate board meetings to running errands for Louisa. In his dotage he was still mindful of his duties: for instance, that a gentleman must sometimes be seated with people he didn't care for at dinner parties and serve as an escort to the interminable merry-go-round of social events during the season. When these services weren't required he was permitted to roam about the men's bar and croquet court of the nearby Mangrove Club – all of which and much, much more Julietta explained to Philip in the course of the afternoon.

The sound of high-pitched laughter and of chairs scraping the mossed flagstones filled the courtyard as guests flocked to their seats. A chorus of acclaim erupted when waiters appeared with trays of mint juleps, presented in ice-cold silver tumblers; followed by squeals of dismay at the discovery of a foot-high hornet nest inside the bougainvillea. Hannah and Carlotta were seated between Mrs Vine and her daughter to help keep the peace, Sunny half mad with longing as silver tumblers flew past, the waiters having been instructed to keep them out of her reach. Mrs Vine, who had issued the order with Louisa as her co-conspirator, sat back smugly while stroking a furry creature that kept trying to crawl from the depths of her Louis Vuitton knitting bag.

Having prepared a rousing speech on behalf of the pearl collection, it was Louisa's custom to wait for her guests to have something to drink before asking them for money. She had stayed up late obsessing over the seating plan and had put the two youngest people together at a table nearest the Shell House. Philip was the first to take his seat, and was somewhat relieved when he saw Julietta's name in a flowing script on the place card next to his. He stood up when she arrived and politely held out her chair. The girl, flattered by the attention, whispered something in his ear. Philip inclined his head towards her to hear better, and when he looked up again, he noticed Hannah's gaze fixed on them like a blowtorch.

He couldn't see her eyes, only the sun glinting off the dark blue mirrors of Hannah's sunglasses as she turned to Carlotta in the seat beside her. He watched them conversing, the widow listening intently to what Hannah was saying. Something told him that they were talking about him. But there was no divining who had initiated the subject, or what any of it meant.

TEMPEST

Even before the garden party had broken up the north-east portion of the country had begun shutting down ahead of the predicted storm. Aerial images on television showed it swirling across the Atlantic towards the East Coast even though, so far, not a single snowflake had appeared in the sky above the oncology wing of Manhattan's Memorial Hospital. Irritated that the cancer clinic was about to shut in his face, Thaddeus Caulfield grudgingly donned his anorak, scarf, mittens and sheepskin hat and locked his office. Lingering indecisively in the hospital corridor, he had no idea what to do with himself.

The sky turned more threatening as he trudged uphill to an address on East 76th Street at which he lived during the week – or rather slept, since he spent nearly every waking hour at the clinic. Without Hannah, Jesse or his work, Thaddeus wondered how he would make the long weekend pass. As the first snowflakes drifted down over Manhattan the familiar neon sign outside the local Korean grocery grew gradually harder to read. The doctor often stopped there for a takeaway, and the large family that ran it knew him by sight. Finding them all together (though there seemed to be much more than one family involved in running the shop) made him miss his wife and son more.

The all-weather plastic cover draped over fruits and vegetables displayed on outdoor stalls shivered in the wind, making the predicted storm feel suddenly real. Inside the warm bosom of the grocery Thaddeus dallied over the aromatic foods bubbling on trestles at the self-serve counter, wondering whether to stock up for possibly much more than one meal if the weather worsened. He ladled stir-fry vegetables, pork, beef and spicy chicken into tinfoil containers, adding to his shopping basket two types of noodles, a carton of Samuel Adams beer and a tub of vanilla ice-cream. The doctor was secretly fond of foods that he would never recommend to his patients, and the coming storm gave him an excuse. He exchanged obligatory bows with the grandad, who spoke no English and was peeling vegetables into a bucket behind a half-drawn curtain. Grinning through his missing front teeth, the patriarch, with bushy white brows and a smart goatee, always managed to slip some memento – a rice cake or packet of Yakgwa cookies – into Thaddeus's pocket.

By the time he stepped outside again, swirling eddies of snow had transformed Lexington Avenue into a white prairie. The streetlamps had become nests of light and what traffic remained crawled through an eerie silence broken by the distant rumble of subway trains from beneath grilles in the pavement. Manoeuvring the icy outcrops exposed by the wind, it took Thaddeus much longer than usual to reach his apartment block. He stomped the snow from his boots as he entered the lobby, saluted the doorman and took the elevator to the seventh floor. It always felt too warm on the higher floors of the centrally heated pre-war building, and he began shedding his outerwear as soon as he stepped through the door. Looking about the sparsely furnished apartment in which he too often slept on the Chesterfield sofa, medical journals and week-old newspapers scattered on the floor, the doctor's eyes fell on a framed photo of Jesse and Hannah in the swimming pool. It was a picture he loved, and he couldn't understand why it should make him feel so dispirited. Then he realised why: and that not going home this weekend also meant Jesse would miss the usual dose of serum Thaddeus had administered by injection for the past ten years.

Would skipping a single dose matter? he wondered, standing in the window whited with snow. Hearing none of the familiar traffic noises from outside, the cheerless silence deepened his anxieties. Not just about his son, but the risks associated with his company's expansion to a new facility on the East River, meant to take place on Monday. Addison had warned against the dangers of expanding before the serum had received full FDA approval, but Thaddeus insisted that the level of research required to get the approval couldn't be reached without a much bigger and better-equipped laboratory. His brother had acquiesced in the end, and even helped him to obtain the necessary bank loan. But in the ghostly silence of the storm Thaddeus became seized with indecision.

On an impulse he decided to go and visit the site – now, before he was snowed in. Rushing about the apartment, he searched for long johns, corduroys and a thick flannel shirt to wear under his heaviest cowl-neck sweater. He rummaged on his hands and knees through the floor of the hall closet until he located an old pair of snowshoes from boarding school days in Vermont. Thaddeus had lived in the same apartment since he arrived at Memorial Hospital as an intern, and it was filled with odds and ends from his past that ought to have been thrown out long ago. He began to sweat inside the heavy clothes, but couldn't leave without calling home. Pressing the automatic dial on the cordless phone, he cradled the instrument on his shoulder while he laced up his boots.

The phone rang a long time before the answering machine came on. Even a recording of Hannah's voice had a soothing effect, and he left a brief message. The doctor wondered where they could be. Perhaps, he thought the English lad had taken up his suggestion and invited them to the new turtle facility. Thaddeus tried to remember the lad's name but couldn't: only that he had trained at Oxford and that Jesse believed he was some kind of prince. The doctor smiled, thinking about his son's world, filled with magicians, monarchs and outlaws, and in which his own special role was that of head magician.

Downstairs in the lobby he congratulated the doorman for staying at his post during a nor'easter. But he ignored the man's warning not to venture out. It wasn't in Thaddeus's nature to waver once his mind was made up, and he stomped somewhat clumsily but with purpose across the lobby in his old snowshoes. The doorman tried to hold the door open for him, but the wind was too strong and Thaddeus finally left through the service entrance. The snow was accumulating quickly, and Third Avenue, a broad and normally busy thoroughfare, was silhouetted on both sides by white mounds that bore, more and more faintly, the outline of cars buried underneath. Coming to a traffic light swinging drunkenly from a wind-tossed wire strung across the road, Thaddeus felt as if he could almost reach up and touch it. I am Gulliver in the streets of Lilliput, he thought as he strode in his snowshoes through the white prairie, labouring with his bulky frame against the gale.

He struggled to recognise once-familiar landmarks, among them the old New York Foundling Hospital that was now a Woolworth's. The shopfront windows shone dimly through a netting of white, illuminating broad patches of a winter landscape that made the city feel like open country. Thaddeus thought of his son again when he passed an elaborate Lego construct of the World Trade Center Twin Towers in one of the shop displays. Gliding past it in his snowshoes he remembered his long-ago walks and talks with Hannah along this same stretch of Third Avenue during the first winter she and Jesse had spent in New York. The doctor's face, seared by the icy wind, turned redder as he thought back on their clumsy courtship, with Hannah living in his apartment while Jesse underwent treatment. They had married after three months in order to solve problems with her visa. But Thaddeus had never entirely understood, either then or now, the little Hannah had told him about her past: the parents she hardly mentioned or who Jesse's father had been. In the end, none of it had mattered: all he had ever asked of her was that she stay.

They didn't sleep in the same bed until after Jesse's cancers had been cured and they had moved to Palm Beach. It was in the vast pink house filled with sunlight and living essentially apart while Thaddeus commuted to New York that they finally, in a manner that still made the doctor blush, came together as man and wife. It had resolved a number of issues, if not the thorniest ones, ending Thaddeus's dream of having a large family. Tests showed that the gene that had caused Jesse's ailment was transmitted through the mother, placing any future children – especially male children – at risk. Thaddeus coped with the news as any decent man would. But as a clinician he clung to the hope that science would find a way to isolate the mutation, and that the father's DNA also played a role.

At 82nd Street he was nearly toppled by wind gusting off the East River. Wrapping his arms round a lamp post, he waited for it to subside. Looking over his shoulder at the way he had come, the doctor could no longer see his tracks. The storm eased somewhat by the time he reached Cherokee Place, but the snow was still coming down hard, erasing the street signs. Fortunately, he recognised the iron fencing around the perimeter of the turn-of-the-century facility that would soon house the new Pandorex laboratory. At one time families of tubercular patients being treated at Memorial Hospital had been lodged in the same building – in the days before there was penicillin and being diagnosed with tuberculosis was the equivalent of a death sentence. Like cancer still is, Thaddeus thought. But all that was about to change. And Dr Caulfield, whose serum had been derided by the medical community not so long ago, was the one who would change it.

He had staked everything on it – his career, reputation and finances. Not to mention the finances of private backers among his friends, family and neighbours. The firm, as Thaddeus well knew, was hardly out of the woods. Once the new facility was in place they would need additional money to hire technicians, lab assistants and office staff. In order to lure the most highly qualified personnel, Addison had suggested that they offer shares in the company in lieu of salary until the serum was approved and Pandorex became solvent. The core group of scientists who had stuck with Thaddeus from the beginning were all banking on the success of the final Phase Four clinical trials now in progress. In the mean time, he had been using his own money to make up the cash shortfalls and, most recently, had taken out a mortgage on his home to give the company a one-time, interest-free loan to cover the cost of expansion.

Thaddeus had planned to discuss all this with Hannah over the weekend. He hadn't done it earlier because he felt sure that she would back his decisions. But he was about to take a much bigger risk, one that even his brother was worried about. As legal counsel and managing director of Pandorex, Addison had dissected the issue from every angle, warning that any unforeseen setback to the FDA's expected approval could adversely affect the value of the stock, hampering Thaddeus's ability to repay the loans.

If lawyers ran the world, he reflected, rather than move forward it would only remain more as it was. But developing a cure for cancer was about taking risks, not steering clear of them. The phrase 'who dares wins' popped into his head. The doctor couldn't remember where he had heard it or in what context; only that, this time, he meant to win.

TO THE REEF

Marta had just folded the linen napkins into squares on the ironing board, singing softly to the coming day, which, like the days and weeks preceding, only stretched as far into the future as Jesse's health permitted. His weekly home-school kit from the Florida Department of Special Education had arrived that morning, meaning a lesson day indoors and pizza for lunch. Marta would bake brownies to relieve the tedium, the only interruption to it today being the annual termite inspection scheduled for later in the morning.

'I'll get it,' Hannah called, hearing the doorbell. Lifting Jesse, she went to answer it. But instead of the termite inspector they found Philip standing on the doorstep.

Wearing a blue and white striped T-shirt over his bathing trunks, his nose peeling and a rucksack bulging over his shoulder, he gave his neighbours a sunburned smile. 'Like my new flip-flops? They were on special at Greene's – three pairs for ten quid.'

'Dollars,' Hannah corrected him.

'Cool,' Jesse murmured and slid down his mother's leg to inspect the new sandals.

'They certainly made a splash at the pearl collection,' Hannah observed frostily.

Philip grinned. 'That was your fault, by the way – for telling me never to leave home without a pair of flip-flops.'

'Or sun cream.'

'We'll need a fair bit of that for our outing.'

'Outing?' Hannah raised an eyebrow.

'To the reef.'

'Said who?'

'Mrs Vine told me it was all arranged.'

'But Jesse has lessons this morning…'

'We can do those any time,' the boy cried. 'Three cheers for Mrs Vine!'

The road tapered to a strip of asphalt between the ocean and intercoastal waterway as the small travelling party made its way to the northern tip of the Island. Philip led the way on his bicycle, Hannah and Jesse trailing him in the open-top convertible. When the road ended and it seemed they could go no further, Philip parked his bicycle in the shade of a tall banyan tree and Hannah pulled up in the car beside him. She lifted the cooler with their provisions from the back seat and the three set out together on foot.

Philip had been coming to the reef nearly every day to harvest algae samples, and he knew a shortcut to the beach. With Jesse bouncing on his shoulders they followed a sandy footpath partially overgrown with dense foliage, the trail so narrow in places that they had to walk single file. Then, all at once, a marvellous scene opened up before them like a foreign country, amid a sunlit stretch of dazzling, powder-fine sand and crystal-clear blue water. Hannah caught her breath, astonished that no one had ever mentioned how close the reef was to their home. At the very least it seemed that Thaddeus, who had grown up on the Island, must have played here as a boy. At last she grew calm, spreading their beach towel on the sand and placing the sun umbrella and cooler packed with food and cans of soda on top.

Philip fitted a diving mask over Jesse's goggles and gave mother and son a quick snorkel lesson. Padding in their flippers like ducks along the shore, Jesse shrieked with joy when Philip and his mother lifted him by the arms between them and splashed into the shallow blue water.

'Let's go Dolphin!' he cried. At low tide the adults could almost have waded the entire distance to the reef. But they would have missed the thrill of swimming past schools of butterfly fish and purple eels; and a giant hawksbill so well camouflaged by the reef that even Philip almost failed to spot it. Jesse wanted never to leave his undersea kingdom, resisting with all his might when it came time to head back to shore.

'The reef will still be here tomorrow, and the day after, and the day after that,' Philip coaxed.

'But what if I'm not?'

'Course you will.' Philip tousled the boy's wet hair. 'Dolphin says so.'

They ran to the beach blanket that had become an oasis in a desert of hot sand. Hannah changed Jesse's bandage and distributed Marta's egg and cress sandwiches, while Philip labelled the vials of algae he had collected from the reef and placed them inside the cooler. Jesse, his eyes shining, made up stories about the giant hawksbill he had petted at the reef.

'I'm pretty sure that was one of Princess's family. They're waiting for her to get better and come back to them.' He chattered non-stop until his store of energy suddenly gave out. Laying his head on his mother's lap in the middle of a sentence, he fell sound asleep.

Hannah pried the uneaten portion of the sandwich from his hand and angled the beach umbrella over him on the blanket. Without Jesse's prattle the atmosphere grew hushed, the ocean still, silver-edged cloud banks sprouting like silent animation on the horizon.

'Jesse will never forget this outing,' Hannah said. 'And neither will I. What a palette of colours we saw – as if the reef were showing off.'

'Actually, it was. Producing vibrant colours is a sign that the corals are struggling to recover algae they need to survive. When the partnership with algae is thriving the coral is typically of a brownish hue. But when there is any kind of trouble – such as environmental stress or higher than normal water temperature – internal photosynthetic production declines and the corals risk starving. To get the light-sensitive algae to return, they try to attract attention by emitting super-bright colours.'

Hannah had a faraway look in her eyes. 'They teach all that at Oxford?'

'Not all of it. The truth is, I did quite a lot of independent research while I was there and hope to do a great more here.'

'I've always regretted not finishing my education,' she said pensively. 'It's wonderful to meet people who are passionate about their work.'

Was this what had attracted her to Muir – and to Caulfield? 'Actually,' Philip said, to show that he was different, 'for a long time I didn't give all that much thought to marine biology.'

'Really? Yet something made you decide to come here.'

Philip wondered if this was the moment to tell her. Would she ever speak to him again? 'I couldn't pass up an opportunity to work at such a world-class institute.' It didn't sound very convincing, even to Philip's ears, since the institute was brand new. 'Or one so well funded,' he added quickly.

'That's for sure. Everything on the Island is well funded!'

Hannah leaned back on her elbows, threw her head back and gazed up at the sky. Her wet hair glistened in the sun, the damp swimsuit hugging her body.

'And you?' he said. 'What are you passionate about?'

'Jesse is my only passion.'

'No hobbies?'

'Well, I do like poetry.'

Philip remembered the poems inside the beach cottage, and those other poems he wasn't supposed to know about. 'Do you read or write poetry?'

'Both.'

He asked who her favourite poets were, and she named several. But she didn't name Muir.

'Actually, I read quite a bit of poetry...' Philip cleared his throat. 'If you ever feel like showing me any of your work, I'd love to read it.'

'I didn't think biologists read poems.'

Philip shrugged. 'Some of us do.'

For a long time neither of them spoke. The sun rose higher, the sky a flawless Florida blue. 'It's hard to imagine a blizzard only a few hundred miles up the coast,' Philip said.

'I hadn't heard,' she said absently, running her fingers through Jesse's hair. He stirred drowsily and, lifting his head, asked if Philip was ready to go.

'You want to go home already?' Hannah asked.

'Not home – to the institute. Dolphin promised to show it to me. We're going to ride there on his bicycle.'

Hannah glanced sharply at Philip. 'I think we've had quite enough excitement for one day.'

'He didn't invite *you*. He invited *me*,' Jesse pouted, and crawled to Philip's side of the blanket.

Hannah, trembling, stared at them in silence.

CREATURE FROM THE
BLUE LAGOON

It wasn't until she walked into the kitchen and saw the message light blinking on the telephone that she remembered her husband was due back from New York on the afternoon flight. Afraid that he had already arrived and was waiting at the airport, a wave of relief swept through her when she listened to the message.

'Sorry, darling, but the flights have been grounded and I won't be home after all. You had better let Carlotta know that I can't come to the Refugee Ball.' There was a pause, Thaddeus's disappointment palpable. 'I'm just heading out for a quick walk before I get snowed in and will call you again in a while.' After another, much shorter pause, he said: 'I love you.'

Hannah pressed another button on the cordless phone and called Carlotta. When Malachi replied that madam had gone to the hairdresser, she explained that Dr Caulfield was snowbound in New York and couldn't come to the ball – to which the butler's response was, as Hannah had feared: 'But you will be there, of course.'

She wanted to say no but couldn't. The Alonsos had been early backers of Thaddeus's research, and the Cuban Refugee Relief Fund, founded by Ernesto, was precious to their hearts. For thirty years, Carlotta had begun planning the next annual fundraising ball practically from the day the previous one had ended. Not turning up at the last minute would disrupt her seating plan, with potentially disastrous repercussions.

'Yes, of course,' Hannah said.

Unlike Carlotta's hairdresser, who catered to women over seventy and set their hair in metal rollers under a hood dryer, the new spa at The Breakers hotel had become hugely popular with young Islanders. Appointments were hard to get, and Hannah had booked her pedicure and hair style several weeks in advance of the Refugee Ball. With ambient music playing softly in the background and the smell of essential oils in the air, Hannah grew instantly more at ease. A part of her was still under the spell of the undersea adventure Philip had organised, making her feel almost nostalgic when the stylist leaned her head back in the basin and rinsed the salt from her hair.

Later, sitting in a plush white-leather armchair as she waited for her nails to dry, Hannah thought about her mum. Was she still working at a hotel spa in Northumbria, or had she moved to one of the big cities in the west as she had always talked of doing? Was it normal that neither of her parents had tried to find her after she left home? More likely, as the unwanted child of their youth and only real link between them, Hannah's departure had also set them free. In the years since, her memories of life with these two people had become almost indistinguishable from the grey sky and grey-brick houses that had made up their village. Hannah never spoke of it, not even to Thaddeus, and considered it a blessing that people on the Island – even very famous people – rarely talked about their pasts. As a result, no one had enquired, either directly or indirectly, about Hannah's history. And Louisa, who would have liked to ask, had been strictly forbidden from doing so by her fear of what she might learn.

Her thoughts were interrupted by two women wandering about the salon in white terry slippers and robes, silver foil in their hair as they gossiped. Lingering over a selection of the season's latest nail-varnish colours inside a glass cabinet, they fawned over the display.

'Makes you wonder how safe it is living here,' mused the somewhat younger of the two. Turning to one of the attendants, she asked whether there had been any update on the injured bicyclists.

Hannah moved to the edge of her seat.

'They say the alligator got away. And there's no word yet on the state of the bicyclists.'

As they neared the water's edge plovers scattered in front of them like handfuls of pebbles tossed in the air. They stood a long time looking at the ocean, Philip scanning the horizon while Jesse waited eagerly for what would happen next.

'Think we'll see it?' he asked.

'It's a near perfect night for it. To the extent that the Belt of Venus can ever be seen.'

'But you've seen it. You told me you have.'

'Only that one time, on the plane coming over from London.'

'What was it like?'

'As the sun lowered in the west so the curvature of the Earth's shadow became projected in a rainbow of pinks and blues across the sky. It's a phenomenon that occurs every evening at dusk, but conditions have to be exactly right for it to be visible from the ground.'

They waited while the minutes ticked. Then, all at once and with a ferocity characteristic of the tropics, the sun dipped beneath the sapphire blue rim of the ocean and was gone.

'Did we miss it?' Jesse asked. 'I don't always see right.'

'It's probably to do with that storm up north. Never mind, we'll see it another time. I promise.'

The evening folded like a warm garment around the last two figures on the beach. Jesse, lifting his face to his friend, kissed him; so lightly on the cheek that Philip thought he had imagined it. 'I love you Dolphin,' he said.

Hannah ran to the door. It was locked, and the windows were dark except for the glow of a monitor next to the giant sea turtle silhouetted on the cot. Walking round the side of the building, past Mrs Vine's old tennis court and croquet lawn, she saw Philip's bicycle leaning against a tree. Reasoning that they couldn't have gone very far without it, the only place left to look was the beach.

At last she spotted them: Philip cantering like a filly in the first pale flush of moonlight and Jesse riding on his shoulders. The boy pretended to be pulling the reins to make Philip trot this way and that, their laughter rolling like a beachball across the dry evening sand. Hannah, stifling her cries, stood motionless, waiting for them.

AND THE CEILING PARTED...

Wearing a dead man's tuxedo – there had been at least half a dozen to choose from in Ernesto's old closet – Philip stood with Carlotta in front of the Florentine Fountain, waiting for their picture to be taken. It was the same spot from which Hannah had begun her frantic search for him and Jesse a few hours earlier, with the same contingent of valet parking attendants clad in loose-fitting uniforms to keep them cool, dashing about like players on a football field.

This was Carlotta's moment to outshine her rivals, and she was determined to make the most of it. Indeed, she was so busy trying to see who was standing where and with whom that she missed a step leading into the hotel lobby. Saved from landing face down on the marble floor by a quick reflex action on Philip's part, the widow's full cheeks turned crimson as a photographer from *The Shiny Sheet* entered her path at that very moment for a close-up of 'Doyenne of the Cuban Refugee Ball Arriving at the Gala' – as tomorrow's caption would read.

Fearing some further mishap the doyenne clung to Philip's arm, comporting herself like royalty with an immense diamond-encrusted ruby, emerald and sapphire dragonfly brooch pinned to the shoulder of her Galanos ball gown. Gleaming on her wrist was a graduated freshwater pearl and diamond cuff, topped by one of the orchid corsages Eduardo presented each year to his mother. With her hair coiffed in tight little cauliflower buds, Carlotta, who shared a birthday with Queen Elizabeth II, was trying very hard to look like her. (Fortunately, the widow had never seen any pictures of Queen Elizabeth I, to whom she bore a much closer resemblance on account of her receding hairline.) Blissfully unaware of this, Carlotta regarded with a touch of vanity her reflection multiplied tenfold in the mirrored lobby of the hotel as Sir Philip escorted her on his arm through the long, fresco-ceilinged corridor to the Ponce de Leon ballroom.

He was still recovering from the speed with which his presence had been commandeered at the gala. Carlotta had pounced on him the instant he had returned to the house, insisting that Philip take Dr Caulfield's place at her table. 'None of the eligible men I tried are free at such short notice,' she cried in despair.

Now, the main topic on everyone's lips was the alligator attack on Lake Trail, and that the cyclists – a pair of Latino gardeners for one of the estates – were at this moment undergoing emergency surgery. A cry went up at the ball to hold a special collection for the hapless victims, to cover their medical expenses and provide for the families. Carlotta took to the cause with absolute conviction. It was enough for her that the victims were Latino, and she hastily made a last-minute addition to the benefit auction, offering use of the family's yacht, *The Carlotta A*, to the highest bidder.

Every mention of the alligator attack replayed in Philip's mind the look on Hannah's face when she had discovered them on the beach. Handing Philip the car keys she had asked him to drive home, while she sat mute in the seat beside him, cradling Jesse as if he were an infant. Squashed together in the front seat, Philip had never felt so close to anyone.

It was hard to believe that after all that Hannah would come to the ball. Yet here she was, standing across the ballroom in a family circle that included Louisa Caulfield, Dixie Wainwright and the Sloans. She wore a midnight-blue silk gown cut on the bias, her hair braided and pinned up around her head like a chaplet. Philip traced with his eyes the nuances of Hannah's body inside the gown, blushing when he realised what he was doing. Small and statuesque, wearing a single strand of pearls and no make-up, out of all the women in the ballroom no one seemed more beautiful.

As Hannah turned to profile, the pearls round her neck, which had appeared relatively modest from the front, were shown cascading halfway down her backless gown. They glowed against skin that had just been in the sun, the outline of her bathing suit showing through the spaghetti straps and scooped back of her gown. Standing beside a Doric column like a figure from antiquity, Hannah smiled at Addison Sloan as he handed her a cocktail.

'Some women have no shame,' Carlotta scoffed, following Philip's gaze. 'Sunny wears those ghastly sequin belt buckles to parties because she thinks they make her waist look smaller than small. She got drunk at last year's ball and I've warned Addison to keep a sharp eye on her tonight.' Relaxing her grip on Philip's arm, Carlotta indicated with a nod of her flat chin that it was time to proceed to their table.

Philip could have no further doubt that his role tonight was to serve as Carlotta's 'walker' – a term, he learned, applied to escorts, occasionally paid for their services, who accompany single ladies past a certain age to important social events. Since charity functions depended on the largesse of such women – dubbed 'swords' (for single, widowed or divorced) – walkers had become integral to the Island's social life. Until tonight Philip had been of the opinion that Julietta was making all this up – never imagining that he would become a player in the charade.

Stone crab cocktails and canapés floated on silver trays, bon mots flying like sharpened arrows through the packed ballroom and the noise level so high that only certified lip readers could have understood what was being said. But there were some things that didn't need to be said: for instance, that even best friends were potential enemies and that deciphering which among them was about to switch sides was part of the game. Among the unspoken rules was the age-old system for keeping people apart who didn't get along (or had once been married to each other) and another system for keeping the old guard at a safe distance from the parvenues – creating areas of light and shade, rich and richer, that were rarely allowed to intersect.

The tinkling of a bell sounded through the din, signalling that a five-course feast was about to be served. The bud lights on the Murano glass chandeliers began to pulse and the double doors to the dining and dancing arena parted, admitting dozens of guests. Thinking that it was an optical illusion, Philip noticed the ballroom ceiling begin to lift, opening like two halves of a drawbridge. Soon all heads were bending backwards to watch them lift higher and further apart until the two halves stood perpendicular to the sky. Clouds, floating on the back of the night, could be seen breaking away from each other, making the sky seem to draw nearer. Lowering his eyes from the ceiling, Philip saw Hannah standing next to him.

'You seem to be everywhere today,' she said, smiling as she looked up at the sky. Hannah's neck, bare shoulders and arms had the quality of alabaster in the dimmed lights, and the pearls falling down her back had the cool radiance of stars in the ceiling. 'Anyway, I'm glad you're here. I was too distraught earlier and didn't – couldn't – thank you properly for taking such good care of my son. I hope I didn't seem curt...' She broke off, knotting her fingers. 'But even just thinking about what might have happened...'

'Don't think,' he said. 'It didn't happen. Nothing happened. Jesse is safe and we're here.'

Carlotta, who was hanging on Philip's other arm, seemed miles away as she chatted with the mayor, who had come to pay his respects to the doyenne of the ball – and get his picture taken.

'So, how do I look in a tux?' Philip asked.

Hannah assessed him judiciously. 'I suppose like every other man here. Though I will say that yours is a wee loose round the waist,' she said, tugging playfully at his cummerbund.

'It was the only outfit I could find at such short notice – with compliments of the stone-faced immortal who once owned it.'

'Stone-faced immortal?'

'For he is lost to such revels as we on earth…' Philip said without thinking. It was a line from one of James Muir's poems, a lament over the statue of a Roman god while the poet, languishing in the arms of his lover, delights in the pleasures of her touch. Philip froze, wondering whether Hannah would recognise the poem.

She gave no sign that she did. Still smiling, she waved to Armando, who had arrived before them at the head table. Attired in a morning suit with padded shoulders to make him look slimmer, wearing a flamboyant polka-dot bow tie and his long hair slicked back in a ponytail, he greeted Hannah with an embrace.

'How's my big sister?' he asked, nibbling at her bare shoulders. Philip glared at him but was reassured a moment later by the appearance of Armando's stunningly pretty girlfriend, wearing a low-cut bustier and pleated silk taffeta mini skirt.

'She won second place in the Miss New Jersey swimsuit contest last year,' Armando bragged, showing off his prize to the table.

The chandeliers pulsed with renewed urgency, propelling guests post-haste to several dozen tables draped in floor-length organdie. The ballroom exploded with cheers when legendary bandleader Tito Puente mounted the stage in a white tuxedo. The ageing but still robust musician bowed to a standing ovation and opened the show with '*Oye Como Va*', playing his signature timbales as guests stampeded to the dancefloor. With the ceiling gone and stars and candles now the only illumination, the vast hall took on the aspect of a raucous cloister garden. From beneath the arches of the surrounding indoor colonnade, hung with swags of fir and fairy lights, peeked lush plantings of potted palms, hydrangeas and asparagus ferns dusted with gold. An upper balcony – remote and half-lit by church candles inside waist-high cut-glass cannisters – sheltered beneath a vaulted ceiling garlanded with pale-blue gauze and star-shaped indigo lights.

Philip, looking round the table to see if he knew anyone, discovered that, in fact, he knew everyone. In addition to Carlotta and Hannah, the Sloans and three generations of Alonsos, Louisa Caulfield had brought Dixie who, after the first round of drinks, sat grinning like a marionette, his chin submerged in a stiff collar that had grown too big for his neck. Due to his wealth and advanced age Dixie didn't strictly qualify as a 'walker', although he served the purpose, when he had to, in nearly every other sense. He had been widowed three times and each of his wives — robustly wealthy Mayflower descendants — had died of the same type of cancer, making him a matrimonial risk that Louisa had so far been unwilling to take.

'I suppose everyone's heard the latest findings about glyphosate,' Armando said, looking daggers at his father.

Eduardo, swallowing the full contents of his wine glass, signalled the waiter to pour him another. 'Yeah, so what?' he barked.

'So, all the data shows that Roundup has been leeching into the water supply. It's even been detected in the plasma of manatees.'

Sunny fixed her eyes unhappily on the immense centrepiece of Persian mountain violets and roses blocking her view of the drinks trolley. 'Roundup sounds like the way this ball was put together,' she mumbled.

'Very funny,' Armando snapped back. 'Roundup ought to be banned. Period.'

'Together with the entire human race, I suppose,' Eduardo added.

'What is Roundup?' Philip whispered to Hannah.

'A common pesticide. It's used on lawns and in a really big way on sugar-cane plantations,' she whispered back.

In the awkward silence that followed, the band music booming in the background provided a much-welcomed distraction. As conversations slowly began to reignite, Philip, turning to Carlotta, noted with regret that Mrs Vine was missing from their group. In a very short time he had become fond of his benefactress, as moved by her concern for plants and animals as he was charmed by her witticisms.

'I'm afraid that Vanessa has been blacklisted until further notice,' Carlotta replied. 'She brought her chauffeur to the Red Cross Ball just before Christmas. The silly goose thought we wouldn't recognise Jerzy out of uniform, but of course everyone did.'

Philip wanted to say that, by inviting him, Carlotta had in a sense done the same.

'Afterwards,' she continued without pause, 'when Louisa upbraided her for behaving like the *nouveau riche*, Vanessa replied: "That's all well and good for you Mayflower blue bloods, but the rest of us unwashed masses would rather be *nouveau* than no *riche* at all!"'

Carlotta described the exchange with gusto, indicating that, at least on this occasion, she had sided with Mrs Vine. Smearing her roll with butter on both sides, she wolfed it down as if she feared The Breakers might run out of bread. It was typical of Carlotta to eat fast. As the youngest of eleven children she had learned early what one had to do to keep from starving. But at parties like this, where survival was a more subtle juggling act and people preferred to drink rather than eat, and talk instead of listen, Carlotta did nothing but eat and listen. Her ears were continually on fire, silently gathering information that she could later use against them.

Tonight, her intended target was her grandson's fiancée, as the former Miss New Jersey swimsuit contest winner turned out to be when Armando, tapping a silver fork against his wine glass, made the announcement to the entire table. Eduardo finally seemed pleased with his son, Patsy looked down at her plate and Carlotta, with her lips pressed together, vowed privately to do whatever it took to stop the waitress at the Dune Dog Dive Bar from ruining the family. Taking a few quick sips of the Tootsie Roll cocktail that had magically appeared at the side of her plate of foie gras and toast points, Carlotta tried to put the tragedy of Armando's impending nuptials out of her mind by computing the amount of money the numbers tonight would bring in for the cause dearest to her heart.

The musicians took breaks during courses, and Tito Puente, responding to a flurry of requests, promised to play his award-winning '*Mambo Gozon*' after the silent auction. Stepping down from the podium, the bandleader walked through the glittering orbit of silver trays and candlelight to the head table and, bowing to Carlotta, thanked her on behalf of refugees everywhere. His comments were followed by a crescendo of applause that seemed to go on and on while the whole ballroom rose to toast Carlotta. Philip, trying to keep out of the limelight, pushed his chair away from the table and gazed up at the sky in the ceiling.

'A penny for your thoughts,' Hannah said.

'I was just thinking about – about the beach at night,' he improvised. But what he was really thinking about was being alone with Hannah on the beach. 'And the distraction the lights and noise of the ballroom pose to the turtle nests. Do they hold parties here often?'

'Several times a week during the season. It's a huge source of revenue for the hotels. On a more cheerful note,' she added, 'Jesse loved every moment he spent with you today. It's all he could talk about when we got home.' Hannah checked a tiny gold and diamond wristwatch that Philip had thought was a bracelet. 'I expect Julietta has already put him to bed. But first they must read from *The Little Lame Prince*. We can't turn out his light without reading a few pages.'

'What will you do when the book is finished?'

Hannah explained that the book had been finished a dozen times. 'Then we go back to the beginning and start over. Do you know the story? The book was a children's classic when I was growing up.'

Philip didn't know it. It occurred to him that, despite his father being a poet, neither of his parents had ever read to him.

'It's about a little lame prince exiled to a tower. One day he discovers a magic cloak and uses it to fly to places he would otherwise never see.'

Philip listened attentively as Hannah described the tale. When she finished he asked whether she had written any stories. 'I mean for Jesse, based on his favourite characters.'

She seemed surprised by the question. 'I've never thought about writing fiction.'

'Why not? I could serve as a consultant on all matters related to the sea.'

Carlotta returned to her seat and, on cue, waiters sprang from doors and behind curtains to serve the next course. Across the table Sunny had just discovered that the differently shaped goblets surrounding her plate were all filled with ice cubes and water. 'I'll just be a minute,' she said and rose from her seat.

'No you won't,' Addison whispered and pulled her back.

Looking more and more agitated, Sunny jumped to her feet, her sequin belt buckle gleaming as she leaned her elfin figure over her plate and grabbed Philip's wine glass.

'Don't be a selfish prig,' she said loudly. 'We brought you here to clean up our beach, dammit, not drink all our wine!'

Seeing his shock, Hannah reached for Philip's hand under the table and squeezed it. The others, however, felt they were getting off easy. Sunny might, after all, have taken off her clothes. Fortunately, Tito Puente had returned to the podium and the orchestra resumed playing. Philip, still reeling from Sunny's assault, asked Carlotta to dance.

'Too much fast beat for my old bones,' she demurred, fixing her eyes gloomily on Sunny. 'Ask me again when Tito plays a slower tune. But I imagine Hannah wouldn't mind a twirl round the dancefloor.' Inclining her head towards Philip she confided that Dr Caulfield didn't dance. 'But since he can't be with us tonight I should think it would do Hannah a world of good to go for a spin.'

'Shall we?' Philip said, turning to his right.

They rose from their seats as 'Five Beat Mambo' turned up the heat in the ballroom. Fuelled by Michelin-star food and five-star gossip the dancers let themselves be seized by the music, popular Latino tunes rolling over one another as their bodies grew entwined, making it hard to tell who was dancing with whom. This was what Islanders kept in shape for in their gyms and on the golf and tennis courts: the reason they returned, season after season, until the final moment when they silently dropped out of sight. One of Hannah's shoes came off in the tussle and she got down on her knee to search for it. By the time she rose again a vaguely familiar man with a Cheshire cat smile and flabby cheeks had slipped in between her and Philip.

It was the head vicar at Gethsemane-on-the-Sea. He had ditched his cassock for an Armani tuxedo, the sole concession to his divine calling being the requisite clerical collar instead of a bow tie. Spiriting Hannah deeper inside the jungle of tuxedos and ball gowns, he deposited in her place an elderly man wearing a much younger face and a great deal of make-up. Philip sprang back from the man's hideously distorted features. Then he remembered something he had overheard at the pearl collection: to the effect that, no matter what age you are, the main thing at parties is to look twenty years younger.

It was past two in the morning when Eduardo swung the Bentley into Hibiscus Way. Philip saw Hannah's white convertible parked in her drive, silently congratulating her for managing to slip away from the ball early. Carlotta, resting her stiff hair on Philip's shoulder in the back seat, drowsily hummed the old Cuban national anthem that Tito Puente had played in her honour at the close of the evening.

On his way to the annexe Philip stopped beside the softly illuminated infinity pool. He stretched out on a canvas chaise longue, hands locked behind his head as he gazed up at the sky and recalled the events of the day. It seemed to him that of all its astonishing twists and turns, the most astonishing by far was the shift taking place between him and the strange new world he had entered: or perhaps, Philip thought, only between him and Hannah Caulfield. In a place of heady fragrances and giant toads that seemed to hop straight out of a fairy tale, attitudes had a curious habit of shapeshifting. For example, the way Hannah seemed so at ease around people the young woman writing to his father would have found laughable. Philip certainly found them laughable, yet also somehow more human than the same kind of people back home, for whom pretence was not just a game but a way of life.

He unbuttoned his stiff collar and picked apart the bow tie, breathing in the scent of flowering night jasmines, their white, starburst-shaped blossoms splayed open to the moon. He remembered how his bow tie had come loose when he and Hannah began dancing, and how nimbly she had reassembled it, her cool fingers brushing against his neck. Closing his eyes, Philip felt again the touch of her hands.

JULIETTA RALLIES
THE TROOPS

Hannah reached her arm to the nightstand, catapulted from a deep sleep by the sound of the telephone. Lying next to her in the bed, his gold hair spread on the pillow, Jesse gave a yawn and turned over on his side.

It was the first of several calls from snowbound Thaddeus in New York. Bored and with nothing to do, he asked about the ball, the weather and how Hannah and Jesse were planning to spend the day without him.

'We haven't decided,' Hannah said drowsily.

She would have liked to go back to sleep, but her husband's calls kept coming, one after another.

'What are you making for breakfast?' he asked.

Hannah and Jesse had by then gone down to the kitchen and the Looney Tunes cartoons were putting on their usual Saturday morning performance in the family room. Hannah, cradling the cordless phone on her shoulder, emptied the dishwasher and made toast while listening to her husband complain about the weather in New York. 'I didn't make any provisions for breakfast,' he grumbled. 'And now all I have is leftover Asian stir fry. What are you having?' he asked for the third time.

'It's hard to think about food after last night,' Hannah said. 'I'll see what Jesse feels like in a bit.'

'Just don't let him do anything too strenuous this weekend.'

'What do you mean?' she asked, lowering the shade above the sink. Having slept late, the sun was already streaming full over the counter.

'Only that, without his weekly injection Jesse's condition could deteriorate quickly. You don't have to keep him indoors or anything, but do keep an eye on him.'

'Actually, he seems rather better than usual.'

It occurred to Hannah that this was a chance to pause the serum and see how Jesse did without it. Saying nothing further about it to her husband, she ended the conversation and went to the family room.

'After breakfast we'll go out on the beach to see if there are any new turtle nests. You'd like that, wouldn't you?'

Jesse shook his head, his eyes glued to Road Runner, who was darting across the large screen television. 'It won't be the same without Dolphin.'

'But he might be there now, waiting for us.'

'No he won't. Julietta is bringing a group from her school to the institute and they're spending the entire day.' Jesse rubbed his nose. 'Want to know what else Julietta told me last night? But you must keep it secret.'

Hannah smiled and raised her right hand. 'You have my word, poppet.'

'Julietta and Dolphin are going to be married as soon as she gets out of school. And we're all invited to the wedding!'

Hannah said nothing, the smile gone from her face. 'Is that so?' she mused.

Philip petted the turtle affectionately when he noticed one of its fins protruding over the edge of the cot. 'You're longing to return to the sea, aren't you? It won't be long now.'

He loved early mornings at the lab, when he could work without being interrupted and sunlight streamed through the east-facing windows: the only sounds coming from Princess's heartbeat on the monitor and ever-present rise and fall of waves on the beach. Philip had just entered the turtle's vital signs in the log when, seeing a shadow in one of the windows, he looked up and saw Julietta, accompanied by half a dozen girls, peering at him through the glass.

He had almost forgotten that Julietta was bringing a group of volunteers from the Day Academy, and now here they were. My foot soldiers, Philip thought, his heart leaping as he spread open the door and shook the girls' outstretched hands. They were dressed to the nines, in Lilly-print sundresses and volumes of Woolworth's make-up, fawning over Princess with their new 'bedroom eyes' look while Philip tried to tell them about his new environmental initiative.

'And we can do it right here, starting with our own offshore reef. Measuring subtle shifts in the ocean's saline levels will help us predict not just the degree of stress these changes have on the corals' ability to survive but on the global ecosystem they produce...'

For more than an hour Philip expounded on the intricacies of harvesting coral samples from the reef and seeding them in the lab. One by one, the girls' bedroom eyes glazed over and they began whispering: about Princess and how cute the Englishman looked when he was trying to be serious.

'It would mark the beginning of South Florida's first coral research station,' Philip continued, raising his voice to be heard above the titters, 'and will require continual and highly precise monitoring – not something I can do all on my own.'

'But you're not on your own,' Julietta championed. 'You have us!'

A collective cheer went up, effectively ending the session. The teens filed out the door and Philip, seeing his foot soldiers about to disperse to more profitable Saturday activities, sprang after them. Then, like an answer to a prayer, the stampeding girls were stopped in their tracks by Mrs Vine's Silver Shadow blocking the drive. Chugging like a vintage locomotive it proceeded to the outdoor picnic table where the widow, bundled in a diaphanous violet-tinted robe and veiled raffia hat, slid like a dollop of warm butter from the creamy interior.

She approached the group with her usual slow steps, using her folded parasol as a cane and accompanied by the dutiful Jerzy carrying three large cardboard parcels stacked on top of each other like hatboxes. Another cheer erupted when the chauffeur placed them on the picnic table and, lifting the lids, produced several dozen *paczki*, a homemade Polish version of jam doughnuts dusted with powdered sugar. Hurrying back to the Rolls, Jerzy returned with several Thermos flasks filled with ice-cold lemonade.

Philip turned to Mrs Vine. 'You saved the day!' he cried.

'Like Jesus feeding the five thousand,' she purred, offering him her cheek. 'And by the look of this bunch, Jesus arrived just in time.'

The teenagers mobbed the picnic table. Some sat on benches and others on the old croquet lawn, downing doughnuts and copious amounts of lemonade; while Philip, standing a little aside with Mrs Vine, continued to discourse on his coral reef initiative. 'It would mean an additional outlay of funds to purchase a seed bank.'

'Oh, that's nothing,' she said, waving her hand dismissively. 'I can always throw another ball. Speaking of which…' The widow lowered her voice, taking Philip's arm. 'I heard that you were at Carlotta's jamboree last night – and that my daughter managed to make a scene.'

'It wasn't exactly a scene,' Philip said tactfully.

'But enough of one to turn me into a laughing stock.'

Philip assured her that no one he saw was laughing.

'If Sunny gets drunk enough at a party she's likely to toss that silly rhinestone belt buckle in someone's face!'

Philip said he believed Sunny's husband hadn't allowed her to drink. 'That's what led to the outburst, and she stomped out before the auction.' Trying to think of something positive to report, he said: 'A number of people mentioned how sorry they were that you didn't come to the ball. You're quite the Island celebrity, you know.'

'Oh, I know, I know. But I'd still like to hear what they said. Out with it!'

'It was mainly to do with your witticisms,' Philip said, skirting the narrative of how she had brought Jerzy to the Red Cross Ball.

'Such as?'

'That all courtships end in court.'

'All except mine! Go on, what else?'

'Well,' Philip tried to keep a straight face, 'that men past a certain age want only one of two things from a woman...'

'A nurse or a purse,' she finished.

The teens started clapping and Mrs Vine, holding court, gave a small curtsy (or as much of one as she could manage) and said: 'You know, we girls say all sorts of things in our youth to establish how clever we are. But they are hardly meant to be a prescription for living.'

One of the teens raised her hand. 'Is there such a thing,' she asked deferentially, 'as a prescription for living?'

'There most certainly is,' cried Mrs Vine, her tired eyes flashing. Stripping the veil from her face she gave her audience a radiant smile. 'It is to make sure that you always get carried away when it seems like the last thing to do; and to positively never – ever! – look back.'

Seated on the pillion behind Philip, with her arms wrapped tightly around his slim waist and the heels of her espadrilles skimming the pebbles on Lake Trail, Julietta Alonso dreamed of a future filled with moments exactly like this. The classmates she had brought to the institute that morning had signed up to volunteer every Saturday for the remainder of the school term, and Philip had felt sufficiently indebted to offer Julietta a lift home on his bicycle. With a moist and gentle breeze from the Lagoon in their faces, he made little or no response to Julietta's repeated attempts to engage him in conversation.

'I wonder how many other gators are still lurking along this trail,' she said when they arrived at the duct-tape barrier surrounding the area where the alligator attack had taken place. There were dark stains on the gravel and around a section of sand that had dislodged when the victims were dragged into the bog. 'It's blood,' Julietta gasped as they dismounted.

Philip kept a sharp lookout on the dense grasses growing along the water as they walked the bicycle round the perimeter. 'Let's get out of here,' he said, remembering Doc Preston's lurid depiction of how alligators entrap their victims.

They got back on the bicycle and Philip began to whistle, looking suspiciously at the bushes as he pedalled. 'What's that you're whistling?' Julietta asked, rubbing her chin on his shoulder.

'An old English country ballad about a young man meeting a tragic end while hunting.'

Not to be outdone, Julietta said: 'Speaking of tragic ends, I don't suppose anything compares to the blood Sunny Sloan's got on her dirty little hands.'

What now, Philip thought. 'How do you mean blood on her hands?' he called over his shoulder.

'Her own daughter is what I mean.'

'It's hard to picture Sunny Sloan having a daughter.'

'I'm afraid she did. And as good as killed her. It was two years ago this month that they found Paula's body beside the pool.'

Julietta had gone to school with little Paula Sloan and had the inside scoop. The girl had been born stout like her father and uncle and looked nothing like Sunny. 'She loved sweets heaps more than she did any of the party dresses Sunny had picked out for her since she was still in the cradle.' Dragged round designer boutiques on Worth Avenue, Paula grew up watching her mother trying on Size Two ball gowns, sipping champagne and God knows what else while the child nibbled on trays of chocolates the shopkeepers served. 'We adored Paula, who was built like a bowl of Jell-O, all fun and giggles and everyone's darling – especially her grandmother Louisa's.'

Julietta's story turned darker, exposing the unenviable lot of girls brought up on the Island. 'The thing is, it's seriously not done at our school for a girl over twelve to carry more than a few ounces of surplus weight. The ideal is the so-called Barbie doll look – twiggy legs and arms, and straight, highlighted hair – and Paula looked nothing like that. She stopped wanting to be everyone's darling and get invited to parties instead. So, on her thirteenth birthday she decided that it was time for her to become svelte. And since no one on the Island was as svelte as Sunny, Paula began paying close attention to her mother's eating habits and exercise regimen.'

'Hang on,' Philip broke in. 'How do you know all this?'

'Everyone knows, for the simple reason that Paula kept a diary – and was writing in it when she fell dead beside the pool. Parts of it were eventually reprinted in *The Shiny Sheet*.'

'So, how *did* she die?'

'According to her journal, Paula had noticed that her mother carried a small plastic pouch in her purse filled with white powder. Sunny had this thing about going to the rest room – to "powder her nose", as if anyone believed *that* – leading Paula to speculate that if a little bit of the stuff worked so well for her willowy figure, then a one-time, much bigger dose would be the very thing to kick-start her own diet. She knew where Sunny kept it hidden and set her plan out in the diary under the heading "My Diet: Day One".

'Sunny drove to Miami on Saturdays – supposedly to practice yoga with some guru but, as it turned out, mainly to buy drugs off him. Addison was playing golf and the maid had the day off when Paula put her plan in motion. She went to where Sunny kept her powders hid and spooned a large quantity of it into a glass of Nestlé instant chocolate. She whipped it smooth in the blender and then stretched out in the sun at the side of the swimming pool, sipping her drink through a straw while scribbling ever more hazy descriptions of what she hoped to look like in a month's time. And there the diary ended. No one was home when the poor thing went into convulsions and Paula had been dead for *two whole hours* by the time Addison returned from golf. The cause of death on the coroner's report was a massive overdose of cocaine. It's still brought up by teachers at our school when they're trying to caution us about drugs.'

'Are there drugs at your school?'

'Heaps.' Julietta giggled. 'Although I will say that no one today would dream of spooning cocaine into their iced chocolate.'

They were nearly home, Philip pensive as they glided past Hannah's house and Julietta regretting the grim mood her story had ushered. 'Think you'll go to church with the Caulfields tomorrow?' she asked. 'Jesse adores you, you know. He told me last night that you two are blood brothers.'

'Would they go to church without Dr Caulfield?' Philip asked.

'Sure they would. Hannah's thick with Fr Leo and often attends his midweek Mass. It seems,' Julietta said, lowering her voice as she slid off the bike, 'that the pair of them are hatching a plan for some kind of miracle to cure Jesse.'

Nothing Julietta had told him so far stunned Philip nearly as much as this news. 'You mean cure Jesse by an act of God?'

'Guess so. Though I should think it will take a lot more than one act. Dr Caulfield isn't very likely to go for it, so I suppose it's just as well he doesn't know what Hannah and Fr Leo are getting up to.'

'But you do. Is there anything that happens in this place you don't know about?'

Julietta looked at him sideways. 'No,' she said. 'Not a thing.'

Philip was among the first to arrive for the eleven o'clock service. He took a seat diagonally behind and a little to one side of where he had previously sat with the Caulfields and dropped down on the kneeler. Resting his forehead against the hard surface of the pew in front of him, he was still trying to come to terms with what Julietta had told him: first the dreadful news about the Sloans' daughter, followed by the revelation that Hannah was hoping for a miracle to cure Jesse. Coming to church quietly on his own, he hoped to understand better Julietta's claim about Hannah and the priest.

At length he heard the sound of feet and of pews creaking. Hannah was among the arrivals, wearing a powder blue, two-piece outfit and a stylish hat, Jesse in his Sunday best. They settled into their usual seat and Hannah slipped on to the kneeler, her lips moving in prayer. Then, very slowly, she lifted her eyes to an oil painting of a childlike Virgin Mary holding the infant Jesus that hung in the south transept nearest their pew. When she finished praying Hannah crossed herself, her gaze totally absorbed in the painting.

The Sloans dashed in at the last minute, hovering in the side door until the procession of choristers, servers, associate priests, vestry and curates had cleared the aisle. Tiptoeing over the stone tiles in a pair of three-inch-high stilettos, Sunny, followed by Addison, squeezed into the pew beside Hannah and Jesse.

Philip was glad that Fr Leo was officiating instead of the head vicar who had made such a spectacle of himself at the Refugee Ball. Despite his limp the Revd Dr Leopold Harris cut an imposing figure, his fiery black eyes sizzling during the Gospel reading. Quoting the entire passage from memory, he addressed his flock with gravity, while the head vicar dozed in a side chair below the pulpit.

'Light within all light,' Fr Leo said as he concluded the sermon, 'soul behind all souls, guide our hearts to discern the face of the Beloved in each child of God.'

Philip stole another look at Hannah as they listened to the priest; and saw an entirely new emotion written on her face.

BRIDGE LESSONS

'I think it's time you dropped all this nonsense about *Sir* Philip this and *Sir* Philip that,' Louisa admonished as she directed Carlotta to a seat at the card table. 'That young man has less blue blood in his veins than I do, charming as he is. I will say, however,' she added judiciously, 'that he also has far better manners than some of the snowbirds this year.'

'Even in flip-flops?' Carlotta teased.

Louisa considered. 'Well, I suppose that could happen to anyone. Why, only the other day Dixie forgot he was still wearing his slippers when we entered the dining room of the Mangrove Club.'

Carlotta knitted her bushy brows. She was far more concerned about the suit of cards she was being dealt than the details of Dixie's latest gaffe.

'Regardless of his good manners, I was frankly surprised that you brought Philip to the ball the other night.' Louisa continued. 'He is, after all, little more than a hired hand at the institute. Speaking of which, I think that my grandson and daughter-in-law have been spending more time over there than seems prudent.'

Carlotta gathered her cards. 'The institute has been a godsend for Jesse, who is finally showing some colour in his cheeks. And Sir Philip – who, by the way, I reserve the right to call by any appellation I choose – has been a wonderful influence on him.'

'Still, with Thaddeus away so much we have an obligation to keep an eye on things. Did you see those two dancing at the ball?'

'If you mean Hannah and Philip, may I remind you that I was the one who suggested that he ask her to dance.'

'Why shouldn't they get on? After all, they're both English,' Sunny observed sensibly (forgetting, perhaps, that her sudden assault on Philip was what had driven them from the table). Sunny was in any case out of sorts, having been recruited by her mother at the last minute to take the place of ninety-four-year-old Mrs Flagg, who was their usual fourth at bridge.

'I pass,' Carlotta said, and placed none of her cards on the table. Louisa, leaning smugly back in her seat, added a seven of diamonds to her burgeoning suit.

The women were gathered in Louisa's pastel drawing room with the seashell wallpaper and all the windows open. Nibbling on finger sandwiches and sipping raspberry-lime rickeys from silver tumblers, the players understood what never needed to be said: that the game they were about to play had less to do with their skill at cards than with revealing neither too much nor too little of what was really on their minds.

Sunny drank thirstily but was unable to detect any gin in her lime rickey. Once again, at her mother's request, alcohol had been omitted from her glass, leaving a much stronger taste of sugar, raspberries and key limes. When needed, the Big Three performed such favours for one another. They had raised their children together, and for decades had been fiercely devoted friends and competitors. In advanced years their agreements were more likely to be due to some disagreement with everyone else, and their rapprochements the by-product of exhaustion.

Louisa held a distinct advantage over her companions (her only advantage, so far as they were concerned), in that her family had always occupied Villa des Coquilles. She outranked them in the husband department as well, having been widowed twice. This was another dubious distinction so far as Carlotta and Vanessa could see, since neither of Louisa's marriages had been a success. Vanessa, too, stood somewhat apart on account of her past in the music halls. Yet over many years she had earned her position as an equal in their tight circle – admission to which had far less to do with looks, style or how much money one gave away during the season than with outlasting the competition.

Mrs Vine was silently fuming that Louisa had put her in the seat facing the floor-to-ceiling rococo mirror. She supposed that someone had to take it, though she'd rather have sat on top of the pianoforte, which would have provided more space for her derrière, and spared her the continual reminder of what she looked like. There had been a time when Vanessa Vine never passed a reflecting surface without stealing a glimpse at herself. These days mirrors were a reproach, announcing to the world that her eyes bulged and the skin around them sagged. It was, in Vanessa's case, the reason for the veils she wore, and possibly a sign of some ailment to do with her heart – a small price to pay in her estimation for all the love that little organ had produced.

'In any case,' Louisa resumed – she never lost her train of thought – 'we have our duties to consider.'

'What duties?' Carlotta passed her eyes over the richly appointed drawing room. 'We have everything done for us.'

'I was referring to our moral duties.'

Mrs Vine began to object, and a minor skirmish broke out. Sunny, seeing an opportunity, quietly left the table.

'We three are the last line of defence between the way Islanders behave and the way they ought to behave,' Louisa lectured, sliding one of her cards under the table. 'Growing old together is the strongest bond between us.'

'But not as exciting as having been young together,' cried Mrs Vine. 'And don't imagine I didn't see what you just did with that card!'

'And I'll thank *you* not to break my Louis Quinze chair again,' Louisa, hearing it creak, shot back.

Sunny in the mean time returned to her seat.

'I pass,' Carlotta said, fanning her cards shut.

'Bid!' Louisa triumphantly placed an ace of spades on top.

All traces of camaraderie faded as the game turned deadly fierce. For a few tense moments everything the women had discussed, or were about to discuss, turned into an aside for the cards being shuffled furiously between the two teams. When the game ended they leaned back reflectively in their seats, the ghosts of themselves as young wives and mothers hovering over the table.

Mrs Vine was the first to get up, her new hip stiff from being seated too long, and followed Louisa to the door. The women's talk was about the next big gala coming up and their plans for the evening. When it turned out that none of them had any plans, Louisa returned to the subject of her family. 'Say what you will, Carlotta, but it seemed to me that the British contingent at the ball was getting on like a house on fire. And that dress!'

Carlotta gave a dreamy smile. 'It did rather remind me of the backless little number Princess Di wore in '85 – in the same ballroom.'

Mrs Vine, still bristling that she had been excluded from the ball, thrust her walking stick-cum-parasol purposefully ahead of her, leaving the women standing in the door.

'Now don't go on worrying about Sir Philip,' Carlotta confided when the others were out of earshot. 'Something tells me that young man has fresher fish to fry than our poor Hannah.'

HOT TIPS AND RUMOURS

Snowploughs rumbled through the streets of Manhattan like tanks in a city under siege, yellow cabs with chains wrapped around their tyres grinding over the whited avenues. As New York painstakingly stirred back to life Thaddeus found himself continually on the phone – with his bank, scientific team and brother in Palm Beach. The more they weighed up the impending real-estate deal in Cherokee Place the clearer it became that an additional influx of capital would be needed to secure the lease. Fortunately, unlike banks in New York, which were still shut due to the storm, the Shearson branch in Palm Beach was doing business as usual. And as luck would have it, Addison happened to play golf with the bank's president on Saturdays.

'Of course, it would be easier to ask Mother for a loan,' he said, thinking aloud. 'She could write a cheque and it would be done and dusted in no time.'

But the brothers knew that asking Louisa for money was a risky proposition. Not because she might refuse, but because she would never let them forget it. A moment or two of silence followed on both ends of the phone line while the brothers considered, and quickly dismissed, the Louisa option.

As it turned out, the loan was approved with astonishing speed. The Caulfield name vouched for itself, and funds were wired overnight to the property association in Cherokee Place. The closing for the transaction was set for the end of day on the coming Friday, with more papers to sign on Saturday; making it very unlikely that Thaddeus would be able to return home for the second weekend in a row. In the mean time, rumours abounded on Wall Street. Chief among them was that Pandorex was investing in a massive new facility on the East River for the final phase of clinical trials because the serum had been tipped for quick approval by the FDA. The profit seekers and high-stakes market gamblers took advantage of the quiet days after the storm to accumulate large chunks of stock. By the time the lease was signed, not on the following Friday due to a technical glitch but late on Saturday, the value of Pandorex shares had nearly doubled.

Over the course of several long and on the whole unsatisfactory phone conversations with his wife, Thaddeus Caulfield felt his grip on their son's treatment slipping. Distance does matter, he thought, as he struggled to convince Hannah that the serum was absolutely essential to Jesse's health.

'But I tell you he's doing fine without it,' she argued.

'And without me too, I suppose.'

Hannah felt like hanging up on him, but instead she said: 'Oh Thad, of course we miss you – terribly. Although,' she couldn't refrain from adding, 'it's not as if we're not used to you being away.'

The doctor had to admit that his family sounded well, the house running smoothly. And yet, for the first time, not all his calls were returned. When Marta answered it was to say that Hannah and Jesse were 'out on the beach' or 'at the institute'. The news should have made him happy. It was, after all, his idea that Jesse become involved with the new turtle facility. Yet, in no small part due to Louisa, the notion that the young marine biologist running the institute might not be the best influence on his family began to needle him.

It wasn't the first time Louisa had tried to drive a wedge between Thaddeus and Hannah. From the moment he had brought his new wife and her son to the Island, Louisa had made no secret of her view that Jesse's infirmity and consequent 'lack of children of your own' was too big a sacrifice for a young man. It was bad enough that Louisa's other son had married the drink-and-drugs-addled Sunny Vine, leading to the loss of a granddaughter in the sort of tragedy that takes the polish off a good family name. And to Louisa, Caulfield and Sloan were wonderful old names. Thankfully, neither of her husbands had lived long enough to disprove it, and she had done her duty by giving each of them a child – the minimum, in Louisa's estimation, that should be expected of a wife. By contrast, the women her sons had married led to a feeling of dissatisfaction with her progeny that Louisa made it a point never to conceal from them.

As Addison's plane taxied towards the gate at LaGuardia airport, passing a line of airplanes waiting to be de-iced, the lawyer counted himself lucky that his flight from Palm Beach hadn't been grounded. He had flown to New York specifically to work out the details of the Pandorex lease, and to prep Thaddeus for an upcoming FDA inspection of the new facility and all-important review of the clinical trial data. Helping his younger brother was something Addison was used to doing, starting on the day Thad's father – Louisa's second husband – had died after a lingering illness from cancer. Louisa had insisted that the entire family be present at his deathbed, and four-year-old Thaddeus had gone to hide in the Shell House. Louisa followed him, admonishing as she tried to pull him out by the ears and accusing the boy of dishonouring his father; while Thaddeus, stuttering and with tears streaming down his face, clung to the shell doorframe and shrieked.

It was the first, last and only time that Addison, who was then fifteen, powerfully built and tall for his age, stood up to their mother. Wresting his little brother away from her he had carried Thaddeus to the boat landing, far from the wail of the ambulance that had come to roll the elder Caulfield into a canvas body bag. The brothers had remained at the dock until the house emptied and Thaddeus finally fell asleep on Addison's shoulder. Louisa withdrew angrily to her room, shuttering every window facing the Lagoon, and didn't come out for two days. When she did, it was with her usual disdain for any form of weakness and something akin to a new respect for Addison.

Thaddeus, however, as became evident from the time he entered school, possessed something even Louisa couldn't touch. He was, simply put, brilliant. Lumbering along with a boyish grin, he had a way of coming up with solutions to seemingly insoluble analytic problems, wowing teachers, colleagues and, in due course, his patients. But when it had to do with family, Addison knew that his brother was nowhere near so sure of himself. In the lawyer's estimation Thaddeus had taken a huge risk by marrying a foreign teenage girl he hardly knew and adopting her son: followed by the even bigger risk of staking everything on the success of a cancer drug that was still essentially unproven. Thaddeus, it seemed to Addison as he removed his briefcase from the overhead compartment of the plane and slid sideways into the aisle, had never needed his protection more than he did right now.

After a full day of prepping for the FDA visit the brothers felt entitled to a big meal at the Good Times Diner on Lexington Avenue and 78th Street. Addison went ahead to secure a booth, stomping the slush from his shoes as he threw his anorak over a coat rack heaving with steamy outerwear. The Greek proprietor standing behind the cash register nodded Addison to the same vinyl-upholstered booth with a crack running down the middle that the brothers had occupied on every previous visit to the establishment – the owner's way of saying, perhaps, that in a city famous for anonymity, one could still be known.

Addison slid inside the high-backed vinyl booth and ordered a cup of coffee. His mouth watered at the oblong plates smothered in French fries and onion rings that were being delivered to the next table. As a young man he'd had a weakness for fast food, fast girls and fast cars, recalling, with some of the same appetite, the thrill of falling in love with Sunny Vine. Pretty, pert and endlessly good fun when she was drunk, Sunny was the Island bad girl. They had played together as children before drifting apart but found each other again after university: Addison to practice law in Palm Beach and Sunny raising hell at all-night parties.

He had always liked the look of her: blonde, petite and unconventional, she was the exact opposite of Louisa. With Sunny he could let his guard down and drive faster. In a rare act of defiance he married her. Addison still remembered their first night on the beach: Sunny stoned and chatty and full of tall tales about who her real parents could have been – unlike Addison's lineage, which was codified like a tombstone in the pages of *The Social Register*. But apart from marrying Sunny and driving the latest model Maserati, Addison had remained a caretaker at heart. He took care of estates and trusts at Sloan, Ritter & Clark as he had always taken care of his little brother. And now he had mad, sad Sunny to attend to, who excoriated herself more violently than the world ever would for the death of their child.

Sipping coffee, his thoughts darkened amid the glare of headlights in the diner window. On the other side of the panelled glass, misty from food sizzling on the grill and frosty on the outside, pedestrians sloshed home from work past waist-high snowbanks dirtied by traffic. Addison watched them, wondering if it had been a mistake to leave Sunny alone in Palm Beach – not because of the pills and powders, which she seemed to have given up, but the harm he still sometimes feared she might do to herself. Hearing a tap from the other side of the windowpane, he saw his brother.

There was only just enough room for the two giants in the narrow booth, the chrome-edged Formica tabletop wedged between them thronged with condiments. 'We sat with Hannah and Jesse in church the other day,' Addison said, ripping with his teeth a packet of oyster crackers and sprinkling them over his cup of corn chowder. 'Sunny sees them a good deal at the turtle facility, and she thinks it's done Jesse a world of good.' He broke off. 'As a matter of fact, I think it's done Sunny a lot of good as well.'

Addison described how his wife, responding to orders from the Big Three, had taken over the student volunteer program. 'Hannah brings Jesse over most days to join the group and he's never seemed better.'

Thaddeus said nothing. From the time his son's tumours had gone into remission he had continued to administer small doses of monoclonal antibodies by injection. Although he had no definite proof, the doctor was convinced that Jesse was benefitting from the serum in other, so far undocumented, ways. Few children born with the same malady lived past their teens, and Jesse, who would soon be twelve, was doing far better than expected. Hearing from everyone he spoke to that his son was recovering at a stage of the illness when his body ought to be shutting down was the surest sign yet that the injections had been having a positive effect. To stop them now, as Hannah wanted, was nothing short of reckless.

'I must get home,' Thaddeus muttered into his chowder, scarcely aware that he had spoken the last words aloud.

THE GOLD-DIGGER'S TALE

Of all the versions in circulation about how Vanessa Vine had snared the mining king of North America, the most popular by far was the one she told herself. She never tried to conceal the fact (as others might have done) that the deed had been accomplished in collusion with a bouncer at Manhattan's 21 Club, who had very likely been paid for his services. Or that the iconic New York restaurant standing a stone's throw from Radio City Music Hall had been the venue in which twenty-five-year-old chorus-line dancer Vanessa Fitzgerald made her debut in the life of Sanford Vine.

She had just landed a break as one of the Rockettes at Radio City and had never been more ravishing – or more determined. The said bouncer, thought to have some connection to Vanessa back in Peoria, Illinois, had tipped her off that the fabulously wealthy – and recently divorced – Sanford Vine had begun frequenting the bar. The bouncer's role was to get the occupant of the bar stool next to Sanford called away to the telephone at the very moment that Vanessa walked into the 21 Club after a dress rehearsal.

All went according to plan. Vanessa claimed the seat on the empty bar stool, crossed her long dancer's legs and hiked her skirt up several inches above her knees. She was very slow about it, as she was about fastening the arch of one of her tap-dancing shoes over the brass foot-rail of the bar. Perched like a bird on the wire, the chorus girl was anything but unaware of the sparkle in her forget-me-not-blue-green eyes as she powdered her nose in the mirror above the bar.

Placidly smoking a cigar as he monitored the redhead's strategic machinations, the mining king, as Vanessa had already begun to think of him, looked regal in a hand-tailored, three-piece suit, silk cravat and diamond-embossed platinum cufflinks. The pair made eye contact in the mirror: he pure silver and she gold; he with money and she full of ideas about how to spend it. What Sanford Vine thought at this crucial juncture remains unclear, though he allegedly disclosed to a few of his male friends, years later over bourbon and cigars, that he had been less taken with the chorus girl's looks than by her smell – a heady mix of gardenia-scented talc and the pure odour of her sweat. It evoked images of bare skin and coconut palms on a sandy beach in the tropics. Sanford, who was nearing fifty and could well afford to buy such a beach – and almost anything else besides – was hooked.

He offered the sumptuous creature a drink; and, when she politely refused, showed her all three of his platinum cigarette cases and asked her to choose one.

'You mean one cigarette or one case?' she said. Winking at the bartender, Vanessa asked for a glass of cold milk. 'I get so parched after rehearsal,' she laughed. Then, inclining her head a bit closer to Sanford Vine, she lowered her voice to a mellifluous ripple and confessed that their meeting had been no accident. 'I contrived it, sir, and have an excellent reason for doing so.'

The mining king respected honesty. It was the greatest of the virtues, he thought, next to hard work and fair play. But what he liked even more was the way this girl half his age cocked her hip against the brass rail and said, in the same rippling voice: 'You see, a little bird from back home happened to mention that you and I, improbable as this may sound, are in the same line of business. And it occurred to me that, with a coincidence like that – I mean you rich and me good-looking, as the song goes…' – here Vanessa paused to hum a few lines from 'Summertime' – '…we might do something really grand if we pool our resources.'

Sanford Vine considered it a bizarre proposal. 'I fail to see how we could be in the same line of *business*, Miss—'

'The name is Fitzgerald – Vanessa Fitzgerald,' she said proudly. 'And the business I am referring to is mining.'

Sanford, looking around the bar, asked her to explain.

'It's quite simple,' Vanessa announced, all the little stars in her eyes shining. 'You own mines in Nevada and I'm a gold-digger.'

Sanford Vine turned bright red, and his cheeks puffed out as he held his cigar breath for as long as he could. Then he exploded in a boisterous laugh that made every head in the 21 Club turn to the bar. When he quieted, his chest heaving and tears rolling down his cheeks, Sanford gave the redhead a silent round of applause. 'I hate to disappoint you, Miss Fitzgerald,' he said, beckoning her nearer, 'but my mines are of platinum, not gold.'

Vanessa smiled. 'Oh, I'm sure we could work around that. My methods, you see, are exactly the same when it comes to precious metals.'

A few insanely short weeks later Sanford Vine proposed marriage. 'On one condition,' he said, drawing a red, gold-edged Cartier box from his pocket. 'That we go live on a gardenia-scented island in the tropics.'

'So long as the island isn't deserted,' Vanessa replied, grabbing the box.

Their married life began with a search for the biggest, most expensive property in Palm Beach. The house the newlyweds eventually found was another match made in heaven. The Villa des Vagues had just come on the market and the couple offered to pay more for the estate than anyone in their right mind would have done. Scouring Europe for antiques and *objets d'art* suited to the villa's ambience, the Vines embarked on a decade-long buying spree that continued long after their house was furnished. In the process – and contrary to expectation – they grew closer and more connected. Having set out to conquer the Island, the couple discovered that they were having much more fun conquering each other. And when it turned out that Vanessa couldn't bear a child they adopted a baby girl and named her Sunny. What else were they to call the tiny cherub with bright-yellow hair and a smile that never left its face?

Sanford doted on his little girl. But to Vanessa's profound dismay, loving a strong-willed child wasn't as easy as loving her pets. However hard she tried she couldn't always hide the relief she felt when Sanford took the girl to one of their private clubs for the afternoon, leaving Vanessa to attend to her growing family of stray animals. It was hardly acceptable in those days for a woman to admit – as Vanessa blithely did, pretending it was a joke – that she would much rather have a handsome man burst into her room in the middle of the night than a child with a tummy ache.

Sunny was still in high school when Sanford's throat began to give out from the bourbon and seven daily cigars. Vanessa – having gone, according to her own dictum, through Sanford's 'purse' – astonished everyone by becoming his devoted nurse. She hardly paid attention to their daughter during his dreadful collapse, leaving Sunny dangerously prone, like many another child raised on the Island, to soothe the pain of growing up rich with almost any form of excess. Sunny imbibed Listerine and sniffed glue when she couldn't find anything stronger and drank her heart out at parties. She was locked out of the house so often at night that she got more used to sleeping with the feral cats inside the colonnade than in her own bed.

It was a huge relief for everyone – except Louisa of course – when Sunny married Addison Sloan. Horrified by his choice, Louisa couldn't understand why, of all the Island girls, her brilliant son should choose Sunny. But what disturbed her even more was that Vanessa Vine scored a decisive victory in their years-long competition by unloading her reprobate daughter on Addison, the most promising young lawyer in Palm Beach.

Left alone in her palazzo, Sanford Vine's widow retreated deeper inside the make-believe world they had created. Every tapestry, piece of art and furniture – not to mention Vanessa's weight in jewels and beaded ball gowns – reminded the ageing chatelaine of her former happiness. She no longer noticed the opulence of her surroundings, only the memories attached to them. In old age she began spending the evenings when she wasn't attending some gala in the stubborn silence of her boudoir, hung with tufted brocade to resemble a Moorish tent. In between the dinner dances and charity auctions she engineered to alleviate her loneliness the widow would spend long periods seated among the cushions in her boudoir with the door to the walk-in safe wide open. Petting her furry companions, Vanessa tried on the precious rings, bracelets and necklaces Sanford had given her, many still in their original satin and velvet boxes. The jewels glittered in the dimly lit oval mirror with a light that briefly eclipsed the parchment-like skin on which they were now mounted: reminding the widow that, given the chance, she would not choose to live life over again – with the exception, perhaps, of those few episodes without which her life would not have been worth living.

With the winter of '91 so very much warmer than in previous years, Mrs Vine's gardenias were set to bloom early and the almond trees were already shedding their bright-red leaves. She loved strolling in the late mornings through her moss-edged coquina paths shaded by an avenue of banyan trees hung with orchid plants. The lavender-tinted Vanda orchid was Mrs Vine's favourite, recalling her start in showbusiness more than sixty years ago as Vanessa the Vampish Vanda. That was when she had still been doing the fan dance at a strip bar in Peoria – a place that seemed as far removed from the scent of lemon, lime and orange blossoms surrounding her half-indoor, half-outdoor swimming pool as the twentieth century was from the Garden of Eden.

The widow paused during her stroll in order to give her hip a rest and crush the orange blossoms between her fingers to release the smell. Rubbing the fragrance on her temples she remembered the cheap gardenia talc with which she had doused her armpits on the day she went to the 21 Club to lay a trap for Sanford. It had been the last time Vanessa was obliged to buy anything cheap, and for some moments she grew lost in thought, the sound of water gurgling from several different fountains muffling the noise of the doorbell. Expecting her daughter for lunch, and surprised that Sunny would ring, the widow hobbled indoors on her parasol and nearly collided with Fr Leo in the foyer.

He had a down-home habit – or perhaps didn't know better – of dropping by his parishioners' homes unannounced. This was usually in order to ask for some small favour or financial assistance for the disabled children. In Mrs Vine's case it nearly always had to do with coercing Gethsemane's biggest donor to start coming to Mass again. Wondering how Fr Leo would go about it this time she began planning her rebuttal as she led him through the front vestibule to the colonnade.

The priest's limp was always worse when the humidity was high, causing him to trip over the ragged edge of a Persian carpet nibbled threadbare by one of the pet pigs. Regaining his balance he laboured painfully to keep up with his formidable hostess. How does she get around so fast? he wondered, aware that Mrs Vine had a new titanium hip and was leaning on her parasol. Fr Leo had so far refused to use a cane, trusting in God for his support. But it was getting harder each day, and he dropped gratefully on a stone bench next to the widow.

Mrs Vine's bottom took up most of the seat. She hoped her visitor would notice that the outdoor table had been set for lunch and realise that he mustn't stay too long. In the mean time she would make the smallest talk she could think of. 'Have one of these, Leopold,' she said, thrusting a plateful of pierogi in front of him. 'Dear Jerzy made them this morning. He says they taste yummy when accompanied with ice-cold vodka but, as you can appreciate, we try not to keep spirits in the house.'

Fr Leo, who was aware of Sunny's 'problem', made an assenting sound. The ocean breeze stirred the droopy, bell-shaped flowers of the angel's trumpet trees – a natural hallucinogen of which youngsters on the Island were not unaware – growing in a variety of pastel colours inside giant terracotta planters on either side of the swimming pool. The sway of their willowy branches, like the arms of ballet dancers in *Swan Lake*, created a continuous play of light and shadow that induced in the priest a mildly trance-like state. Rousing himself, he cleared his throat.

'Out with it, Leopold,' Mrs Vine prompted affectionately as she handed him a glass of iced tea.

'I've come to see you about a notion I have to refurbish the immersion pool at Gethsemane,' he said. 'Full-body baptisms used to be common in the early days of our parish, and the marble pool in the garden served as the outdoor font. The practice has lost favour in recent decades, and it has become a sort of dream of mine to revive it.'

'A divine idea – if you'll pardon the pun.' Helping herself to two of everything from the platter, Mrs Vine said: 'It could become the next big Island craze – with Wall Street types lining up to get baptised so they can have their pictures taken. We could ask Jerzy to begin. I've been dying to see him undressed.'

'Actually,' Father Leo ran his fingers uncomfortably round the inside of his clerical collar. 'I have another motive in thinking this an opportune time to refurbish the pool. It has to do with Jesse Caulfield.'

The widow paused, holding the pitcher of iced tea in her hand. 'Go on,' she said quietly.

'You may recall from when you still went to church that one of the stained-glass windows above the altar is a depiction of Jesus healing the sick man in the Pool of Bethesda. Jesse loves that window, and his mother and I are of the opinion that it would boost morale – not just his but of the entire congregation – if a special healing Mass was to be held on Jesse's behalf at the baptismal pool.'

'Hmmm. And you want me to pay for its refurbishment.'

'It wouldn't take much – not any more than you usually give. But the vestry won't go for it unless you specifically designate the funds for the restoration of the font.'

'I see.' Mrs Vine's eyes narrowed as she studied the priest's face. It had, she thought, especially when he wanted something, the same star quality of Charlton Heston in *The Ten Commandments*. 'Consider it done, Leopold,' she announced after letting him stew for a minute or two. 'There's nothing quite so uplifting as a good old-fashioned miracle now and then. Just tell me to whom to address the letter and the amount of money you think you'll need.'

The priest continued to fidget, trying without success to eat all that Mrs Vine had heaped on his plate. 'I've never understood,' he said, brushing the crumbs from his cassock, 'how someone can donate thousands of dollars to an institution they never visit.'

'I do that sort of thing quite a lot,' she said, refilling the priest's glass. 'And I do, of course, believe in the church. Only not in *that* church so long as *that* vicar remains in charge. You've been at Gethsemane long enough, Leopold,' she added, by way of explanation, 'to have more than an inkling as to why I should feel the way I do.'

He gave a helpless look. The proclivities of the long-sitting head vicar were another open secret that Fr Leo, as a relatively new associate priest, could do nothing about. 'No matter how inadequate the church,' he said at length. 'It is our main link with the divine. Priests are worldlings too, you know. They stumble and fall but those who truly repent deserve to be forgiven – as the Father forgives his children.'

'Oh, I always forgive. But in my long experience of such things, most people want forgiveness without repentance.' Mrs Vine reflected. 'Are you quite certain,' she asked, 'that you have chosen the right profession for a man of your convictions?'

Fr Leo reddened, fixating on the last, half-eaten pierogi at the side of his plate. 'It has never occurred to me to doubt my calling. Although…' He hesitated, knotting the embroidered napkin round his fingers. 'I confess that I feel closest to God when the church is empty.'

'Never mind,' Mrs Vine murmured. 'You are still young and will come to feel a great deal more one with the world.'

'But I don't want to feel one with the world!' Fr Leo exploded. He half rose from his seat, beads of sweat erupting along his hairline. 'I want to be content with nothing – like the Desert Fathers.'

If only I were younger, thought Mrs Vine, I could cure him of this nonsense. 'My dear man,' she said philosophically, 'your calling is to be a pastor, not a martyr.'

Then it dawned on her that Leopold might be one of those celibate priests. 'The Island is hardly what I would call an ideal place for a Desert Father,' she said. 'And the social season is like one of my feral cats in heat.' Turning dead serious, she said: 'Have you considered asking the bishop to move you to a different parish?'

Leopold shook his head. 'It's no use,' he said, flattening the wrinkled napkin against his knee. 'I may be a pastor, but where, I ask, is my flock? I am like the mendicants of old who begged for alms. But instead of alms I only beg people to believe.'

'Believe in you?'

'In God!'

Feeling another wave of affection the old lady wrapped her thick arm around him. 'Beware of the devil, Leopold,' she said, giving him a squeeze. 'My Irish grandmothers used to say that one can always find the devil lurking among the church pews. Satan lusts for saints, not sinners, who, you must admit, he's already got by the throat. Trust me on this, Leopold: Satan will attempt to defeat you through the very thing you cherish most.'

Fr Leo hung his head. For nearly a minute he said nothing, his eyes burning as he stared at water trickling from a pair of marble putti, one at each side of the fountain. 'Hannah Caulfield is an extraordinary woman,' he blurted. 'Pure and good and selfless, like Our Lady.'

Mrs Vine tightened her grip, wondering if Leopold was slightly mad – or in love. Having been acquainted with a number of priests, she had yet to find one that wasn't suffering. Thank heaven, she thought, that women are spared from entering such a profession.

'From what I know of life, those who try to have sole possession of things they have no right to always end up losing in the end.'

'And what is it you think I am trying to have sole possession of?' Fr Leo asked accusingly.

'Of God. And perhaps also of Hannah Caulfield.'

BATTLE SCENES

Hannah stood with her back to the refrigerator, her palms pressed to the door. 'I tell you he doesn't need any more injections. Jesse has been perfectly fine without them.'

'I was only getting a can of beer,' Thaddeus snapped. 'I live here too, remember?'

He was hurt that after more than two weeks apart Hannah didn't appear happier to see him. She had seemed on edge from the moment he stepped off the plane, and nearly flew off the rails when he suggested, a few moments ago, that he administer a higher dose of serum to make up for the injections Jesse had missed.

Hannah slid her hand through a gap in the fridge door and held out a can of Miller. 'All I'm asking is that you hold off a while longer.'

'How much longer?'

'Until the – the healing Mass.'

'The *what*?'

'I didn't want to mention it over the phone. Actually, it's something Fr Leo and I have been discussing for a while.'

'Discussing what, exactly?'

'A healing Mass for Jesse at the outdoor baptismal font. It's to mirror the Gospel story of Jesus curing the cripple that appears in one of the church windows.'

The doctor stared at his wife. 'You're not serious.'

'Jesse adores that window. He prays to it silently during Mass.'

'That's well and good, but the rest – the rest is nonsense!'

'And was it nonsense ten years ago when, against all the odds you cured Jesse's tumours with something no one believed in?'

Thaddeus took a seat at the kitchen table and placed his beer on top: the familiar jingle of the Looney Tunes cartoons in the family room like a death knell to his ears.

'I would do anything for Jesse,' he said, trying to control his agitation. 'And I believe in science more than ever. But this...' – he struggled to find the word – '...is pure superstition.'

Hannah crossed her arms and looked at her husband's profile. She had never seen Thaddeus so unkempt, his stomach bloated after two weeks of eating exactly what he liked. By contrast, the house around them had the ordered feel of a place not entirely lived in. This was common among homes on the Island, whose owners wanted to be able to put them on display at a moment's notice. Unlike his neighbours, Thaddeus's reason was that Jesse's environment should be as sanitary as possible. He obsessed about it, Hannah thought, as much as he didn't give any consideration to his own well-being. She could just imagine what the New York apartment looked like, not having been to it for several years. Yet here at home, for Jesse's sake, Thaddeus insisted on daily cleanings and had ozone-filtered air conditioning installed. Now, suddenly, of all the things Thaddeus obsessed about, nothing seemed as important to him as to continue administering the serum.

'Did Fr Leo tell you to stop the injections?'

'No. I mean, not exactly. He told me to have faith – and that things aren't always what they seem.'

'He can say what he likes, but I say let's continue the serum, which I believe is having a cumulatively positive effect. It's even possible that it prolongs life expectancy in children with Jesse's syndrome. Hannah, this could be a huge finding.'

'My son,' she said icily, 'is not one of your findings.'

'*Our* son,' he corrected her. 'And may I remind you that it was one of my findings that saved his life. Oh, Hannah, please don't tell me that you seriously believe Jesse can be healed by some miracle.' Thaddeus rose from his seat and took a step towards her. 'Well, do you?'

It occurred to him that he had been shouting. Rather than say things he knew he would later regret, he popped the lid from his can of beer, foam sputtering all over the counter, and carried it to the family room.

Having never shown any interest in her mother's animals, it came as something of a shock to Sunny Sloan to discover that she was falling in love with a three-hundred-pound reptile. Coerced into volunteering at the institute by Louisa – 'to keep an eye on things', as the Big Three had finally agreed – and before Sunny could quite get her head around it, she found herself in charge of the student volunteers. Another surprise was that spending Saturdays with them proved far less tiresome than she had feared. She took pleasure in their easy company and in doing mindless tasks around the lab; and found a source of refuge in memories of the happy times with her father, who had taught her to play croquet and tennis on the grounds which had used to be their home.

But Sunny Sloan had never been content with a little bit of anything, and in a very short time she set her sights on doing 'something grand' for the local sea turtles. And the best way to do that in a place like the Island was to throw a party. Not just any party, but a special ceremony to mark Princess's recovery and release back into the sea. 'We could hold it on the beach and invite the whole town,' was how she broached the subject with her mother, hoping that Mrs Vine would fund the event. 'A great big release party to thank the volunteers and raise the institute's profile in the community.'

Mrs Vine, who hadn't heard her daughter excited about anything for a very long time, warmed to the idea. She invited Sunny to lunch at Villa des Vagues to work out the details, the first time the prodigal had been asked to the family home since Paula's death. Jerzy prepared a big Polish repast and another lunch was arranged, then a third and fourth as plans for the beach party got underway. After mornings of physical work at the lab Sunny began to look forward to having something to eat. And when the needle on the bathroom scale she had worshipped since high school edged up a few pounds, it meant less to her each time she looked.

Still, visits to Villa des Vagues came at a cost. They brought back the pain of losing her beloved father and of violent scenes with her mother, practically since Sunny had first learned to talk back. The pets remained a source of division, with the poor creatures arriving in droves from animal rescue shelters, often with their teeth, paws or an eye missing. They panted, nosed and limped through the grounds and dimly lit corridors of the immense palazzo until they were summoned by their mistress to feed and play. Sunny couldn't remember a time when she hadn't been jealous of them. When she suggested to her mother that it was a form of cruelty to animals to treat them like her personal playthings, Mrs Vine retaliated by reminding her daughter that she too had been adopted.

After Paula died Sunny lost the strength to fight back. In face of the nearly universal recrimination that followed the tragedy only Addison had stood heroically by her; insisting to those who were brave enough to talk about it to his face that no one could blame Sunny more for their daughter's death than she already blamed herself. Privately, he was far more open with his brother, confiding as a patient would to a doctor about his fears for Sunny's mental health. Thaddeus's advice was to put the tragedy behind them and have another child.

Addison admitted that he would like to. 'Is that what you and Hannah plan to do?' he asked. 'I mean, to help you get over Jesse when the time comes.'

Only an estate lawyer, his brother thought, could say a thing like that and get away with it.

Having spent the morning elbow deep in soapy water, scouring the sides of the aquatic tank to prepare for moving Princess outdoors, it was somewhat later than usual when Sunny finally set out to meet her mother for lunch. To save time she took the shortcut along the beach and entered the palazzo through one of the doors to the loggia facing the ocean. The house felt strangely quiet as she stepped inside the cavernous, dimly lit dining room with beamed ceilings. The curtains were kept habitually drawn on account of the rare tapestries, and it therefore took Sunny several moments to notice, indistinctly among the shadows, a large, stone-still figure seated in one of the high-backed Moorish chairs against the wall. She approached the figure gingerly, ready to raise the alarm in case it turned out to be an intruder. But it was only her mother, the old woman's face ashen, rouge running down her cheeks in a flood of tears.

'I just lost one of my beloved cockatoos,' she said, breathing heavily. 'And the other is sure to die of grief without its partner. Jerzy discovered it inside the azaleas – murdered by a bufo toad.'

Seeing the grief etched bluntly on her mother's face, Sunny felt a stab of jealousy that she should have more compassion for her parrot than she had ever shown to her. When the circumstances of Paula's death had become known Mrs Vine had responded by turning a cold shoulder to Sunny. At the funeral they had faced off from opposite sides of Paula's white lacquered casket on which Mrs Vine, her face wrapped in a black veil, had placed a fragrant bouquet of gardenias. She didn't wait to hear the vicar's sermon and never entered the church again.

'Bufos only spray poison in self-defence,' Sunny said. 'And that cockatoo has been trouble since the day it arrived.'

Sunny knew it was the exact wrong thing to say to her mother. Still, she couldn't resist. Seeing the old lady flex her fingers, she sprang back, lifting a hand protectively to her cheek. But her mother proved quicker and seized Sunny by the wrist, pulling her, in a ferocious display of energy, into the foyer. 'You had better run along, dear,' she said, depositing her in the door. 'I'm afraid I don't feel like lunch today.'

Sunny dithered. She was afraid to leave her mother, in case she had a seizure or fell and broke her hip again. But she was even more afraid of what would happen if she stayed. Hoping that Jerzy might help, she asked where he was.

'Digging the grave in the garden,' replied Mrs Vine, her face a death mask as she shut the pecky cypress door, decorated with bronze hinges and crossbars, in her daughter's face.

Outside, Sunny was nearly toppled by two pet rats darting across the threshold (Mrs Vine always kept animals in pairs so that they should never feel lonely), staggering a little as she walked to the bottom of the drive. Mother probably thinks I've been drinking, she thought miserably, trying to regain her footing.

On the other side of the door the old woman managed half a dozen steps before she collapsed at the foot of the stairs. Cradling an orange tabby cat that had crawled on to her lap, and with tears streaming down her face, she moaned Sanford's name: calling to him softly, over and over again.

Lines of illumination showing faintly round the perimeter of the curtains were the only sign of life in the house next door. Philip spent a long time on his balcony watching it, asking himself what his neighbours could be doing amid so much silence. Even their television wasn't on tonight, the quiet from within pushing its way outdoors. At length Philip went back to his room and lifted from the nightstand the story Hannah had asked him to read.

He punched the pillow, plopped his head down on it and immersed himself in the adventures of Sir Peacock, a medieval knight who follows a mermaid princess to her kingdom beneath the sea. Their son, the young crown prince whose name contains Jesse's initials, grows up half-merchild, half-human and embarks on a quest across the seven seas. Riding on the back of a winged sea turtle he dreams of recovering an ancient spell to merge the kingdoms above and below water into a new world. Philip recognised himself as Sir Peacock, with Hannah as the princess and Jesse the young crown prince. It took him less than an hour to read the story straight through, and when he finished he placed the handwritten manuscript on his chest and shut his eyes.

The door to his terrace was open and the scent of nightshade blooms drifted into the room, making some of the events in the story Philip had just read seem to blur with what had occurred three days ago, when Hannah had first given him the story.

They had spent the morning on the beach, relocating one turtle clutch after another until Jesse's supply of energy ran out and he asked to lie down. Hannah carried him to the beach cottage and Philip followed them a little later, bringing their towels and beach bag. He found Hannah seated at the edge of the daybed, with Jesse asleep beside her. She rose as soon as he entered and went over to her writing desk. Hesitating with her hand on the drawer handle, she pulled it open and, turning to him, held out her story.

'The other night you suggested that I write something for my son.' The paper shook in her hand. 'You offered to advise me on matters relating to the sea…'

Philip nodded and she came nearer. Thrusting it into his hand she said: 'I'm afraid it may not be very good.' She stood watching him expectantly; as if she not only wanted Philip to read it, but to read the first few pages right now.

He obligingly scanned the beginning, the handwriting eerily the same as in the letters the teenage Hannah had sent to his father. 'Lovely opening… really sets the mood…' It was all he could think of.

The smile she gave made Philip want to fall to his knees and confess everything. He also wanted to kiss her. Blushing, he looked down at the floor. Their bare toes, dusted with sand, stood a hair's breadth apart: his coarse as sandpaper and Hannah's shimmering with rose-coloured varnish. Trying to hide his confusion, he asked if he could take the story with him. 'To go through it properly and make some notes.'

'Of course,' she said, her eyes glowing and the clean, salt-water smell of her hair like an elixir. 'Keep it for as long as you like.'

Now, having come to the end of *Sir Peacock*, the sound of wind rustling through the palm fronds fanning his desire, Philip realised that the excitement he felt had very little to do with the story's contents.

Many more than the immediate family had been invited to this week's Sunday brunch. There were several new faces auditioning to fill the usual age-related vacancies, and, by way of introduction, Louisa fully intended to keep them waiting. It was an old initiation rite handed down by her grandmother who had believed that those who are made to wait are also made to feel inferior – putting a hostess on much more solid footing with people she didn't know. Having quieted them with rum punch and Bloody Marys, Louisa signalled to Thaddeus that he follow her discreetly to the Shell House. This was where, as children, her sons had been reprimanded, punished and reprieved on more occasions than any of them cared to remember. Even now, Thaddeus felt some of the old anxiety as he followed his mother to the sacred destination, as if he were being pulled there by the ears. Traces of punitive atmosphere lingered in the way Louisa stood, feet apart and arms akimbo, on the shell floor of the compact structure, her birdlike features only somewhat tempered by the amber-tinted light filtering through octagonal stained-glass windows.

'With Pandorex stock going sky high I wonder if I should buy more shares.' Louisa worked her mouth as she spoke, a nervous habit she had developed at boarding school. 'Mind you, I'm not asking for insider information – what rubbish will they think of next! – only your personal opinion.'

Thaddeus was stunned by his mother's suggestion that she invest more money in his company. 'I have absolute faith in Pandorex,' he replied, trying to recover from the shock. 'The company's prospects are excellent and the stock is poised to rise further – possibly much further,' he added cautiously.

'You've done well, Thad. Everyone thinks so.'

Receiving praise from his mother was something so entirely new that the doctor was left momentarily speechless. It made them both ill at ease and Louisa was soon back on her guard. Complaining of the heat, she hastened to the drawing room, walking a few steps ahead of her son.

During lunch Dixie Wainwright was tasked with entertaining the parvenues lumped together at his end of the Louis Seize walnut table. Confined to Louisa's orbit and increasingly unsure of his actions in old age, Dixie was determined to show that he was still worth keeping. Boring social events like this were the acid test of why Louisa put up with him at all, and Dixie, making a heroic stab at what had so far been a hopeless conversation, repeated how much he had enjoyed doing business with the savings and loan in Winnetka, Illinois.

'But we're from Lake Forest, not Winnetka,' the exasperated couple tried to explain for the third time.

'Well, in that case I suppose you must be enjoying our hometown paper, the iconic *Shiny Sheet.*'

Unable to make sense of his reasoning, the woman sitting next to Dixie observed that the Island's daily newspaper seemed to contain very little actual news. Smiling sympathetically, he assured her that she would come to see things very differently in a few months.

The new arrivals exchanged looks. They had nothing against the old man. What they minded, very much, was being consigned to the company of a crusty has-been who, as was abundantly clear, could do nothing to further their social careers. (But in this regard they were sorely mistaken: for as it turned out, Dixon Wainwright was also chairman of the admissions committee at the nearly-impossible-to-get-into Mangrove Club.)

Hannah, who was sitting near the group, listened to their exchange with downcast eyes. She had hardly spoken to her husband since their row in the kitchen, and for the past two days only Philip's enthusiastic response to her story had kept her spirits up. Why, Hannah wondered, had she never shown any of her writing to Thaddeus? Fr Leo was the only one given that privilege, in the form of a small spiritual poem she had thought he might like. And it had taken a perfect stranger to get her to write fiction.

Yet Philip Godolphin didn't seem a stranger, Hannah mused as she looked out the window at a yacht drifting lazily in the Sunday stillness of the Lagoon. Her initial distrust of Philip's designs on Julietta had receded and couldn't compare to the debt of gratitude she owed him since the alligator incident. Starting then, she had brought Jesse to the institute nearly every day, and his health seemed only to improve. After a weekend of fighting with Thaddeus to keep him from administering any more injections Hannah brightened at the sound of airplanes taking off from the airport in West Palm Beach. For it meant that he would soon leave on his usual Sunday afternoon flight to New York, and the anxiety that he might inject Jesse with something she no longer believed in would go with him.

Moving her eyes from the window to where Thaddeus was seated, Hannah realised that he had been waiting for her to notice him. Checking her watch, she half-whispered, half-mouthed that it was time for them to leave for the airport. The doctor folded his napkin and quietly rose from his seat, without interrupting the flow of conversations around him. Walking round the table to Hannah he placed both his hands on her shoulders. 'You stay here,' he said coldly. 'Addison is coming with me and we'll take his car.'

Kissing the top of Jesse's head in the seat beside her, Thaddeus didn't look at his wife again and went to the door.

Hannah watched him leave, feeling the distance between them widen: and that Thaddeus was still simmering with anger that the ampule of serum sat unopened in their refrigerator.

Using his walking frame Jesse crossed the terrace outside his room and rested his chin on the sun-warmed balustrade. All through the dull lunch at his grandmother's house he had been thinking only about the Belt of Venus, and that the best time to see it would be now, just before sunset.

'What are you looking at, poppet?' Hannah followed him to the terrace and leaned her elbows on the balustrade beside him.

Jesse remained silent, gazing restlessly as far into the horizon as his weak eyes could see. 'I don't really understand it,' he said at length.

What Jesse didn't say was that it no longer mattered what he did or didn't understand. He was here on such a brief visit, after all, that it almost didn't seem worth the time to try to understand anything. 'Dolphin knows,' he exclaimed suddenly. 'He knows the way.'

Twenty-four hours later, Addison, Thaddeus and their four-member scientific advisory team appeared on the Financial News Network in a question-answer session about Pandorex. A retinue of Wall Street analysts flung questions at them over the phone and in the studio about the latest round of clinical trials, each of which Thaddeus addressed with absolute conviction. Elated by the cordial reception they had received, on the way back to Cherokee Place their small group decided to celebrate with dinner at the posh Primavera restaurant that was only a few blocks from the new facility. Addison, who insisted on picking up the bill, ordered a vintage Barolo while they reminisced about the worst and best moments of their seven-year-long journey since Pandorex was launched at forty-four cents a share.

'And tonight, gentlemen,' Addison said, raising his glass in a toast, 'the stock has closed at forty-four dollars!'

The toast was followed by others, with more wine and banter so that Thaddeus didn't get back to his apartment until after ten o'clock. He called home as soon as he walked through the door, wondering if Hannah and Jesse had seen him on television.

'Where's Hannah?' he said, startled to hear Julietta answer. His immediate thought was that, without injections for nearly three weeks, Jesse had been rushed to St Mary's.

'She's gone to fetch pizza, and Jesse and I are blowing soap bubbles. Wait, I think I hear them now. Hannah, is that you?' Julietta shouted, without bothering to put her hand over the receiver.

'Hello, Pa.' Jesse picked up the phone, the sound of the girl's shrill voice, so like Carlotta's, in the background.

Thaddeus looked at his watch, 'Who's *them*?' he demanded, fuming that Jesse was still up.

But the receiver seemed to have been placed on a hard surface, bringing to the doctor's ear unfamiliar background noises punctuated by bursts of laughter.

'Who's *them*?' he repeated, shouting to be heard. Thaddeus was about to ask for Hannah again when the line went inexplicably dead.

STATE OF GRACE

'But it *is* my fault, I tell you. I'm the one carrying the gene that caused Jesse's illness – a rare chromosome found among people in the north of England, passed down by a mother to her sons.'

Hannah and her spiritual advisor were seated beneath the thatched roof of the summerhouse in the church garden, surrounded by a profusion of angel's trumpet trees in bloom. Hannah spoke candidly with Fr Leo in a way she could never have done with anyone at Louisa's table. Only the priest, enduring constant pain and standing a little apart on account of his faith, seemed to understand her anguish.

'We are each of us God's masterpiece,' he said, placing his hand reassuringly over Hannah's on the bench between them. The sun blazed overhead and his touch was pleasantly cool in the heat of midday. 'The best of who we are isn't in what we have, but in what we have given up. And you've given up so much.'

Fr Leo's remedy was to pray harder: for a cure if possible and, failing that, for deliverance.

Praising her husband, Hannah described again how he had found a cure for the cancers that had nearly ended Jesse's life. 'He has been trying to prolong his life by giving him a series of experimental injections. And yet, as anyone can see, my son's underlying condition remains.'

Not far from where Hannah and the priest were seated stood the old immersion pool that Mrs Vine was paying to refurbish ahead of Jesse's healing Mass. At a depth of four feet and made out of white and pink-veined marble, the baptismal font that hadn't been used for five decades was waiting to be cleaned and have fresh water pumped into it. A long piece of black rubber hose lay coiled on the bottom.

Looking at it, Hannah said: 'The steps are much too steep for Jesse to navigate by himself.'

'Once it's filled with water, buoyancy will make it easier. He can swim, can't he?'

'Oh yes. It's what Jesse loves best, because it means not having to use his legs.'

But surely, Hannah thought, this wasn't about swimming. Then she saw something that made her hair stand on edge, as one end of what she had supposed to be a piece of rubber hose lifted its scaly head and flicked its tongue – exposing a deadly moccasin snake.

'Someone will have to accompany him,' she said firmly.

Fr Leo reflected on this complication. 'The font was originally built for full-body immersions, as adult baptisms were then, and sooner or later a candidate is bound to come along. We could perhaps combine the rituals so that Jesse is not by himself.'

'I can't wait that long. My husband wants to resume the injections, and I'm terrified that he will do it behind my back. We had to stop them while he was snowbound in New York, and Jesse seems to have improved without them.' Hannah paused. 'It might also have to do with my son making new friends and spending more time outdoors.'

Hannah's cry for help pierced the priest's heart. What use am I, he thought, if I can't deliver even a small measure of hope to one of my flock? Considering all possibilities, and his dreams for the font, he said: 'Perhaps the young Englishman could accompany him into the water. I noticed, with disappointment, I might add, that he doesn't take Communion with the others. That's normally a sign that a person hasn't been baptised.'

'You mean that Philip might be a candidate for immersion?'

'I don't see why not. We could hold a double ceremony – a baptism and healing Mass combined.'

Pressing her hand, Fr Leo lowered his lids. Hannah waited for him to say a prayer, but after a lengthy pause he asked instead if she knew what her name meant.

Still thinking about the moccasin snake, Hannah said that she did not.

'It means *the favoured one* in Hebrew – bestowed on a devout biblical woman so beloved of God that He blessed her with a son.'

Hannah nodded. 'You have no idea what I went through to give Jesse life. When I was still a girl...' she began, and quickly stopped. The last thing she wanted was for this to turn into a confessional. 'I was very young when I had Jesse and had to fight to keep him,' she said and gently withdrew her hand. 'Then I was told he wouldn't live.'

Fr Leo's lids fluttered. 'The biblical Hannah prayed in silence, without words. And when the Lord blessed her with a son she dedicated her child to Him.'

Now Hannah too lowered her eyes. For a few seconds she had a feeling of weightlessness, as if she were being lifted to meet the priest's voice. 'Jesse was the Lord's gift to you, just as he is,' she heard him say. 'The healing Mass is not meant to make him whole, and therefore less dependent on God, but to bring a sacred meaning to his infirmity.'

Hannah's eyes sprang open. 'You don't expect him to be healed?'

'Your son is already healed. The ritual is about getting us to view his condition as a blessing rather than an affliction. The problem these days,' Fr Leo said, apparently starting a new thought, 'or rather, one of the problems, is that we live in a world where, no matter what direction we turn in, we see only our own image instead of God's.'

Hannah looked at him in astonishment. Lowering her gaze to the empty pool she noticed that the venomous snake was done sunning itself, the top of its tail slithering beneath the matted palm fronds strewn along the bottom.

Her thoughts spun faster as she drove back to the institute to pick up Jesse. Hannah knew next to nothing about Philip's background and religious beliefs, or how he might react to the proposition that he be baptised. He might, for instance, be deeply offended; or happy enough to accompany Jesse into the font for no other reason than to help him navigate the steps. Would asking him to undergo baptism, possibly not for the first time, be construed as taking a liberty?

But as Hannah parked the convertible at the side of Mrs Vine's old croquet lawn a new and more troubling thought occurred to her: that there could be no healing Mass without Thaddeus's consent and that he was, at the moment, violently opposed to the idea. Her thoughts grew more confused as she walked to the outdoor tank – where Princess had been moved to recuperate – and didn't immediately register that Jesse was no longer where she had left him.

Sunny, standing on top of a stepladder, was drawing a long pole through water inside the tank, collecting debris in a mesh basket attached to the end of it. She wore what had become her work uniform, a check shirt tied at the waist over pencil-thin white capri trousers and rubber-soled ballerina flats. Without make-up and her hair pulled back in a short ponytail, Sunny didn't look much older than the teenager assisting her from the foot of the ladder. The girl, who had been helping her empty the net into a bucket, looked up, the metal braces on her teeth glinting in the sun. Hannah caught her breath, stunned by the girl's astonishing likeness to Paula.

'Where's Jesse?' she called to them.

'Mother stopped by on her way to feed the cats,' Sunny called back. 'She thought he looked a bit tired and said she would take him home. Philip went with them.'

Hannah checked her watch and realised that she had spent more than two hours with Fr Leo. Thaddeus's warnings sounded in her ears as she drove home, her apprehensions turning to panic when she pulled into her driveway and saw no evidence of

Mrs Vine's Shadow. Marta had left for the day and her car was gone as well. The house, when Hannah opened the door, struck her as deathly still.

She found no one in the family room or kitchen, and the upstairs was as quiet as the rest of the house. Marta had tidied up Jesse's room, and his bed was neat, the toys put away and the unfinished Lego towers and fortresses silhouetted like ghost towns in the waning light. A butterfly mobile swayed gently from the ceiling as Hannah flung open the French door to the balcony and did a quick visual search of the pool area and rear of the house. Then, amid the gathering darkness she noticed through the foliage a glimmer of illumination coming from the beach cottage.

Peering through slats in the plantation shutters she saw Jesse asleep on the daybed, his head resting comfortably on a pillow and a blanket over him. The light Hannah had seen was coming from the lamp on her writing desk, and Philip stood over it, his back to the door. What was he so engrossed in? she wondered. It wasn't until he straightened and turned over one of the sheets lying on top that she realised that he had been reading her poems.

Hannah cleared her throat and stepped inside the cottage. Philip gave a terrific start when he saw her. 'I was looking for something to write with,' he stammered. 'To jot down a few ideas for *Sir Peacock*.'

Insects attracted to the light streamed through the door and Hannah, saying nothing, shut it softly behind her.

'I shouldn't be reading your poems without asking,' Philip apologised. 'But I couldn't help it. Having so enjoyed the story you wrote I wanted to see more of what you'd written.' He waited for her to speak, and when she didn't, he said, hoping it would please her: 'I'm surprised that you haven't published any of your writing.'

'My poetry is too private to share with strangers.'

He began apologising again, and this time she cut him short. 'Never mind. You're not a stranger. In fact, you've become a friend, above all to Jesse.'

'I feel the same.' Philip gave a sigh of relief. 'By the way, *Sir Peacock* is such a fantastic yarn, I have only two suggestions – for an undersea cave with crystal stalagmites and a wacky scientist in a submarine.'

'Jesse will like all that.'

'I'll write it down clearly when I get back to the house.' He glanced at his watch. 'But I had better leave now. Carlotta insists that we all sit down to dinner together.'

'Yes, they're such a tightly knit family.'

'Amen!' Philip laughed.

Contained in that one word, Hannah saw her opening. 'Speaking of which,' she said, taking a step towards him. 'There's something I've been meaning to ask you – a favour, actually. It's to do with Jesse's healing Mass. Have I mentioned it?'

Philip shook his head, listening with polite interest while Hannah described Fr Leo's plans for the outdoor font.

'He wants me to carry Jesse into the pool and bring him out again?'

'Actually, that was my idea. You're the only one I trust... But I'm afraid there's a catch – or rather a bonus, depending on how you view it.'

Hannah had never seemed lovelier, with a hint of mischief in her eyes. 'Fr Leo feels that only someone who is also taking part in a sacred ritual should enter the pool.'

'Sacred ritual?'

'Such as baptism.'

It took Philip a few moments to grasp what she was saying. 'What, me – get baptised – at my age?'

Hannah nodded. Yet what she was asking seemed almost laughable. Why not? he thought, if it means that much to her.

'Sure. Jesse and I can be saved together!'

Overcome with gratitude she flung her arms around him, the touch of her lips like a feather. They pulled apart in confusion, but not before a spark of something had passed invisibly between them. Quick as a quiver Hannah was at the other end of the room. Standing over the sleeping child she held her breath; waiting for she knew not what.

A minute or two passed. To Hannah they seemed an eternity, the noise of insects growing steadily louder. When at last she turned, the door was open and Philip gone, her poems face down on the desk.

He still couldn't understand why Fr Leo felt that an interview was needed. Or why he had asked him to bring proof of identity. As a result, on his way to their meeting Philip had to stop at the First National Bank to retrieve his passport, which he had placed in a safe deposit box, along with Hannah's letters and other personal documents that he didn't want anyone to see.

'Counselling is standard among adult candidates,' Fr Leo had said over the phone. 'To make absolutely certain they understand the meaning of the sacrament they are about to receive.'

Philip had his own reasons for consenting to the meeting. He was eager to find out more about this lame preacher who held such sway over Hannah; and hoped as well that talking to a priest might help resolve the disturbing thoughts he had been having about her.

There was a line at the bank and he was late for his appointment. The bell tower was already chiming the quarter hour by the time Philip parked his bicycle and entered the church by a side door. Peering inside the parish hall and administrative office, he finally located the priest in the Sunday school classroom. Fr Leo was seated at one of the small desks, wearing lightweight khaki trousers and a short-sleeved shirt with a clerical collar, leather sandals on his misshapen feet and his broad shoulders stooped over a notepad. Philip knocked on the open doorframe, waiting to be asked in. But the priest continued scribbling, perhaps to admonish him for arriving late.

'Just a minute,' he said impatiently when Philip knocked a third time. 'I'm in the middle of a sentence.' Then, without looking up,

Fr Leo indicated with the tip of his pen that Philip take a seat at one of the little desks opposite him. 'So,' he said when he had finished writing. 'You've come to talk about your baptism.'

Philip wanted to remind Fr Leo that he was the one who had asked for the interview, but thought better of it. He'd had some experience of clergy during his years at a Church of England primary school in Highgate, and knew how touchy they could be when they were preparing their sermons. Despite his parents' reservations about sending him to a church school, Philip had quite enjoyed his time at St Michael's. He sang in the choir and attended chapel in the morning. But these activities had meant little more to him than making music and rhyme, and prayers were a problem. They still were, for it seemed to Philip that God ought to know what lay in a man's heart without having to hear him talk about it.

'Spread out the sky... as a molten looking glass,' Fr Leo murmured.

'Excuse me?'

The priest flinched, as if he'd forgotten that Philip was still in the room. 'It's a line from the Book of Job that I am using in my Sunday sermon – as a parable for those who seek to do and possess everything except come face to face with themselves.'

'Like the Islanders, perhaps?'

Fr Leo nodded, knitting his black brows.

'Regarding this baptism,' Philip began, 'and in case you're wondering, Jesse is the reason I'm doing it.'

'Only Jesse?'

And Hannah, he wanted to say. But Philip couldn't think of a way to explain to a man like the Revd Dr Leopold Harris the circumstances of his case. Or that curiosity about his father's lover and their child was what had brought him to the Island; and that from the moment he had seen Hannah crossing the beach towards him – or looked into Jesse's blue-grey eyes, so like his own – nothing had gone as expected.

'I should think it's as good a reason as any to get baptised at my age.'

'Baptism is a holy sacrament.'

Philip shrugged. 'Actually, until I came here I never went to church unless I had to.'

'And what changed – here?'

'The neighbours invited me.'

'Ah, that is often the way. Yet you came back, the following week, by yourself.'

'I did.'

'The second time you seemed more – how shall I say – more reflective.'

'You were watching me?'

'I watch everyone. And in your case I felt as if – and please correct me if I'm wrong – you were communing with the unseen something on which our lives depend.'

'Unseen something––'

'On which our lives depend.'

Philip hesitated. 'I suppose I was.'

'And was it a new feeling?'

'Entirely new.'

'That puts you far ahead of my congregation,' Fr Leo said bitterly. 'I ought to have guessed what lay ahead of me here when I delivered my first homily. It was about Jesus's advice to the wealthy young man – that it is easier for a camel to pass through the eye of a needle than for a rich man to enter the Kingdom of Heaven. After the sermon the head of a large investment bank came up to me to complain. "I think what Jesus meant," he corrected me, "is that it's not about how much money we have, but about how we use it. And here on the Island, rather than lose the Kingdom of Heaven, people would have a needle built for them that's big enough for a camel to pass through."'

Philip found the episode amusing but, seeing how unhappy it made Fr Leo, said nothing.

'Another parishioner,' the priest continued, 'writing anony-mously, of course, complained that during my sermon about the Day of Judgement she had the impression I was eyeing her from the pulpit the entire time, and that some of her friends noticed.' Fr Leo shook his head. 'I really don't know why I'm telling you all this.'

'Maybe it helps to talk about it. I imagine snowbirds would much rather have a vicar they can invite to parties than one who tells them the truth.'

'Indeed. Oh, how I long for a good fight.'

Moved by the recollection of an Old Testament reading from his schooldays, Philip, hoping to impress the priest with his biblical knowledge, suggested that they organise a fight. 'We could wrestle like Jacob and the angel,' he said, smiling.

'Jacob was wrestling with God!'

On the other side of the open window a soft rain began trickling down from a clear blue sky, so fine that the air outside appeared more misty than wet. 'Every young man I've known,' Fr Leo said, 'was spoiling for a fight. I do not exclude myself, by the way. Now that I am older I try to conserve my energy.'

'What do you conserve it for?'

'To wage war with the devil.'

'Another snowbird?'

Fr Leo finally smiled. 'Returning every season on the dot. Though half the time it isn't the devil but some poseur trying to stand out from the crowd – or a geriatric of unsound mind.'

'Yes,' Philip agreed, thinking of poor Dixie Wainwright.

'And yet the fidelity of a few matters more to God than multitudes. As you have seen, Gethsemane is packed on Sundays. But it means nothing. Only Hannah Caulfield is faithful, and exactly as she seems.'

'You know her rather well, don't you?'

Fr Leo paused, looking at the rain. 'I don't think I've ever known a woman like her.'

During another, somewhat longer, pause, Philip realised that the priest had said all he was going to on the subject. Taking out his passport, he handed it to him. 'You asked me to bring some proof of identity.'

'Ah yes. Thank you for reminding me.' Fr Leo drummed his fingers on the desk while he perused the document, scribbling something on a scrap of paper before giving it back to Philip. 'It's a formality, so the bishop can issue your certificate of baptism.'

It occurred to Philip that they hadn't really discussed the baptism. 'What exactly should I expect?'

'There will be two parts – a short healing Mass for Jesse and a rite of baptism for you, during which the oil of chrism, pleasantly scented with balsam, is applied to the forehead and other organs of sense.'

'Organs of sense?'

'The nostrils, ears and breast are anointed with holy oil in a physical representation of the gift of the Holy Spirit. It is called the Rite of Chrismation.'

Philip gulped. 'Did you say cremation?'

'Heavens, no.' Fr Leo laughed heartily, explaining in a few words how he would apply the holy oil, followed by immersion in the pool. 'Given the warm weather lately, I expect you'll quite enjoy it.'

Feeling easier, Philip stood up and went to the door. For all his bluster to a packed audience on Sundays and ministry for the disabled, the Revd Dr Leopold Harris struck him as quite a solitary man.

On his way out, Philip stopped in the garden where the immersion ceremony was to take place. He circled the pool into which fresh water was being pumped through a hose, ash from the sugar canes carpeting the upper steps. He tried to envision how, dressed in the light garments Carlotta had been sewing for them, he would descend the stairs with Jesse on his arm. Lulled by the sound of water gurgling from the hose as it rose steadily higher inside the marble pool, he took a seat on the bench that Fr Leo and Hannah had occupied a few days earlier. In the midday heat the angel's trumpet trees' bell-shaped flowers that had bloomed during the night lay matted on the grass around him, leaving a honeysuckle-sweet odour.

For a long time Philip remained seated with his eyes closed, palms open and resting on his knees. Half-dreaming in the quiet garden he didn't notice Fr Leo, who had changed into a cassock, leaving the sacristy on his way to midweek Mass.

The priest felt a twinge of resentment when he saw the young man occupying his prayer bench. Then he softened. My words, he thought, his heart expanding as he stole silently across the lawn, have meant something, after all. Becoming aware of a sharp pain in his hip, Fr Leo thought he heard, beyond the coo of mourning doves on the roof of the summerhouse, a voice saying: *Where two or more are gathered in my name, there I am in the middle of them.*

His decision was made before nightfall. There was no further doubt in the priest's mind what the Lord had been whispering in his ear, the reason He had brought him to this spiritual wasteland in the first place. To evangelise in the devil's own playground was the sort of achievement that had been the provenance of saints, martyrs and Desert Fathers – and now, God willing, Leopold Harris.

It was while he lay prostrate on the cold, hard floor before the high altar that the answer had come to him: together with the conviction that more than the ordinary means would be needed to save the snowbirds' souls. Fr Leo would in this instance be aided by his past, harkening from all that long way back in Lake Charles, Louisiana where his father had been a fire-breathing Baptist minister. The senior Revd Harris's popular revival meetings had portrayed the battle between good and evil as a terrifying struggle between the devil and the Lamb of God, his sermons peppered with the whiff of folk tales and local legend. The young Leopold had been sufficiently alarmed by his father's methods to decide to pursue a more traditional line. Funded by one scholarship after another that eventually took him from the bayou to the Harvard Divinity School, he found only disappointment. Unable to fit into a humanist mould that seemed to elevate man above God, Leopold struggled in a strange new world he feared more than he scorned. At the same time, he dared not refuse his calling and headed south again to begin his ministry. To his dismay he discovered that, once again, God had assigned him to a place where people worshipped only themselves. With the exception of Hannah Caulfield, he despaired of leaving any mark on his new flock. And now, suddenly, an opportunity presented itself that recalled his father's style of conversion when all else failed.

It was past midnight by the time he left his two small rooms at the rear of the church and crept into the garden. The rest of the vicarage, a vast 1920s house bequeathed to the church by a wealthy parishioner, was occupied by the head vicar and his revolving entourage. Tonight, they were being quieter than usual, and the vicarage stood dark as Fr Leo, carrying a small wicker basket and a pair of shears, walked to where the night-blooming angel's trumpet trees grew in profusion. Hell's Bells was what they had been called back in Lake Charles, on account of the flowers' hallucinogenic properties. Their smell, subtle at first, grew more powerful as Fr Leo snipped the droopy pastel flowers that seemed to glow in the moonlight, and placed them in the basket. Then he returned to his lodging and soaked the petals in hot water, leaving them to steep overnight.

'An angel went down into the pool so that whosoever stepped in was made whole of whatever disease he had. But one man with an infirmity that had lasted many years could not even make it into the pool and appealed to Jesus to help him. "I have no man," he said, "to put me into the pool." And Jesus said to him: "Rise, take up thy bed, and walk." And immediately the man was made whole.' Fr Leo, attired in a ceremonial gold brocade cassock, paraphrased from the Gospel of St John. He motioned the guests to form a circle around the immersion pool where Philip and

Jesse, wearing identical white linen garments, stood at the top of the marble stairs. The priest approached them with a slow step, holding the vial of holy oil, and dipped his thumb into it. First he marked Jesse's forehead with the sign of the cross; then, beckoning Philip to kneel before him, he dribbled the oil on the crown of his head, letting it trickle from his forehead down the sides of his nose to his chin. Guiding his thumb over the young man's cheeks the priest cupped his palms over his nostrils and said: 'You are now sealed with the Holy Spirit.'

Philip inhaled the oil's intoxicating sweetness, feeling as if he were both inside the pool and levitating above it. When Fr Leo proclaimed that he was being reborn into the spirit through a second birth Philip lifted his eyes to where Hannah stood, her face radiant as she watched him descend into the water with Jesse, their garments billowing.

After the ceremony guests crowded round the candidates to congratulate them. Everyone agreed that, with his white robe, beard and longish hair, Philip had been the very image of Jesus healing the sick – forgetting, perhaps, that Fr Leo had done the healing. Planter's punch and petit fours were distributed by strolling waiters, courtesy of Louisa, and Jerzy treated everyone to Polish baptismal pastries in the shape of crosses. Addison, wearing a pink bow tie and a poplin jacket slung over his shoulder, ambled over to his brother at the hors d'oeuvres table.

'How do you like my new suit?' he said. 'With Pandorex stock going through the roof I treated myself to the Brooks Brothers spring special.'

'I still can't quite believe it,' Thaddeus mumbled, swallowing his third devilled egg. 'We have only two more weeks till the end of the trials and then, if all goes well, we can begin mass-marketing the serum.'

'Have you heard anything further from the FDA about their site visit?'

'Not a word. Maybe they forgot about us.'

'The government never forgets,' Addison said. 'But I will say that they're running out of time if they plan to act.'

Thaddeus shifted his weight uncomfortably to the other foot. 'We're going to need capital for the expansion, and I'm considering taking out another loan – a short-term one, payable at the end of six months with my Pandorex shares as collateral.'

'That's quite a lot of risk for you to shoulder alone.'

'It's my company, after all.'

'And you're the largest shareholder.' Addison winked, his face ruddy after an early morning game of golf. 'Pretty soon my kid brother will have more money than us lawyers.'

While they were talking Addison kept looking over the sunhats and elaborate hairstyles with a watchfulness honed by years of having to keep an eye on Sunny at social events. When at length the lawyer spotted his wife she was seated primly with the Big Three inside the summerhouse. Wedged between Carlotta and her mother-in-law, Sunny sat holding in her hand what Addison hoped was a glass of water instead of vodka. Carlotta, looking regal and taciturn next to her on the curved bench, cradled a Tootsie Roll cocktail in her palms. Rubbing his chin, Addison joked with his brother about how Carlotta had contrived to obtain it.

A few feet from them Hannah was attempting to extricate Jesse from the well-wishers and coax him into a change of dry clothes. Philip, his eyes shiny, responded cheerfully to Julietta's barrage of questions about his experience at the font.

'How did it feel to be filled with the Holy Spirit?'

'Out of this world,' Philip replied without hesitation.

Seeing Hannah about to leave, he excused himself and followed her and Jesse to the sacristy where they had left their clothes. Hannah replaced the waterproof bandage on Jesse's arm while Philip changed behind a tall screen the clergy used to don ceremonial vestments. He remained animated, talking excitedly as he put on a new suit and tie that he had bought for the occasion. Jesse, responding to Philip's mood, teased his mother while she pinched and pulled at the elastic tube socks to fit them snugly over his feet.

'Were you afraid?' Jesse asked. 'I think I was when we first entered the pool.'

Philip, boasting that he had grown up next to a big London cemetery, said that he was afraid of nothing.

Jesse's eyes widened 'Was it a cemetery with ghosts?'

Hannah, kneeling beside Jesse, remained very still; her hand resting on the floor. She seemed about to say something when Julietta pounced through the door. 'Hurry up in there. The photographer wants to take a group photo.'

'Coming,' Hannah called back and, lifting Jesse in her arms, followed Julietta into the garden.

'Wait, Ma, please wait,' Jesse pleaded, tugging at her sleeve. 'I have to…'

'Not now,' she silenced him as they took their place between Thaddeus and Fr Leo at the front of the assembled group.

Everyone faced the camera with a smile pinned to their face, Hannah's pensive as Jesse continued to fuss in her arms. Watching them through her veil, Mrs Vine wondered what Hannah would think one day in the distant future when she came across the photo that was about to be taken. How much about this day will any of us remember? reflected Mrs Vine. Or remember only that none of it would have been possible without Philip Godolphin.

Amid clicks of the camera, the photographer squatting on the grass for a deep angle shot, Jesse renewed his efforts to escape.

'Hush,' Hannah chided. 'We'll be done in a minute.'

Feeling something warm trickle down her arm, she realised that he had wet himself.

'I love you,' he said in a small voice, trying not to move.

PANDORA'S BOX

The doctor stood in the doorway, hoping against hope that she would climb back up the stairs and tell him that it had all been a mistake. He felt numb, listening to the wind gusting against the east-facing door of the facility and cold air sweeping up through the old mosaic-tiled stairwell. Finally he closed the door and returned to his desk. The familiar laboratory sounds that he had grown to love – of snow sifting against the windowpanes, animals scurrying about their cages and hum of diagnostic equipment – all suddenly irritated him. One of the bulbs inside the strip of fluorescent lights in the ceiling that had been flashing throughout the meeting brought his nerves close to breaking point.

Thaddeus had almost stopped expecting a visit from the FDA site investigator when she suddenly turned up unannounced that morning. Of short stature and wearing round horn glasses and a grandmotherly smile, she had nodded appreciatively during the doctor's presentation of the scientific protocols used in the clinical trials. When he finished his exposition the site investigator read off a series of questions that bore no resemblance to those Thaddeus had rehearsed with his brother. Then, just before concluding the session, the investigator dropped the bombshell she must have arrived with: informing the doctor in a calm and dispassionate voice that, based on the data submitted, the FDA had no choice but to request additional and more detailed results before it could recommend approving the serum.

To his peril, Thaddeus began arguing with her: that the results hadn't been interpreted correctly and the FDA's assessment was too focused on the methodology used to collect the data. The investigator wasn't amused. 'In that case,' she said with a smile that had turned ice cold, 'you had better show us, clearly and conclusively, the error of our ways.'

The unanswered question was how to address the FDA's queries without at the same time raising doubts in the eyes of the public about the effectiveness of the serum. Wall Street had been poised for fast-track approval and anything less wouldn't seem good enough. It would, moreover, take at least a year for a fresh cross-spectrum of data to be gathered and uniformly assessed. The value of Pandorex stock would very likely decline in the interim – and would almost certainly plummet on Monday when the FDA planned to announce a delay in granting its approval – making it extremely difficult for Thaddeus to repay his loans.

'What now?' he muttered, his voice tinny against the bare, freshly painted walls of the new facility. His hand slid across the desk to the telephone and he dialled a number he knew by heart.

'I'd like to speak to my brother,' he told Addison's secretary.

'Mr Sloan is in court today. He said that if you called to tell you he would stop by your house this evening.'

The site investigator's visit had lasted more than three hours, and Thaddeus had already missed his usual midday flight to Palm Beach. If he lost any more time he would miss the five o'clock direct flight as well. Worrying about it, he began to pace the office, boardroom and connecting corridor. In the laboratory, the doctor's favourite place, he paused nostalgically over the microscopes, plasma-measuring equipment and score of instruments sitting on long metal work tables. The results coming in from cancer clinics participating in the trials had been gathered, discussed and tabulated in these rooms by Thaddeus and his chief scientists. Their small group had been so confident of their findings that only last week they had given up their positions at Memorial Hospital in the expectation that FDA approval was imminent.

Thaddeus began pacing the facility, while sleet ghosted the turn-of-the-century windows and the ancient pipes clanged their heart out inside the waist-high radiators. He hadn't told Hannah about the three-million-dollar loan he owed on the facility, or the mortgage he had recently taken out on their home, fully expecting that he would never need to if things had gone as planned. The loan had been secured on the basis of vast amounts of Pandorex stock he had accumulated over the years, often in lieu of salary. On paper he was worth millions and would be worth twice that amount once the serum was approved and marketed. But all that would change on Monday when the FDA was set to make its announcement.

Would Hannah be upset? She rarely concerned herself with matters that didn't relate to Jesse, yet something had changed between them lately that made the doctor far less sure of her reaction. Or what she would say when she learned that he had staked their financial security on a serum she no longer allowed him to give Jesse. Thaddeus still remembered their last dreadful argument, after which he had agreed to the healing Mass as a way of smoothing things out. But as a scientist he considered it a dangerous proposition to start putting hope in faith healers. Lifting the heavy Truman glasses from his nose he placed them on the desk and rubbed his eyes. At forty-three he felt suddenly old – at any rate, too old for Hannah.

Fridays were a half-day at the firm, but due to the weather only Thaddeus had come in that morning – and the dreaded site investigator. The deafening silence in the normally bustling facility, punctuated by periodic gusts of wind howling off the East River, raised Thaddeus's anxieties to a fever pitch. He looked again at the written summary, in which the FDA listed its reasons for postponing approval until further data was provided. Reading the fine print drained the last remnant of colour from his face, shining a bright light on something that hadn't previously occurred to him or to any on his scientific team: the possibility of a link between heightened mortality among patients with pre-existing cardiac issues and others taking part in the same trials. Thaddeus had assumed that these deaths, due to heart failure, would have occurred even if the patients hadn't been given the serum to treat their cancers. But it was equally possible – as the report suggested – that the infusion might have caused the cardiac arrests. Only a whole new round of experiments could determine the answer. Thaddeus slumped deeper into his chair as he reread the final paragraph – recommending that the trials be halted while the cardiac deaths were examined more closely.

Sweat poured from his armpits as he reached for the phone again and dialled another number he knew by heart. But unlike lawyers and bankers, stockbrokers always somehow managed to answer on the first ring.

'Shouldn't you be on your way to sunny Florida?' Tim chuckled when he heard his client's voice.

'Too much paperwork.' Thaddeus spoke slowly, carefully, trying to control the tremor in his voice. 'I was wondering how Pandorex shares have been trading today.'

Even before Thaddeus finished speaking he could hear the click-click of the Quotron keyboard as his broker checked the latest stock quotes.

'You'll like this,' Tim said. 'Forty-five dollars bid.'

The news should have made Thaddeus happy. But at the moment nothing made him happy. He didn't know what to do – with Addison in court and only three hours left before the close of trading on Wall Street. The sound of phones ringing and the ticker-tape machine in the background served as a reminder that time was money on the trading desk. And Thaddeus had no time to lose.

'Is that all?' the broker asked after a half minute of silence.

'I've never sold any of my shares...'

'Why should you when they only keep going up? Just the other day I put some in my kids' college fund.'

Thaddeus felt briefly gratified that Pandorex might fund an education – or help build someone's house – and that one day everyone who had invested in his company would be rewarded. But to make that happen he had to be in a position to meet his loan repayments and all the other expenses that stood between the current setback and success. It broke the doctor's heart to sell any of his stake, but he had to limit his losses – now, while the stock was riding high, and sell only enough to settle the bank loans and mortgage.

'Actually, I've been thinking of skimming some profit from my position. You know, to help pay the bills.'

'Not a bad idea from a tax perspective. How much were you thinking of selling?'

'Oh, I don't know.'

But Thaddeus knew exactly how much he needed to sell. 'Any suggestions?' he asked innocently.

Tim cleared his throat, sniffing a commission. It wasn't greed, exactly, but more in the manner of a connoisseur savouring a fine dish. 'It's not for me to say what you should do,' he said apologetically. The securities industry had been under much closer scrutiny since the market crashed in '87 and the last thing he wanted was to appear to be pressuring his client.

'I guess a hundred thousand shares then,' Thaddeus said. 'Haven't I got close to five hundred thousand?'

'Five hundred, eighty-three thousand according to my Quotron. Consider it done, Thad. But you'll need to get someone in your legal department to sign the SEC regulatory form.'

'We don't have a legal department – just Addison, and he's in Palm Beach today.'

'Your chief financial officer will do. As president of Pandorex you would be what's considered a principal, and the industry regulates the amount of stock people in your position are allowed to sell.'

'Says who?'

'Says the Securities and Exchange Commission. It's to make sure principals aren't acting on insider information.'

'But I *am* an insider.'

'Precisely. I'll fax you the form – or would you rather think about it a bit longer?'

'No! I mean yes, do fax it to me.'

Simon Allen handled the payroll and accounting for the firm, and was the likely person to sign. But along with everyone else, Simon hadn't come in today.

'OK, fine,' said Thaddeus, his mind racing. 'Fax me the form and in the mean time go ahead and sell a hundred thousand shares. Do it so it settles before the end of trading.'

The doctor expelled a long breath. However temporary, he had found a reprieve. Listening for the double beep of the fax in Simon's office, he hurried to it and stood over the machine. The form that eventually sputtered out was a standard document with space at the bottom for the signature of Financial or Compliance Administrator. Could Thaddeus be considered one of these in his capacity as head of the firm? He had never understood legal jargon or the business aspects of running Pandorex, and he wondered whether he might somehow get hold of Addison at the courthouse. But that would hold things up, and Thaddeus had to get this settled before the end of the day. If he hurried, there was still a chance he could make the five o'clock plane.

Slamming his fist against the metal-top desk he vented all the rage that had been gathering inside him. 'Damn, damn, damn!' he screamed, startling the mice and rabbits in their cages. They cowered, whimpering, while Thaddeus ranted against government regulators trying to restrict what he could and couldn't do with his personal assets. Furious, he marched over to the filing cabinet where the weekly payroll and company accounts were kept and rifled through them, studying Simon's oblong signature at the bottom of each. He carried them to his desk and laid them out, copying and recopying the signature on an old prescription notepad until it began to resemble Simon's. Then he transcribed it one last time, with today's date, on the form sent by his broker, and faxed it back to him.

Grabbing his coat and briefcase, Thaddeus switched off the lights and secured the lock. He sloshed ankle-deep through the wet snow to the corner of First Avenue where a cavalcade of yellow cabs sped past him with their Off-Duty lights on. A turbaned Sikh finally took pity on the heavy-set man with his coat unbuttoned and pulled up alongside him at the curb.

'To La Guardia airport,' Thaddeus said as he dropped thankfully into the back seat. 'And you better step on it.'

Carlotta Alonso had noticed for some time that Hannah's interest in what she was saying had lapsed. Still, she liked the sound of her own voice too well to let it stop her from talking – and liked even more watching her granddaughter and Jesse splash about the pool.

'Marco! Polo!' they shouted, tossing a bright-red beach ball back and forth to each other. From beyond the border of palm trees the sound of waves grew suddenly much louder.

'My husband's flight from New York has been delayed,' Hannah worried aloud, unaware that Carlotta had been in the middle of a sentence on an entirely different subject.

'Maybe he should have stayed in New York,' Carlotta said, looking at the sky.

'That's what I told him, but he wouldn't hear of it.'

'Thad misses you,' Carlotta commiserated, dangling her stout legs over the side of the pool. For some years now she had made it a point never to disrobe fully or go swimming when other people were present. 'How will he get here from Orlando?'

'Drive, I guess.'

'Should we send a car to fetch him?'

'He said he would rent one at the airport. I had better check the house phone in case he left a more recent message.' Hannah scrambled to her feet. 'May I?'

Nothing was allowed in Carlotta's house without asking her permission. She granted it with an indulgent nod and Hannah went inside, leaving her to oversee the children.

In the large, hacienda-style kitchen, Malachi had begun marinating steaks in advance of the family barbeque. Eduardo, who was officially master of the grill, refused to have anything to do with its preparation or clean-up, his chief contribution being to strut about in a three-quarter-length chef's apron, sipping a daiquiri and flipping steaks in the air.

'Looks like it might not be such a good evening for our barbeque,' Malachi reported.

He spoke with the authority of a career diplomat, having been in service to Carlotta since she was a bride. Rail thin, patrician-looking Malachi had emigrated from Cuba with the family and lost his wife at nearly the same time that Carlotta's Ernesto departed the world. Ever since, rumours had abounded that faithful Malachi was to Carlotta what Mr Brown had been to the widowed Queen Victoria. And while no one in the family believed the gossip, it was in many ways an accurate description of a bond between the matriarch and her manservant that had ripened over many years.

Finding no further messages from Thaddeus on the answerphone, Hannah dialled the number of Delta Airlines and listened to the automated arrivals update. 'Midnight,' she sighed, and replaced the receiver on the wall. 'My husband's plane is still sitting on the runway at La Guardia, waiting to depart.'

'At least the planes are taking off,' Malachi said in the consoling voice he used with the women of the house.

Distracted, and with one hand resting on the wall phone, Hannah looked up and saw Philip enter the kitchen. He had been diving at the reef and his sun-streaked hair was still damp, his bare arms and legs burnished a deep rose gold. 'What a pleasant surprise,' he exclaimed. 'Are you staying for dinner?'

Before Hannah could reply, the sky on the other side of the French doors exploded in a peal of thunder that shook the house to its foundation. It was followed a moment later by a piercing shriek from the swimming pool.

Philip turned pale and charged through the French doors. 'Stay clear of the water!' he screamed.

The sky lowered and raindrops the size of bullets pummelled the rear of the house. The wind tore off Carlotta's hat, and they found her crouching like a rumpled sack at the side of the swimming pool, her arm reaching out to Julietta who was making a clumsy attempt to climb out of the pool with Jesse on her back. Philip bundled the boy under one arm and dragged Julietta with his other into the shelter of the loggia. Malachi rushed to the side of his beloved mistress, his skeletal frame nearly buckling beneath her weight and force of the wind, his uniform drenched. As soon as they were all safely inside he bolted the doors to the loggia where, in less than two minutes, rain accumulated several inches deep, water spewing from the gutters and overflowing the drainage ditches.

There was no sign of Eduardo, who had gone to the polo grounds in Wellington, or of Patsy, who played backgammon at the Bath & Racquet every afternoon. Wrapped in towels and feeling brave in the wake of their adventure, the small group reconvened in the kitchen to watch Malachi pan-fry the steaks Eduardo had been meant to grill outdoors. The large country-house stove was powered by propane, and the skillet simmered uninterrupted while the electric lights flickered.

Carlotta basked in letting Malachi play head of the house. 'This feels like a celebration,' she announced, instructing him to decant a bottle of her son's best wine.

The lights finally gave out, leaving a reddish-blue flame over the stove while Malachi rummaged round the butler's pantry in the dark. A minute later he made a majestic return, holding a lit candelabrum in one hand and crystal decanter filled with rusty-red wine in the other. Amid the winking radiance of a dozen candles, the years melted from his face and his rheumy eyes shone.

The wine brought giggles to Julietta's conspiratorial asides with Jesse, who was seated beside her on one of the chrome and vinyl chairs positioned round the centre island. Exchanging elfin smiles they passed each other food from their plates and Julietta annoyed Hannah by letting Jesse take sips of her wine. The Alonsos loved eating in the kitchen, the relaxed mood enhanced by the sense of isolation imposed by the storm. Talk was of one thing and another and finally settled on the upcoming turtle release. Since the success of the immersion ceremony at Gethsemane the week before, Islanders had begun looking forward to the release as their next big outdoor event.

'I hope it brings in bags of money for the institute so Phil won't have to leave us,' Julietta said, tipsy enough to voice her deepest concern.

Carlotta, musing privately that her granddaughter might yet turn into the beauty of the family, knew that no such thing would be allowed to happen. One or another of the Big Three, or some combination of them, would write a cheque to ensure that Sir Philip's contract was renewed. In the mean time, she considered it more exciting – and more in keeping with her plans – to leave the young people guessing.

'You're not really leaving, are you?' Jesse, looking crestfallen, tugged on Philip's elbow.

Hannah rose from the table. 'Of course he isn't,' she said and went to the phone. When she returned it was to say that Thaddeus's plane was being rerouted to Orlando. 'The recording said that it's not scheduled to land until after midnight.'

'In that case, Miss Hannah, we're not likely to see the good doctor before morning,' Malachi said, his bass voice deepened by the widow's wine.

Suddenly, like an indoor flash of lighting, the power in the house was restored and the lights, air conditioning and appliances came back on. Carlotta's squat chin and Julietta's oily nose showed once more, and Malachi, who might have passed for a man in his prime by candlelight, turned old again. Only Hannah seemed more beautiful, with Jesse resting his head drowsily on her shoulder.

The table fell silent. Was it really over? they wondered, their private reveries interrupted by the ticking of the electric Westclox above the stove. Then, as if on cue, noises at the front of the house announced that Patsy and Eduardo had returned from their clubs. Carlotta grimaced, issuing a litany of instructions and insisting that Philip accompany Hannah and Jesse home. 'The lights are still out in many places and there could be looting in the streets.'

Julietta laughed. 'That only happens in Havana!'

'Don't be so sure,' her grandmother warned, shooing everyone out of the kitchen. 'Now run along, dears, it's past Grandmalita's bedtime.'

Half of Hibiscus Way was still without power and Hannah's house stood dark. She led the way, with Philip, who was carrying Jesse, wading behind her through a shallow lake that had formed at the bottom of the drive. Hannah pushed open the front door, the wood swollen heavy with the damp, and climbed the stairs to the first floor. Philip followed, walking a few steps behind her through spacious rooms with tall ceilings and doorways that seemed to communicate silently with each other. Hannah spread open the wide double doors to the master suite and they entered Jesse's room through the large connecting bathroom. Philip stole a look at the king-size bed, Hannah's red bathing suit drying over the side of the bathtub and her silver brush and comb set on a ledge beneath the looking glass.

Jesse's room was a Lego sanctuary of castles, bridges and fortresses in various stages of construction. Its population of G.I. Joes, miniature cavalries and armoured knights dominated a large area of the floor and built-in shelves. Jesse's bed was tucked into a corner guarded by walls on two sides, and Hannah walked over to it and pulled back the coverlet. She signalled to Philip that he should lay the sleeping child on his side, lifting her son tenderly but firmly away from the edge of the bed and positioning a pair of pillows protectively around him. With so much rainfall and no ventilation the air in the room felt dense and very close.

Philip was perspiring but Hannah remained composed, her movements controlled as she folded Jesse's clothes and placed them on a chair. She pulled a light sheet over him and Philip, standing beside her, tucked the edges under the mattress. They moved swiftly and without words, as if they had rehearsed this, the atmosphere becoming softly illuminated as power returned to a few more houses in the neighbourhood. Philip longed to kiss her – this time really kiss her. Then, without him having to do anything, they embraced. He began to say that he loved her but she stopped him, closing her hand over his mouth. They drew irresistibly nearer, the heat in the room rising like a fever.

'Not here,' Hannah murmured through the steady rise and fall of Jesse's breathing. The silence deepened, quivering with excitement as they backed slowly into the other room.

PART THREE

The Belt of Venus

BLEEDING HEARTS

Skirting the viburnum hedge, Philip experienced the thrill of the cat burglar as he slipped through a gap in the foliage and stole up the wooden steps to the annexe. The lush fragrance of blooming nightshade, heady and acrid as rolled tobacco, revived some of his feeling of euphoria at the baptismal font. As then, it seemed to Philip that there was no past, only future, and that the world was being made new. Standing on the terrace outside his room he lifted his feverish face to the gigantic March moon showing through a rift in the clouds and thought about Hannah.

He wasn't bothered that she hadn't said she loved him. Or that he still hadn't revealed his identity and the real reason he had come to the Island. There would be a time, perhaps soon, when she would be ready for the truth, but that time wasn't now. He entered his room as the first flinty lines of dawn streaked the grey and still somewhat turbulent sky. In the shadowy half-light he stopped dead halfway to the bathroom, having become suddenly aware of a dark figure standing next to his bed. Clenching his fists in self-defence, he approached slowly.

'I know where you've been,' Julietta hissed in a voice dripping with venom. 'And I'm going to make sure everyone knows.'

The doctor watched his wife as she lay sleeping. Power had been restored to the house only moments earlier, and the master suite had a peculiar hothouse atmosphere. Neither Hannah nor Jesse made any response when he bent over to kiss them, as if they were drugged. Loath to wake them and exhausted from his long drive and lack of sleep, Thaddeus tumbled into bed beside his wife.

But sleep wouldn't come. He kept turning over in his head that the FDA announcement would be made on Monday and that, starting then, he would have to endure days, possibly weeks, of interrogation from analysts, scientists, patients and their families. Not to mention investors, friends, family and, crucially, Louisa. With so little of the weekend remaining, Thaddeus wondered whether he would have done better to stay in New York.

He said Hannah's name softly, hoping she would wake so that they could talk about what was weighing on his mind. But she lay still, hardly breathing it seemed. Maybe, thought Thaddeus, glancing at the spongy light in the window, the general torpor of his home had something to do with the storm system that continued to linger offshore. Thinking about the weather, the clinical trials and his own unhappiness, he realised that Hannah's eyes were open. He brought his face nearer, but there was no spark in her – no embrace or questions about his flight and solitary night ride across the state.

'Are you all right?' he asked, raising himself on his elbow. Hannah seemed feverish and he instinctively touched his wrist to her forehead to check for a temperature.

She drew back. 'I'm drained by this heat. We couldn't leave Carlotta's house for ages and there was no power all night.' Hannah's explanations came out in a hurry. When they ended, her head sank back on the pillow and her eyes closed again.

Thaddeus wanted to hold her, but she stopped him. He swung his legs over the side of the bed and went to the bathroom. From where he stood he could see into Jesse's room and his son, rolled up in a sheet, lying on his side. Glancing through the other door at his wife he noticed with a stab of disappointment that she hadn't moved from the position in which he'd left her. Hannah must be unwell, he concluded and ran the shower.

Looking in the mirror he rubbed his thumb over the reddish stubble on his chin. 'Maybe I'll grow a beard,' he thought. 'Like that English fellow everyone's so crazy about.'

Nothing went right at breakfast. Thaddeus didn't feel as if his family were sufficiently excited to see him after what he had been through to reach home. Hannah remained quiet, her manner guarded. Was he imagining it, Thaddeus asked himself, or was she still eyeing him with suspicion each time he went near the refrigerator, where the ampules of serum were stored? Feeling the extreme tension in the air he wondered whether he was unconsciously passing his anxieties about Pandorex on to his family.

Addison arrived at a few minutes past nine, bringing Sunny with him. They were dressed for their Saturday pursuits: Sunny in dungarees for a day with student volunteers at the institute, and the lawyer in a polo shirt and pink Bermuda shorts for eighteen holes of golf.

'I just got in a couple of hours ago,' Thaddeus explained. 'My plane was rerouted to Orlando, and I drove from there.'

'Rotten luck. I planned to come by last evening, but it was raining too hard. Then the lights went out. We'd almost forgotten how much fun that can be.' Addison grinned, his arm around Sunny's waist. Lowering his voice, he turned to his brother. 'I had a message from my secretary that you called yesterday. I thought it might have to do with that FDA site visit.'

The question chilled Thaddeus. He didn't want to talk about it in front of his family, though it hardly seemed as if anyone was listening.

'I said,' Addison repeated, 'did the FDA investigator pay you a call?'

'I'll tell you about it later.'

'Tell us now!' cried Jesse, taking a giant bite of blueberry pancake. He had no idea what his father and uncle were discussing, only that the house seemed suddenly full of secrets.

'It's to do with business,' Thaddeus replied. 'I'm only allowed to talk to lawyers about it. Shouldn't you be getting ready to meet your turtle friends?'

'We aren't going today,' Hannah cut in, pouring coffee into their mugs.

'Whyever not?' asked Sunny.

'I'm feeling a bit off. Jesse too. I think it's something we ate at Carlotta's last night.'

Sunny gave her nephew's plate a puzzled look. She had never seen him so ravenous. 'If you're not well,' she said, patting Hannah's arm, 'I'll take Jesse over there while you get some rest.'

'No,' Hannah said. 'We'll be fine.'

'I suppose you know best. But in that case I'll tell you the big news now. I had so wanted to host a party at Villa des Vagues after the release ceremony, but Mother insisted on holding it on the beach. She hated the idea of opening her precious palazzo to strangers – never mind that half the Island's stray animals live there – and now at last she says that she will.'

'What changed her mind?' Thaddeus asked.

'The lights went out! And Mother, it seems, is afraid of the dark.'

'Hard to believe, isn't it?' Addison chuckled. 'After all these years of Vanessa Vine being afraid of nothing.'

'She became terribly agitated when the storm broke,' Sunny continued, 'and I couldn't very well leave her in that pitch-dark mausoleum of a house. So I brought her home with me – lock, stock and Jerzy – along with a few of her best beloved pets and a pot of goulash.'

'And come morning,' Addison reported, 'the old dame tells us that she'd had a change of heart and would be thrilled to host the entire town for the biggest-ever bash at Villa des Vagues.'

Hannah listened without taking part in the conversation. Her sister-in-law, who rarely uttered more than a few syllables, couldn't stop talking. But there were a few things Sunny didn't report. Among them was that, while sitting up with her mother in the dark, speaking softly as to a child until the old woman had quieted, Sunny described something she had experienced at Jesse's healing Mass: 'I saw Paula' – Sunny was absolutely certain of this – 'among the teens standing round the immersion pool.'

Mrs Vine did not dispute it. She merely nodded her heavy, wigless head resting on the pillow before quietly falling asleep. Sunny then tiptoed across the hall, lingering in the door of Paula's old room before she crept into bed with Addison. Sheltering in each other's arms they talked and talked – about what they had lost and what they might still have together.

When they rose in the morning and Mrs Vine offered to host the party, Sunny couldn't wait to share the news with the youngsters at the institute. She had a particular affection for one of the girls, the gawky teenager with pimples and a smile – braces and all – that were so like Paula's. Anticipating the impact of her news about the big bash, it was the look on this girl's face that Sunny looked forward to most.

At the other end of the kitchen Addison stood huddling with his brother, their voices hushed and foreheads creased. 'Are you trying to tell me that the FDA has refused to approve the serum?'

'*Postpone* was the word she used. It's to do with the way we collected and interpreted the results.' Thaddeus broke off. 'What they're asking for will mean re-launching the clinical trials.'

'But that could take months!'

'More like a year, according to my calculations.'

'Pandorex stock will tumble.'

'I know. But as a clinician my top priority has to be the patients' safety. I've been thinking about this non-stop on my way from New York and, as much as I hate the delay, it's better that we address the thorniest issues now, before any lives are lost.'

'But these people's lives are already lost!' Addison, trying to keep his voice down, drew his brother into the family room so the others wouldn't hear them. 'Every patient enrolled in the clinical trials is terminally ill. The goal is to prolong their lives, even if only by a little.'

It came as a huge relief to Thaddeus to share the news with his brother. He even felt a kind of happiness that he would now be required to go back to his first love, which was clinical research. He considered the amount of time he had spent recently with lawyers and Wall Street analysts as a waste of his talents; and promised himself that, starting now, he would leave the business side of things to Addison.

A crack of light showed through the low cloud cover in the window. Little more than a sliver, it promised the return of sunshine to a place that had begun to feel almost unimaginably bleak without it.

The sun finally broke through at nearly the same time that the Silver Shadow pulled up in front of the institute. A smile crossed Jerzy's usually impassive features when he noticed that the group of volunteers was the biggest yet: congratulating himself that the growing numbers had more than a little to do with the trays of pastry he delivered punctually every Saturday.

Mrs Vine, who was still recovering from the night she had spent in her daughter's guestroom, remained for a few minutes in the back seat of the Rolls. She rummaged inside her knitting bag, looking for the vintage (everything she owned seemed to have, with the passage of time, become 'vintage') diamond and onyx Cartier compact with which she periodically measured the valleys and troughs of her face. These days, checking the mirror was a way of gaining assurance that she still existed. Jerzy, of course, would have been delighted to reassure her. He might even go so far as to insist that she was beautiful. Like a faithful, well-trained pet, a good chauffeur-cum-valet could hardly be expected to do less. For that reason alone Mrs Vine trusted neither Jerzy nor her pets, however delightful they were to have around. Only Sunny − volatile and difficult as she was − could really be relied on in this regard.

Turning one cheek and then the other to the tiny looking glass, Mrs Vine studied the two women shown in its reflective surface. Her features had a peculiarity that made her look nothing like the same person in profile as she did from the front. It had been a huge asset on the stage, and Sanford had loved the duality – 'like getting two women for the price of one' – he had joked. Now, lifting her eyes to the car window – through which Vanessa Vine watched her daughter raking the old tennis court on which she had learned to play the game with her father – she realised with a pang of regret that she had only ever shown one of her faces to Sunny. The spider's web of wrinkles and purple bags under her eyes were always somewhat less apparent in the miniature mirror dusted with powder. But Mrs Vine knew that they were there and, taking no chances, lowered the veil over her face. Lumbering from the rear door of the Shadow with somewhat more difficulty than usual, she called her daughter's name.

'You know, Pa, we could use a super-duper doctor like you at the turtle clinic,' Jesse observed as he watched his father pour kerosene over a small pyramid of charcoal they had just piled on top of the Weber grill. 'Why don't you join us the next time we head over to the institute?'

Thaddeus frowned at the briquets that wouldn't light. 'I spend quite enough time in clinics already,' he said. 'And know nothing about marine life.'

'We'll teach you. Come to find, turtles aren't so different from humans. Dolphin says—'

'You had better use these,' Hannah cut in, handing her husband a fresh bag of charcoal. 'The others are still wet from the rain.'

The afternoon had turned glorious, and the bleeding-heart vines, espaliered on a wooden trellis sheltered by the loggia, had suddenly bloomed; their velvety leaves cradling an abundance of small, bell-shaped white calyxes with blood-red centres.

Thaddeus gulped his third beer. 'Jesse has a point,' Hannah said as they watched the briquets simmer. 'A doctor of your calibre could lend a huge impetus to the institute by bringing the local medical community on board.'

'You want me to sit on another board?'

'Not sit but push for stricter regulation on the disposal of medical waste.'

Thaddeus tossed his can of beer in the bin. 'I'd like to petition for less regulation, not more. It seems to me the government is getting a bit too involved in our lives.'

Hannah studied her husband critically over the rim of her glass. She didn't like the stubble growing on his chin and was about to say so. Thinking better of it, she said: 'Waste from hospitals and laboratories is leeching into the ocean. If we don't do something soon it will wash up on our doorstep.'

'Ma's right. You should have seen the needles and all that stuff they hook me up to at the hospital that was inside Princess—'

'I don't want to hear about it.' Thaddeus clasped his hands over his ears. 'I can't take any more.'

Jesse stared at his father. For a horrifying moment it sounded like a man howling. Hannah, smelling charred meat on the fire, rushed to put out the flames.

Julietta stayed in her room for a week. She took meals there and allowed only her grandmother to come inside. When Patsy and Eduardo tiptoed past their daughter's bedroom and listened at the door, the two women could be heard talking.

Philip kept his distance, hoping that Julietta wouldn't make good on her threat. And that if she did, her reputation as a fantasist would in this instance work against her. Who, after all, would believe such a story about him and Hannah? At times even Philip didn't believe it, wondering if he had dreamed it. But he knew that he hadn't: and that even if some people chose to believe Julietta – as Carlotta undoubtedly did – he would devise a way to keep them guessing. Islanders, he reckoned, had been doing that about him since he arrived.

The doctor had lain awake much of the night, his jaw clenched as he mulled over all that awaited him once the news broke the next day.

Pandorex stock would take a nose-dive at around midday, when the FDA was scheduled to make its announcement, followed by recriminations from investors and families of patients enrolled in clinical trials that would now have to be paused. Becoming aware of a movement on Hannah's side of the bed, Thaddeus saw her throw off the covers and run to the bathroom.

He sprang after her, holding her forehead while she retched violently in the sink. He shut the door to Jesse's room and helped her wash and return to bed. Then he lay down beside her, while the room around them gradually filled with light. At length they heard the tap-tapping of the little walking frame and Jesse crept into bed with them, laying his head on his mother's pillow. Hannah's breathing slowed and she seemed to be asleep, her hair mingling with her son's on the pillow: her profile grave and beautiful as Thaddeus bent over to kiss her.

Checking the clock on the nightstand he dressed and packed his travel case. He thought of calling Addison to say that he couldn't accompany him to New York because Hannah was unwell. But that would be to saddle his brother with the onus of fielding questions about the data that only a scientist could answer.

'Pa has to leave,' he whispered to Jesse. 'You take care of your Ma, OK?'

He met Marta coming through the door on his way out, a heavy winter coat slung over his arm. 'Hannah isn't well,' he told the housekeeper. 'Please keep an eye on her and call me if she isn't any better by tonight.'

A motor sounded in the drive and Addison gave his usual double honk. Afraid that it would disturb Hannah, Thaddeus sprinted towards the car.

Chaotic days followed, with the Pandorex board debating how to respond to the FDA's queries and barrage of questions coming from investors and Wall Street analysts. Only one thing appeared certain: the clinical trials would have to be halted and then re-launched, with Thaddeus making an on-site visit to every cancer clinic that had been conducting the trials.

The doctor embarked on his travels with a mixture of anxiety and hope – anxiety about what he might discover and hope that the original findings would be vindicated. Alone at night in one forgettable hotel after another he wished that there was some way to erase the look on Jesse and Hannah's faces when he had fallen apart at the barbeque. And yet, the more he thought about it the more it seemed that Hannah's feelings towards him had changed even before that scene – in ways a busy man less in love with his wife might not even have noticed.

Wrestling with the challenges facing Pandorex, Thaddeus had little time to dwell on the personal side of his life. On a more positive note, his visit to medical centres from Pittsburgh to Kansas City, Chicago to Denver and, finally, up and down the West Coast convinced him that discrepancies in the collection and recording of data from the clinical trials – and not the efficacy of the serum – was what had led to the FDA's queries. Putting in place a new protocol to eliminate the problem, however, proved far more complex than Thaddeus expected, as one week turned into two, then three, since his travels began.

He tried not to look at newspapers or listen to the news, blocking from his mind the negative fallout about Pandorex that was spreading like a forest fire through the financial community. Instead, he focused all his energy on the doctors, scientists and patients assisting in his task. The sheer amount of work involved and difference in time zones made it difficult to call home at a reasonable hour. But the real reason Thaddeus didn't call was because he was afraid of what Hannah and his mother would say about the precipitous decline in the family fortunes. He didn't feel like giving explanations until he had more data – and was in no mood for Louisa's recriminations. Having devised a roadmap for the new clinical trials he dared not look up until it was established. Then, very early one morning at a clinic outside of Spokane, Washington, the doctor was urgently called to the phone at the nurses' station.

'You had better get on the next plane to New York,' Addison said in a voice that didn't entirely sound like his own. 'We're holding an emergency meeting of the board and we can't hold it without you.'

'But I'm in the middle of—'

'No questions, Thad. Just do as I say.'

It felt like an ambush. The entire seven-member board of Pandorex – scientists as well as officers – were assembled round the conference table when Thaddeus walked through the door. A soft spring snow powdered the east-facing windows, adhering in clumps to the panes and dimming the light as the doctor lugged his old leather briefcase, swollen with documents, to where his colleagues sat waiting. He had sprouted a reddish beard and shed several pounds during his travels, looking different enough from the man they had known to give them pause.

'Mind telling me what this is about?' he said wearily.

Addison rose from his seat.

No one spoke.

Thaddeus placed his briefcase on the table and lifted from inside a wad of folders with the latest data. He passed his fingers affectionately over the soft leather case, a graduation gift from his brother when he had finished first in his class at medical school. Looking up, Thaddeus caught a glimpse of his reflection in one of the darkening windowpanes and almost didn't recognise the bushy lumberjack looking back. Exhausted from his trip, he dropped into his usual seat at the head of the table.

For a long time the only sound in the conference room was the clanging of the ancient radiators. Finally, Addison spoke. 'Whatever made you do it?' he asked.

The first thing Thaddeus noticed was that his brother was twirling his college fraternity ring round and round his little finger. It was a nervous habit when he was deep in thought – or deeply upset. But Thaddeus too was upset, his eyes stinging from the long flight and strain of reading charts. He needed a hot bath, not another meeting.

'Do *what?*' he snapped.

Addison reached inside a yellow manila folder sitting on the table and pulled out a document. He slid it towards his brother without looking at him and waited for his reaction.

Thaddeus instantly recognised the compliance form he had sent to his stockbroker on the day he sold his shares of Pandorex. It was a faxed version of his own fax and the print had shrunk to the point of being barely legible. Even so, he was able to make out Simon Allen's signature at the bottom – or rather, the signature he had copied.

'This document, which you sent to your financial broker, was reviewed some time later by his firm's compliance department. It's routine at investment houses to go back over each week's trades for signs of anything out of the ordinary – for instance, when a large chunk of stock has been sold by the principal of a publicly held company.

'Such trades are flagged in case news comes out about the company,' Addison continued in the same, maddeningly even tone of voice that he used with clients. 'If a red flag is raised the brokerage firm is legally bound to inform the Securities and Exchange Commission of the trade – as happened when you sold a hundred thousand shares of Pandorex shortly before the FDA announced its intention not to approve the serum.'

Addison paused to give time for what he had said to sink in.

'What on earth made you forge Simon's signature?'

Thaddeus mumbled his way through an explanation that, heard aloud in a silent room, sounded as false as the premise on which it was based. 'I would have asked Simon to sign the form if he'd been in the office.'

'And if I *had* signed it I would now be in the same fix as you!' the CFO cried. 'Can you honestly tell those of us here – your friends, colleagues and your own brother – that it was pure coincidence you decided to sell a large chunk of stock immediately after what you learned from the FDA investigator?'

'I only wanted to make sure that there would be enough money to service my loan. I wasn't thinking...' Thaddeus's voice trailed off.

'Oh Thad, you never think.' Addison sighed.

'But he does think, a great deal, about cancer.' The scientists rushed to Thaddeus's defence. 'There would be no Pandorex without him.'

All heads nodded in agreement. 'Look, no one expects Thad to know the ins and outs of securities regulation. But he made one hell of a poor judgement call and I expect the SEC to launch a full inquiry,' Addison lectured. 'Once they get started on something like this no stone will be left unturned. And the timing of the site investigator's visit coincides too neatly with his sale of the stock. Even if it didn't, forging a legal document would constitute a crime. Simon, by the way, was prepared to say that he had signed this form without being aware of the facts. But I advised against it because he cannot swear to it under oath without perjuring himself.'

Silence settled like a wet blanket over the table while the board considered the likely fallout from news that the CEO of Pandorex had sold his stock at the first sign of trouble. 'This,' Addison warned, 'could be the final straw that shreds what remains of investor confidence.'

'What about *our* confidence?' Simon bristled. 'I thought we were in this together! All our employees, down to the lab assistants and janitor, have invested in Pandorex because we believed in it and hoped to make a profit. What made you feel more entitled to avoid the risks than the rest of us?' Simon, who could no longer control the tick in his shoulder, glared at Thaddeus. 'The stock is trading at less than a quarter of its value three weeks ago, and if the SEC launch an investigation it will tank.'

The reproach on the faces of colleagues who had worked alongside him for more than a decade shook the doctor to the core. He thought of his mother and a dozen others, at the Mangrove, Bath & Racquet and Shore clubs, who had also invested in good faith. Finally, there was Hannah. Coming on the back of all the distance between them he wondered if their marriage could survive this.

Turning to his brother he said: 'I'll do whatever you say – anything to keep this from getting out.'

Addison's legal opinion was that the only way to avoid a civil action by the SEC against the entire company was for Thaddeus to admit quietly what he had done and why, plead for clemency and offer to pay the fines. 'Forging a legal document and trading stock on insider information are serious offenses subject to censure and fines. But lying about it is what usually sends people to jail.'

'Jail.' Thaddeus repeated, feeling a sickish taste in his mouth.

MRS VINE TAKES CHARGE

Hannah pressed her cheek to her son's forehead. It felt unnaturally cold in the midday heat, and she checked his pulse next. Averting her eyes from the black and blue bruise on the bandaged arm where the fistula had been re-opened during dialysis, she adjusted the pillow under his head. Jesse had felt so well lately that Hannah had begun to hope the dialysis could be stopped. But when she called the hospital to say that they wouldn't be keeping the appointment, the nurse reminded her that Jesse had missed one session already.

'You'll have to get permission,' the nurse cautioned, and put Hannah on hold.

The attending doctor came on the line. 'Missing a second treatment would lead to a build-up of potassium and phosphorus and could bring on a sudden heart attack – or even death.'

When Hannah remained quiet the doctor put her on notice. 'The hospital cannot take responsibility for something like this. And no parent with a conscience should either.'

Afterwards, Jesse seemed much more tired than after any of his previous sessions, and he fell asleep in the car on their way home from the hospital. Now, seated beside him in the shade of the loggia, Hannah's thoughts turned to Philip. Was it possible to love two men at the same time?

'Oh yes,' she cried. 'Yes, yes, yes!' Covering her face, she burst into tears.

For some moments Hannah remained in the same position, with Jesse asleep beside her. When at length she lowered the hands from her face she saw Mrs Vine standing only a few feet from her, running her fingers through the little red and white blossoms of the bleeding-heart vines climbing the walls of the loggia.

'Are you all right, dear?' the old lady said, hobbling towards her. 'I passed you and Jesse in the car earlier and didn't think either of you looked very well.'

Wearing her usual regalia – a flowing kaftan and wide-brimmed hat with a matching veil – Mrs Vine dug inside her knitting bag and produced a small round cake wrapped in tin foil. 'I brought you this,' she said, without waiting for an answer. 'To help keep up your strength in these trying times.'

'I don't understand,' Hannah said, accepting the cake.

'I only meant that, with the clinical trials halted and Pandorex stock taking a tumble, you're probably in something of a state. I lost fifty thousand dollars the other day. Not that I mind, terribly. Still, I hate to think what Thad must be going through.'

Hannah hadn't heard about any trouble at Pandorex. She hadn't read the papers or spoken to her husband more than a few times, quick calls he had made from pay phones at hospitals and airports. She was aware that Thaddeus had been asked to inspect the various sites at which the clinical trials were being conducted, but he had said nothing to her about them being suspended.

'You know, my dear,' Mrs Vine said after a brief pause. 'It's become quite apparent – at least to me – that you and Thad are leading almost separate lives.'

Behind the veil that concealed much of her face it was hard to know in what spirit, exactly, the widow's observation had been made. 'Mind you, I'm not one to pry.' She slipped her arm through Hannah's and led her away from the sleeping child. 'Back in Peoria I thought nothing of carrying on with several men at once. And I dare say that on the whole it did me a world of good. But these things are hard to navigate and it's best to outgrow them as soon as we can.'

She knows, Hannah thought, and nearly dropped the cake. Did everyone? Such things happened on the Island, without any clue as to how word had got out.

'Ma,' came a small voice behind them. Turning, they saw Jesse trying to sit up. 'I'm hungry.'

'And I've brought you just the thing, my precious,' exclaimed Mrs Vine. 'How does chocolate marzipan torte sound? It's one of Jerzy's family recipes.' Lifting the parcel away from Hannah, she gave it to Jesse. 'I'm afraid I can't stay to have any with you. We're going on safari this afternoon.'

Jesse peeked through his fingers at the visitor. 'To Africa?'

'Better than Africa, my child. We're staying right here on the Island to hunt the bufo toads. Jerzy has a way of spying them out in the bushes and he's fashioned a slingshot to take them out.'

'Sylvester!' Jesse shrieked at the top of his voice.

Fearing that the boy might be having a seizure, Mrs Vine grabbed her parasol. 'Good heavens,' they heard her exclaim as she shuffled out the door.

'Sssh.' Hannah smoothed Jesse's hair away from his eyes. 'Look over there – behind the camelias. What do you see?'

'I can't see anything,' he wailed.

'It's Sylvester,' she said, pointing to something dark hopping towards them across the loggia.

Jesse brightened at the sound of the familiar thud over the tiles and lowered the knuckles from his eyes. Remembering Mrs Vine's cake, he asked for a piece.

Hannah was struck by how much worse her son's eyesight had become. It was nearly two months since his last injection of serum, Thaddeus's warnings ringing in her ears. Then she remembered what Mrs Vine had said about the Pandorex clinical trials being paused and the stock plummeting. But what had the old courtesan meant by her florid advice on the subject of lovers? Was she just posturing, as Mrs Vine loved to do, or did she know something? And if so, who had told her?

Addison explained the situation as tactfully as he could when Hannah called him a little while later.

'Thad has been in a race against time, gathering data at trial centres all around the country, to salvage the company and the hopes of dozens of end-of-life patients waiting to receive the serum.' Saying nothing about his brother's financial woes or pending SEC investigation, he added: 'Your husband, Hannah, is fighting for his life. Thad has never needed you more than he does now.'

Two days later the doctor returned home. As he stepped off the plane he almost walked past his wife and son, who had been waiting for him at the gate.

'Over here!' Hannah called, waving.

He stared in disbelief at the sound of her voice. Seeing Hannah standing behind a wall of people in the crowded terminal he cut a line through them, encircling her and Jesse in a wide embrace. Jesse tugged on his father's beard to see if it was real and asked to ride on his shoulders. Is this what they call happiness? Thaddeus thought: the small, unimportant moments that will remain for ever etched in my heart?

That night, lying next to Hannah in the big bed, he made his confession. He told her about the loan he had assumed on behalf of the company and how he had tried to sell enough stock to cover it. He wasn't sure how much Hannah understood about insider trading and didn't go into the particulars – for instance, that he had forged Simon's signature. His voice became choked with emotion while Hannah listened patiently to his stream of regrets. For a long time after the doctor finished they lay quietly together, side by side but without touching. Then, slowly, firmly, Hannah rolled over on the bed and they drew nearer, their entwined bodies silhouetted by moonlight.

On the other side of the viburnum hedge Philip lay wide awake in his bed. For three weeks he had hardly slept, wondering why

Hannah didn't call or try to see him. And there was little chance of it now that her husband was home.

Living in the same house with Julietta was growing unbearable. The girl's aloofness was tiresome, Carlotta's glances even more calculating than usual. Patsy and Eduardo were out too much of the time to notice the change of atmosphere in their home: for instance, that Philip was no longer having dinner every night with the family. Staying till late at the institute, he would eat supper at the counter of Green's Pharmacy, and was gone again by the time the family got up in the morning.

The town library became his refuge. Housed in what had been the Island's first schoolhouse, the historic one-room, wooden-framed structure looked out of place between the much newer First National Bank and Post Office. The library was staffed by volunteers who didn't always turn up, and books circulated on an honour-based system. Philip went there in the early mornings when the place was nearly always empty. He loved the sound of the floorboards creaking beneath him as he entered and the mouldy smell of woodwork and decades-old books on geography, botany and local history. But what Philip valued even more than the library's holdings was the IBM word processor and printer that someone had recently donated and on which he began composing letters of inquiry to marine life institutes around the world. To make sure that no one got wind of what he was doing he leased a post office box for any responses he might receive. When Philip noticed that he had been assigned P.O. Box 1979 – the year of Jesse's birth – he felt the hand of destiny at his back. He was as sure of it as he was that Hannah had always been meant, not for his father or Dr Caulfield, but for him.

As on every other Saturday, he arrived at the institute well ahead of the volunteers. He fed Princess her usual bucketful of crustaceans and went down to the beach to check for overnight nesting activity. But this morning there were no nests: and in their place Philip discovered two massive hawksbill turtles lying unresponsive on the sand. There were deep parallel gashes in the carapace of one of the turtles and raw flesh hung from the mouth of the other. Philip had just begun checking their vital signs when he heard someone calling him. Looking up, he saw Sunny Sloan running towards him across the sand.

She fell to her knees beside the turtles and helped Philip examine their wounds. Sunny shook like a reed, and Philip, who had thought that he was prepared for anything, found that nothing in his experience had prepared him for this.

'Looks like they were mangled by a boat propeller,' he said. 'I'll stay here to keep them hydrated while you corral the volunteers. We're going to need help moving them indoors. Also, get a hold of that vet who operated on Princess. His name is Preston – you'll find his number in the Rolodex. Hurry!'

To Sunny's greatest surprise the first call she made was to her mother. Mrs Vine had been about to leave her house to feed the feral cats when her daughter's cry for help changed the course of the entire day. 'Leave it to me,' she said, trying to quiet Sunny. There was no telling what she might get up to when she was upset. 'I'll round up the paramedics from the hospital.'

'They have regulations about treating animals.'

'We'll see about that. The ER is named after Sanford, isn't it?'

Sunny flipped through the Rolodex and phoned the vet next. 'I'll be away at a conference until next Tuesday…' began the recorded message, and she hung up.

She had better luck reaching out to the volunteers, most of whom were still at home or in bed. They formed a chain of phone calls, one to another, and when the last call had been made Sunny went to her car. Backing on to County Road she had no idea where she was going or what she meant to do. Her tongue was dry as sandpaper and the old craving for a drink hit her hard. Only something with a kick to it would dispel the scene she had witnessed on the beach and that had continued playing in her mind. It revived images of finding her little girl dead, Addison and two police officers kneeling over Paula's lifeless body as Philip had kneeled beside the hawksbills. For the love of Paula, don't let me fail again, Sunny prayed, her breathing shallow and temples throbbing.

No one would know if she made one small quick stop at home. Addison was at golf and the maid off on Saturdays. As Sunny drove faster she didn't notice the light at the intersection turn red. Screeching to a stop, she backed her car a few feet short of the pedestrian crossing. It was early enough in the day that the streets were empty, and Sunny's foot moved to the accelerator. Checking that there were no pedestrians, she sped through the intersection.

This was her last chance: the only way to make good on the promises she had made to Addison on the night of the storm. Ever since, nursing in secret the new life growing inside her, Sunny saw it all slip through her fingers.

Hannah was drying the breakfast dishes and Thaddeus crawling on all fours about the family room, Jesse riding on his back as the outlaw Jesse James, when their sister-in-law burst through the door.

'Get up, Thad,' she cried, bringing a pause to the room. 'We have a huge medical emergency on our hands.' Speaking with a calmness that astonished no one more than it did Sunny, she explained the situation. 'The vet is out of town and you're the only doctor I know.'

Jesse, seeing his aunt's shadow in the doorway, stared in bewilderment as he tried to connect it with the new authority in her voice.

'But I haven't a clue how to treat animals!' Thaddeus protested.

'Although you're happy to experiment on them when it suits you.'

The doctor picked himself up off the floor and looked sheepishly about the family room: at Hannah, holding a dishtowel over her arm, Jesse pale and strangely silent as he looked imploringly at his father. 'OK,' he said. 'Let's go have a look.'

They followed Sunny to the institute in their car, the first time Hannah and Jesse had gone there in over a month. But by the time they arrived the turtles were no longer on the beach and the facility appeared deserted.

'Where are they?' Sunny asked the volunteers who had gathered in the mean time.

'Mrs Vine came by in a U-Haul van and transported them to her villa.'

Sunny's mouth fell open. 'My mother – in a *van?*'

The doctor's eyes rounded in horror as he entered the tapestried dining room. The two biggest reptiles he had ever seen outside a text book lay flippers to head on Mrs Vine's oak dining table padded with bloodied sheets and towels. The dozen or more high-backed dining chairs with lion's-claw feet had been moved against the wall like judgement seats, and the Moorish chandelier, suspended by a chain-metal cord, dangled from the beamed ceiling.

Thaddeus's immediate impression was of some arcane ritual about to take place. But on closer inspection he noticed at one end of the long table a full suite of modern surgical equipment, lamps and portable monitors that transformed the musty dining hall into a makeshift emergency ward. 'They wouldn't let us into the hospital so I made them bring the ER here,' explained Mrs Vine.

Philip came over to shake the doctor's hand. 'I'm afraid they won't last the day without immediate surgical intervention. Please help us.'

Thaddeus circled the table; his shoulders stooped and welts of sweat forming on his hairline as he considered his dilemma. If it came out that he had been treating animals without a license it would only add to his list of offenses – and possibly cost him his medical license. It was reckless to continue. But as Thaddeus was about to open his mouth to say so, he saw Hannah and Jesse standing to one side, their eyes pleading.

'I don't know the first thing about turtle anatomy,' he said, turning to Philip. 'But if you'll guide me, I'm willing to give it a shot.'

The two men assessed each other frankly: aware how much they needed each other and how much more the hapless victims lying on the table needed them both. Rolling up his shirtsleeves, the doctor instructed Jerzy to boil as many vats of water as the kitchen would hold, and then set to work.

An armadillo scurried across the driveway, startled by the tall human form walking with heavy footsteps from the car to the door of the house. Thaddeus dropped down on the shallow front steps with his head bowed over his chest. He heard wind rustling through the tall palms, like upside down broomsticks sweeping the night; waves echoing along the shore. Cradling his head in his hands, he wept.

Both hawksbill turtles died while he had been working on them: first one, followed almost immediately by the other. As if hastening after each other, trying to punish him. It had certainly felt like another failure, coming at the heels of so many others and cutting open wounds that were just beginning to heal. Filled with recrimination and self-doubt, Thaddeus didn't hear the door open and Hannah's light step behind him. Then, a moment later, her arm around his shoulder as she kneeled on the ground beside him.

'Everything I do these days comes out wrong. I've nearly ruined my company and couldn't even save a pair of reptiles. I was vain enough to feel cocksure that my serum would be approved without a glitch, and arrogant enough to risk your future and Jesse's for the sake of proving I was right.'

'We all make mistakes,' Hannah said quietly. 'But what you did tonight – and I know you went out on a limb to do it – was nothing less than heroic. I've never been more proud of you.'

'I did it for you. The best of me has been you.' He took her hand. 'Say you love me.'

There was no moon and he couldn't see her face clearly.

'I love you,' she whispered, and gently drew him to his feet.

The tragedy shone a harsh new light on the silent killing of the Island's beloved sea turtles. Sunny seized the moment with her usual compulsive energy and placed a death notice in *The Shiny Sheet* paying homage to the hawksbills. Directly below it she issued on behalf of the institute an open invitation to the entire town for a special ceremony, to be held the following week, marking Princess's recovery and release back into the sea. Afterwards, a reception would be held at Villa des Vagues, set to open its doors to the public for the first time since the Second World War, when it had housed a hospital for servicemen wounded at sea.

For Thaddeus it felt like a reprieve. He was home again and Hannah loved him. He had done what he could for Pandorex at medical centres round the country and it was now a matter of waiting for the new protocols to be implemented and the results resubmitted to the FDA. Partly as a way to distract himself he threw his weight behind Sunny's publicity campaign by writing a scathing editorial in *The Shiny Sheet*. In it he cited laxity among regional hospitals in monitoring the disposal of biomedical waste and called on them to form an oversight committee that would keep an eye on how well companies hired to dispose of waste were complying with the rules.

Word began going round the Island that Pandorex couldn't be doing so badly if Dr Caulfield found time to promote worthy causes. 'Just don't start criticising the government directly,' Addison warned on their way to church that Sunday. 'And say a prayer that no one finds out the FDA isn't the only federal agency investigating you.'

But, as the brothers knew, no amount of prayer had ever stopped Islanders from talking.

RELEASE

Carlotta Alonso had begun smoking cigars when she was sixteen, the same year she married Ernesto. No slender cigarillos for her, but the thick brown variety that were a trademark of her family business. Now, as further proof that she was no longer a child, Julietta shared vigorous puffs of her grandmother's cigar as they stood waiting for the release ceremony to get underway. Wearing a Victoria's Secret push-up bra inside a Lilly sundress, Julietta was doing everything but somersaults to capture the attention of the Channel 4 News cameraman covering the event.

It had rained during the night and the sand was hard-packed, a marquee of grey clouds stretching as far across the ocean as the eye could see. Thanks to Sunny's publicity blitz, cars and media vans were parked for a mile and a half up and down both sides of County Road as the expectant crowd thronged the area surrounding the outdoor water tank. Princess, sensing freedom, butted her wing-like flippers against the fibreglass walls of the tank while cameras clicked and people oohed and aahed. They quieted when they saw Philip Godolphin mount a makeshift stage near the tank. Leaner and more rugged in appearance than when he had arrived, his beard full and features more attenuated, he seemed to many to have grown only handsomer on the job.

'Our beloved resident turtle is about to embark on an incredible months-long pilgrimage across the seas,' he said, addressing the crowd through a megaphone. 'Turtles gravitate naturally to invisible forces in the Earth's magnetic compass, an instinct that eventually steers them back to the same stretch of beach on which they entered the world as hatchlings. If that turns out to be our own shore, then you can expect to see Princess here again in about two years. And yet, increasingly, there are those that never return.'

Gasps rose from the audience as Philip described – in more graphic terms than many would have liked – what had caused the hawksbills' violent deaths. At the end of his sombre eulogy all heads lowered for a moment of silence, broken only by the cry of seagulls. Then, with Sunny and the volunteers helping him and the crowd forming a wide semicircle, they carried Princess to the water's edge and gently lowered her.

For a few tense moments the turtle's carapace seemed locked to the sand. Then it made a desperate dash for the ocean, propelling swiftly on its rear flippers while cheers rose from the crowd. Sunny took up the megaphone next, inviting everyone for refreshments at Villa des Vagues. 'We can walk there along the beach, but we'll have to hurry, before high tide floods the steps.'

Some had no doubt come to the release mainly to see the inside of one of the Island's legendary estates. The procession advanced eagerly towards the steep steps leading from the beach up to the palazzo – a marvel in itself since the Island was at sea level and the villa was built on top of a man-made dune ridge to mimic a cliff. People whispered about the house's parading columns, soaring arches and half-indoor, half-outdoor swimming pool. They gazed at its balconies, turrets and towers made of coquina stone, rumoured to come from blocks the architect had sunk for weeks beneath the ocean to give them an aged look. As the tide rose, spectators had the impression that the palazzo was being lifted from the sea.

Carlotta and Louisa insisted on being driven to the reception, despite the short distance. Eduardo had just rolled the Bentley up to the villa's front door when a metallic blue Maserati, coming up from behind, narrowly avoided crashing into him.

'What the…?' Eduardo thundered, cursing in Spanish. Jumping out of the car with his fists up, he made for the driver of the offending vehicle. 'Oh, it's you,' he said, seeing Addison emerge in a pin-striped suit and tie.

'You missed the release,' Louisa chided, helping Dixie from the back seat.

'And nearly killed us just now.' Eduardo added, without any hint of a smile.

Addison, his face white as a sheet, asked where he could find Thaddeus.

'He went along the beach with the others. It's too bad you weren't at the ceremony,' Louisa said. 'It was rather sweet in a way, and for once Sunny didn't make a complete fool of herself.'

Addison bolted through the wide double doors of the palazzo. He knew his way through its vast, always partially shaded rooms, navigating swiftly past a regiment of butlers hired for the event. The mansion had a stale, charity-shop odour that was a feature of old homes on the Island in which the doors and windows were kept habitually open. And Villa des Vagues had never been more open than it was today, oriental urns brimming with two-foot high orchids, birds of paradise and pygmy palms; finger sandwiches and punch bowls laid out attractively on tables in the surrounding colonnade.

Mrs Vine stood greeting her guests in a theatrical pose at the top of the steps leading down to the beach. Addison darted past her, jostling people heading in the opposite direction until he spotted his brother. Grabbing him by the elbow he said: 'There's a plane leaving for New York in an hour and we have to be on it.'

'Maybe you do,' Thaddeus balked.

'It's to do with your case. I don't think I should go into it here.'

Thaddeus glanced at his wife. 'It's all right. Hannah knows everything.'

'Not quite everything. I only just got this news… Your plea for clemency has been rejected and the SEC has issued a Wells letter.'

'Wells?'

'Formal notification of legal action over a violation of securities laws – against you, the company and all the directors – including me. Thad, this could spell the end of my career.'

Hannah, left with Jesse on her arm, watched them leave. What had Thaddeus really done? she wondered as the brothers' stooped figures receded through the colonnade, like a pair being led away to the dock. It certainly didn't seem as if Thaddeus had told her everything. Hannah's thoughts drifted to what it might mean for their future, the party noises growing distant amid the clamour inside her head. Then, closer at hand, she heard Philip's voice.

'Why does my old friend Jesse James no longer come to see me?' he said, walking his fingers up Jesse's back.

The boy giggled, ticklish and overjoyed that Dolphin was teasing him again. 'You better ask Ma about that,' he said accusingly. 'She says she's too busy.'

'I'd like to ask your ma a few things myself.' Julietta, her tresses flowing, stepped out like an oracle from behind one of the parading columns. Before Hannah could do anything to stop her the girl made off with Jesse to where a pack of teenagers stood waiting for them at one of the hors d'oeuvres tables. Jesse erupted in giggles and Hannah, confused by Addison's news and wondering what to do about Philip, didn't have the heart to interrupt their reunion. It also took her a moment or two to realise that Philip was still beside her. And took her completely by surprise when he pressed her subtly but decisively through the thick folds of drapery guarding the entrance to the Moorish hall.

'We must talk,' he said, drawing her inside the dimly lit dining room that had only last week doubled as an operating theatre. Pulling her firmly behind him, he ushered her into the windowless corridor leading to the kitchen and took her in his arms. 'A marine life centre in the Great Barrier Reef has shortlisted me to run their research lab. It's the chance of a lifetime, with a fantastic salary. And so perfect for Jesse – for us. Will you come with me?'

Hannah stared at him, her eyes shining in the whispering darkness as he cradled her face, silencing her protests with his kisses. 'Not here,' she murmured. She was powerless against him. 'Please don't.'

'Where, then?'

'Later. Meet me at the beach cottage...'

Suddenly, the recessed wall sconces on both sides of the narrow passage exploded with illumination. Blinking in the light, they saw an immense figure ambling towards them from what appeared to be a solid wall. Stopping a few paces from Hannah and Philip, Mrs Vine lifted the veil from her face and fastened it to her wig with a long, sharp, diamond and emerald hatpin.

'Pity that they no longer build palazzos like they used to,' she said, tapping one of the wall panels with the tip of her parasol. 'Or with so many secret doors.'

Hannah looked down at the floor, trying to button her blouse.

'But surely there are more congenial places than my kitchen corridor to conduct affairs of the heart,' Mrs Vine pursued. 'The mirador, for instance. Jerzy uses it as a sleeping porch, but if you offered him a little something on the side I'm sure he would oblige.'

The widow saved her most wicked smile for last. Making an unhurried half turn in the direction from which she had apparently come, she cupped a hand behind her ear. 'I hate to spoil the fun,' she said, somewhat less amiably, through pursed, richly painted lips. 'But your son, Hannah, has had his fill of those girls and is calling you. Shouldn't you go see what he wants?'

OPEN SECRETS

Her cheeks burning, Hannah left the party as soon as seemed polite. Every glance in the car rear-view mirror played back the devilish look in Mrs Vine's cabbage-green eyes – and, before that, the heart-breaking expression in Addison's when he had voiced his fears about their future. But in the side mirror – where objects are said to seem closer than they are – Hannah saw with astonishing clarity her means of escape.

She pulled up to the postbox so that Jesse could collect the mail. It was one of his duties each day, and he loved tearing open the envelopes, leaving a small stack of papers with ragged edges for Hannah to sort through later. Done in by the day's excitement, he took less interest in the task than usual and complained that he was tired.

She put him to bed and drew the curtains in his room. Thinking ahead to the appointment she had made with Philip she went down to the bar and poured double the normal amount of gin into a glass of tonic water. Sipping it slowly, she unpacked the weekly home-school kit from the Florida Department of Special Education that had been among the items in their mailbox. What's the use, she thought, tossing the booklets on to the pile, since Jesse was no longer able to follow them. Her thoughts lingered over the possible implications of the legal mess Thaddeus was in: turning the future grim and the opportunity Philip was offering her more thrilling.

Do I dare? she agonised, moving with restless footsteps from room to room.

Another hour passed as the house grew steeped in darkness. Hannah finished her drink and poured another, pacing as she sipped it. At length she went back up to Jesse's room and parted the curtains. Philip's lodgings were less than fifty yards from the terrace and she saw a light showing faintly through the shutters. Was he in there, she wondered? Or had he already gone to the cottage to wait for her?

Her heart beat violently as she remembered the heat of his kisses: how he had promised with touching simplicity never to leave her alone on weekends, if only she would come away with him. Hannah went over to Jesse's bed to make sure that he was sleeping soundly, then went downstairs. She stood undecided in the family room, gazing at the door leading to the rear of the house and the cottage beyond. Without thinking about what she was doing she began compulsively sorting through the pile of mail sitting on the counter. Separating the bills from printed matter and magazines, trying to decide what she would say to Philip, Hannah's eyes landed on a formal envelope near the bottom of the pile. Lifting it to the light she realised that it was addressed to Philip next door. The Alonso's post was sometimes delivered to their house by mistake and the envelope in her hand had the look and feel of an official document.

Should she open it? It was in a sense already opened since Jesse had torn the seal. It occurred to her that it might be the offer of employment Philip had been waiting for, her heart leaping at the triumph of bringing it to him. She pulled it slowly from the envelope, the weight of the paper already hinting at the gravity of its content as Hannah held in her hand a formal baptismal certificate on the Bishop of Florida's letterhead. Below the bishop's seal, typed in a raised Gothic script, she read: 'In the name of God, Father, Son and Holy Spirit, this certifies that Philip James Godolphin Muir has been made a Member of the Body of Christ...'

The words *James Muir* seemed to lift up from the page. The certificate shook in her hand while she went over everything Philip had ever told her about himself. Time and again her suspicions had been aroused, practically since the day they had met. And each time she had brushed them aside. She thought of the cleft in his chin, identical to Jesse's, and his interest in poetry – even quoting from one of James Muir's poems at the Refugee Ball. Then the scene at the immersion pool: with Philip and Jesse, arms clasped round each other and their hair and eyes the same colour, descending into the pale-green water. There should have been no further doubt in the sacristy, when Philip, glib after his baptism, had let it slip that he grew up next to a London cemetery. The image of the boy outside Muir's home all those years ago passed before her eyes. The truth had been screaming her in the face all along, if only she'd had the will to see it.

She read and reread Philip's real name for what seemed like the thousandth time. Then, moving with a quick and deliberate step to the gas stove, she lit one of the burners. Holding the certificate over the bluish flame, Hannah watched it turn to ash.

SACKCLOTH AND ASHES

She lay down fully dressed, waiting for the first orange tint of dawn to lighten the walls of the bedroom. The gin and tonics she had consumed the previous evening made her queasy when she rose to finish packing. Scribbling a note for Marta in the kitchen, Hannah bundled Jesse and their single bag into the convertible and took a last long look at the house as the sun spilled over the roof.

It took a little over an hour to reach the sprawling, low-rise outskirts of Aventura. Jesse, now wide awake and thrilled by the surprise journey, squealed with delight when they stopped for breakfast at a 1950s tin camper-trailer that had been converted into a diner. He loved the bustle and smell of fried foods on the griddle, and friendly attentiveness of the beach-bum regulars eating at the mica-top counter. Hannah barely managed a cup of tea, while Jesse wolfed down a bowl of grits swimming in maple syrup that he kept pouring from one of the plastic cruets on the counter top. Back inside the convertible they cruised south on Collins Avenue with the ocean following them from just the other side of mid-century strip malls and low-rise hotels.

Jesse no longer needed to say anything for Hannah to know when he needed to rest. A new look that was part weariness and part some physical sensation that he seemed unable to express told her everything. His periods of activity were growing shorter and his naps longer. Digesting food after meals tired him, and only an hour after they had eaten breakfast it was time to stop and rest.

In summer there were always plenty of vacancies along South Beach, and Hannah checked into an old Art Deco hotel facing the ocean. It had no porter service, no central air conditioning and only one man on duty at the desk. Casablanca ceiling fans in the lobby seemed to circulate rather than cool the air as Hannah trudged with Jesse and their bag over her shoulder up a flight of steep stairs to their room.

'Deluxe Sea View' turned out to be a small corner suite with a partial view of the ocean. Hannah lay Jesse on the sateen bedspread, the air conditioner taking up most of one window and making so much racket that she turned it off. She opened the sliding door to the terrace and the heat hit her full in the face, misting the pane of glass as she stepped outside. Placing her hands on a metal railing corroded by sea salt, Hannah craned her neck to see the expanse of ocean that separated the two islands on which she had spent her entire life. She thought of her parents and Gran, and of St Cuthbert resting peacefully in his tomb at Durham cathedral: wondering whether he had really heard her plea all those years ago, or whether it was something she had imagined.

They spent the afternoon roaming through the souvenir and five-and-dime shops along Ocean Drive. Hannah bought Jesse a small rubber alligator attired in an old-fashioned bathing costume, straw hat and cat's eye sunglasses. With her son and his new toy mounted on her back, Hannah walked and walked until she could go no further. Drained by the extreme heat, they ate a late lunch at a juice bar on the beach and returned to their hotel.

Hannah finally slept, with her arms wrapped around Jesse as the afternoon drew on. Then, a few hours into the evening, Ocean Drive below their terrace exploded into a night-long carnival of live music and raucous parties. Was this what the world had turned into since she had been away from it? thought Hannah as she lay awake in the sweltering heat. Or perhaps it had always been that way. Jesse heard none of the goings on outside and didn't appear to mind that the leaky air conditioner, despite the loud noises it emitted, did everything but cool their room.

The night clerk, who was still on duty when Hannah checked out early the next morning, was a robust, broad-chested Cuban who could have doubled for Desi Arnaz of *I Love Lucy* fame. He tried to engage the attractive single mother in conversation; while Hannah, her face impassive as she settled the bill, managed to ignore him until he asked her the one question she couldn't answer.

'Where you folks off to?'

'South,' she said distantly.

Desi Arnaz laughed. 'Then you must be heading to the Keys. If you like to snorkel I suggest you stop at Key Largo Dry Rocks – the finest coral reef in America, some say in all the world.'

In a sudden burst of energy Jesse seized on the idea until he could speak of nothing else. 'Maybe we'll see an underwater cave, like the one in *Sir Peacock*!'

His enthusiasm mounted with every mile they clocked south, the convertible's windscreen shimmering with light while Latin rhumbas played on the Miami radio station. Tall condominium towers rose from the early morning haze like graphite pillars, US Highway One narrowing to a single lane in each direction as the sprawling metropolis receded behind them. Lulled by the music and not sure where she was going, for a dozen or more miles Hannah followed a white van several car-lengths in front of her. She got so used to it being there that she didn't immediately register that the rear of the van was growing suddenly much bigger. A moment later it filled her entire windscreen and she slammed on the brake, throwing her weight over the wheel to turn it to the right. The seat belts locked and the convertible wobbled as it slid on to the soft shoulder and ground to a halt.

The van in front had stopped for a contingent of Guatemalans hauling bales of coconuts across the highway. Unaware of how close Hannah had come to hitting him, the driver of the van continued on his way, while the Guatemalans, their faces shadowed by immense sombreros, gathered at the side of the road. Stunned and still in shock, Hannah stared back.

'Are we at the reef yet?' Jesse asked, conscious only of an immense tug on his seat belt while he had been playing with his toy alligator.

'No,' Hannah replied weakly. Swallowing, she felt as if she were going to be sick and got out of the car. 'We hit a roadblock and it may not be possible to go on,' she said, taking deep breaths.

'Oh, but we must,' Jesse cried out. 'We have to and we must!'

Hannah got back in the car, her hands shaking as she manoeuvred the wheel this way and that to dig them out of the gravel. It took several attempts, the tyres spinning while the Guatemalans looked on. By the time Hannah was back on US Highway One the white van was long gone and the coconut bearers had resumed their journey, their squat bodies and wide sombreros in the rear-view mirror melting into the distance.

Signs for deep-sea diving and fishing appeared at the side of the road as they approached the reef. A crudely painted wood marker advertising snorkels for rent caught Hannah's attention, and she followed the sign along a quarter-mile-long sandy drive to a tumbledown shack at the end. A 1960s red Dodge pick-up truck was parked next to the sagging porch, above which appeared another, much bigger hand-painted sign announcing *Bahama's Shipwreck – Best-ever Snorkel Rentals by Day or Hour!* Hannah had just pulled up alongside the Dodge when they heard a ferocious growl from the back of the pick-up.

'Away, you dragon of the deep!' Jesse threatened, brandishing his toy alligator at the grizzly Alsatian raising itself on its haunches in the open tailgate. Hannah screamed and began backing out of the drive when a lanky, bare-chested man darkened the porch of the hut and began shouting at the dog. Wearing nothing except a pair of khaki shorts and a colourful bandana looped pirate-style round his forehead, the long-boned man jumped into the path of the moving car.

'Don't mind the dog, ma'am, he don't bite.'

The man had one lazy eye that made him seem to be always looking somewhere else. Hannah stopped the car, afraid of hitting him, as he walked over to her side and opened the door. 'The Great Bahama,' he announced grandly, 'welcomes you to his humble adobe.'

'Are you a pirate?' asked Jesse.

'I was, once upon a time.' Bahama grinned. 'You folks lookin' to fish or snorkel?'

'Snorkel!' cried Jesse. 'We're going to the reef.'

'Then you've come to the right place. Cause I got plenty of gear to choose from.'

Hannah hesitated, looking from the dog to its owner. 'Hurry up, Ma,' Jesse cried impatiently as Bahama headed back to the shack. 'Or we'll miss the fun.'

What they found inside was indeed a shipwreck, the counter strewn with diving gear and snorkels and the air infested with the smell of dry fish bones and brine. The walls were hung with nautical curiosities, fishing nets in various stages of disrepair and a six-foot-long taxidermy shark suspended by two rusty chains against one wall. Crates of empty Kentucky bourbon bottles and old lobster traps stood stacked like steps on the floor below it, while Bahama, his gaunt face beaming, studied the effect his 'humble abode' was having on the visitors. Digging deep inside one of his pockets he produced a grease-stained tobacco pouch, dipped his thumb into it and smeared the inside of his cheek with snuff.

'You're going to need a boat to reach the reef,' he advised. 'Dry Rocks is a national park now, and it's cordoned off with buoys. If folks don't navigate them buoys right they're likely to get grounded. There's guides at the marina who know their way around, but there's no one better than Phil.'

'Phil?' Jesse glanced at Hannah.

She pretended not to hear him as she rummaged through a rat's nest of snorkels and diving masks. Her final selection required two trips to the car, during which she left Jesse sitting on the counter while Bahama regaled him with tales of Gaspar, the notorious Spanish buccaneer who had once ruled the Florida coast. On her way back to the shack Hannah turned pale when she saw Bahama tottering down the steps of the sagging porch with Jesse on his arm. Terrified that he might drop him, she took her son from him and hurried back to the car.

Phil, who had been somehow alerted to their coming, stood waiting at the entrance to the pier.

'You're not by any chance related to the great outlaw?' he asked when Jesse, now fully in the spirit of the adventure, introduced himself as Jesse James.

'He's my namesake!'

Phil stroked his chin. Winking at Hannah, he said: 'Some folks say that old bushwhacker still roams parts of the South – wherever there's trouble brewin'.'

This is madness, Hannah thought as they followed the boatman to his dinghy. But Jesse had his heart set on going to the reef and she could see no way around it. Thinking ahead to a time, perhaps soon, when he wouldn't have the strength for any more adventures, she lost the will to deny him anything.

The motor sputtered as Phil manoeuvred past a line of buoys encircling the reef. High above, thin white clouds sailed across the sky, the dinghy mirrored on the water's glassy surface. They dropped anchor and Hannah began to remove Jesse's special socks and shoes. Phil politely looked the other way while the boy wriggled into his swimming trunks and Hannah fitted flippers and a snorkel mask over his magnifiers.

'Are you quite sure, ma'am, that you and the kid is up to this?' Phil asked, looking sceptically at the waterproof gauze Hannah was wrapping tightly over the fistula in Jesse's arm.

'I swim heaps better than I walk,' the boy laughed. 'You'll see.'

Hannah had worn a bathing suit under her sundress and dropped lightly over the side of the dinghy. Holding on to the boat with one hand, she grabbed hold of Jesse with the other as Phil lowered him into the water beside her. They snorkelled dreamily through the turquoise sub-atmosphere, swathes of purple and reddish-brown plankton swaying beneath them like an underwater prairie. Lulled by the lack of sound and her own weightlessness, Hannah wasn't sure how much time had passed. Then, suddenly, she felt Jesse tug urgently on her arm. Turning in the direction to which he was pointing she noticed a large object some distance from them on the sea floor. She was surprised that Jesse could see that far – and totally unprepared for what he did next.

Abandoning his snorkel in a move Philip had taught him, Jesse duck-dived straight towards the mysterious object.

Hannah dived after him, terrified that he would run out of oxygen. She tried to pull him with her to the surface, but Jesse pushed her away, buoyancy making it easier to dart ahead of her towards what appeared to be a bronze sculpture. Feeling the tightness in her chest turn to pain, Hannah dragged him forcibly to the surface. But after only a few breaths Jesse dived straight down again. There seemed no stopping him and they quickly arrived at the statue – a nine-foot-high bronze sculpture of Christ, its robe and outstretched arms flowing with algae. Jesse hovered above the figure, his hair floating about him and his eyes, enlarged by the swimming mask, the same clear, underwater blue as those of Philip and James Muir.

Ignoring the pain in her chest Hannah placed her hand on the statue. 'Forgive me,' she prayed silently, without words.

'Bet you folks never seen nothin' like *that*,' Phil chuckled as he hoisted them over the side of the dinghy. 'They call it 'Christ of the Deep', put down there by a sculptor back in the sixties. Not exactly the sort of thing divers expect to see on a visit to the reef.'

Jesse slept on the way back to Bahama's shack, and Hannah left him in the open convertible while she went to return their gear. The proprietor, now smelling strongly of bourbon, counted the money she took from her purse. 'Want a drink?' he said, moving to her side of the counter.

Hannah gave him a cutting look, trying not to show her fear as she backed out of the shack. Bahama stumbled after her, spitting a clump of tobacco on the sand while she escaped ahead of him to the car. For Hannah, far worse than the leering man or his dog's hideous growls was the waxy pallor on Jesse's face as he lay curled up in the front seat. She jumped in beside him and pressed her foot to the accelerator, charging in reverse to the bottom of the sandy drive and on to the highway.

Why didn't Hannah come to me about any of this? Fr Leo wondered as Philip concluded his narrative. He still couldn't decide how much of what the young man had been telling him had actually happened, and how much was make-believe. All the same, Hannah Caulfield had abruptly gone to New York to be with her husband, taking Jesse with her, and had done so without telling him. And now these bizarre revelations from another parishioner whose soul he had gone to such lengths to save.

They were in the same room as before, surrounded by the miniature desks, easels and children's Bible-study materials belonging to the Sunday school. Philip had arrived in an agitated state and without an appointment. After repeated attempts to locate Fr Leo in the rambling church premises he had finally discovered him measuring vials of holy oil in the ambry, a walk-in cupboard the size of a broom closet. The priest had looked startled and a little embarrassed to see Philip enter, ushering him quickly to a nearby room.

For some time after Philip's narrative ended neither of them spoke. Finally, taking a long inhale, Fr Leo said: 'If I understand you correctly, all this took place after I removed your sins through baptism?'

Philip nodded.

'Is that any way to thank me?'

'I wasn't thinking about how to thank you. When I was with Hannah I forgot everything – and with Jesse I became a prince.'

'The prince of turtles.'

Philip nodded again, looking so wretched that, despite his anger, the priest felt moved to help him somehow. It seemed to him that the young man had grown thinner since the last time he'd seen him, his anguish real. 'I don't pretend to have all the answers, but one thing I do know is that everything which happens to us is part of God's plan. My role as a priest is to help people hear the small still voice and abide by it.'

'But how do we know, when we hear that voice, that it's God speaking and not something we made up?'

'We know because the things God says are frequently not what we want to hear.'

Fr Leo's eyes travelled to the ambry and he got up to close the door. For a few moments he stood with his back to Philip, enduring in painful silence the tyranny of his calling. Mrs Vine had warned him about the devil's tricks, but he had pressed on regardless: as if the Holy Spirit needed his help.

Returning to the classroom, Fr Leo tried a different tack. 'I can see,' he said in the consoling tone of voice he used with the bereaved, 'that you have a fine analytic mind. I personally hold science in high regard. I mean, it always gets one from A to B, and so on. But it doesn't get one to heaven.'

It was one of Fr Leo's favourite themes, and he began to expound on it. But to Philip it seemed insufficient. 'You mentioned, when we last spoke in this room, the unseen reality on which our lives depend. Being a scientist makes it hard for me to imagine such a reality.'

'It might help to think about the process of discovering God as not unlike the discovery of the atom – or algebra.'

Philip gave a puzzled look and the priest continued. 'The unseen, like atomic particles or a mathematical algorithm, already exists as an underlying reality, even though we can never actually perceive it. Only when we discover it operationally do we realise that it is not only true but has always been true.'

Feeling a stabbing pain in his leg Fr Leo shifted his weight uncomfortably in the little seat. 'Are you quite certain,' he said slowly, 'that what you told me earlier is true? Or is it something that you – you wanted to be true?'

Philip understood perfectly what was being asked of him. He considered his answer carefully, trying to decide what Hannah would want him to say. She, after all, was the reason he had approached Fr Leo in a last desperate attempt to win her back. Hearing thunder in the distance, he turned his head to the window.

The priest bent forward to rub his bad leg. He was obviously in pain, the child's seat too small for him. But the greater pain, as Philip could see plainly, would be for him to be forced to accept that Hannah was like other people.

'Only the bit about my father was true. The rest...' Philip paused, looking past Fr Leo at a sudden cloudburst of rain that wiped any view from the window. 'The rest I made up,' he said, not at all sure that the priest believed him.

'Put Your Tiaras Back in the Vault, Ladies, and Fold Up the Elbow-Length Gloves!' ran the front-page headline of *The Shiny Sheet*. As the Island grudgingly danced itself still, Mrs Vine hosted a grand end-of-season fundraiser that, by every account, topped all the others combined. The gala raised enough money to pay for a new coral seeding station at the institute and extended Philip's contract through to the end of the year.

Seated next to Mrs Vine at the head table, he remembered asking her to dance and very little else about the event. The only person Philip would have liked to be there had been absent, with Hannah and Jesse still in New York while Thaddeus waited to find out whether he would be indicted by the SEC. Rumour had it that the doctor was obliged to place all his assets in escrow pending a decision on his case and that, as a result, the family was on the brink of financial ruin. Only the house in Hibiscus Way was still theirs, Louisa having, in a conspicuous display of maternal fortitude, purchased it back from the government.

Philip admired Hannah for going to be with her husband in his hour of need. He expected no less from her. And despite the negative rumours about the doctor, he could hardly forget Thaddeus's heroic efforts to save the hawksbills. What he couldn't fathom was Hannah's complete silence. On the night of the release ceremony he had waited and waited for her at the beach cottage, but she never came: her house dark and the curtains drawn. At the time, Philip had assumed that her husband had still been at home and that she couldn't get away. But the next morning Hannah's car was gone, and he learned from Marta that Dr Caulfield had left the day before.

Philip followed closely the news about Pandorex. When the story finally broke that Thaddeus Caulfield had been indicted by the SEC, the press vilified him as a man who had betrayed the trust of his employees, patients and shareholders for the sake of profit. Questions about the doctor's personal integrity raised questions about the integrity of his data, causing the FDA to delay approval of the serum a second time. The implication, seized on by the media, that someone who had forged a legal document might also be capable of forging test results, cast further doubt on the drug's safety. A criminal trial was scheduled for the autumn, obliging Thaddeus to resign from the firm he had founded. If he ended up serving a prison sentence – as a well-known financial newscaster suggested was likely to happen – the family would be left destitute.

And Hannah would be free.

The 'Pandorex Scandal' was now on everyone's lips. People lapped up its daily coverage in *The Wall Street Journal*, *New York Times* and all the major news networks. Not to be outdone, *The Shiny Sheet* ran front-page stories that usually opened with: 'Renowned pioneering cancer clinician and founder of the biotech company Pandorex, local Island resident Thaddeus Caulfield, recently indicted by the Securities and Exchange Commission on fraud and insider-trading charges…' So near the end of the season, and with little left to amuse the social set, the Pandorex narrative was all that Islanders could talk about.

'Rubbish,' Louisa scoffed, arching one of her pencil-thin eyebrows higher than the other as she handed the newspaper to Dixie. The octogenarian former banker – who only looked at *The Shiny Sheet* if he or Louisa were in it – had already been appraised of Thaddeus's downfall at the men's bar of the Mangrove Club.

'I don't believe it either,' he said. 'Or rather, I do believe it, but can't imagine Thad knew what he was doing.'

'If he needed money, why didn't he ask me?'

'My dear, that is the last thing I would expect either of your sons to do.'

Louisa wrinkled her nose. 'You make it sound as if this were *my* fault. I suppose we'll never hear the end of it now.'

Dixie patted Louisa's bony wrist, her skin nearly the same tissue-thin texture as his. Trying to reassure his keeper that none of their acquaintances would say a word about it, he concluded: 'Not in front of us, at any rate.'

Louisa gave her heirloom silver toast stand a severe look. She was less bothered about her son's predicament than the possibility of losing her place – top place, so far as she was concerned – in the Island's widow hierarchy. 'Thank God the snowbirds are about to fly up north,' she said, wiping a smudge of marmalade from Dixie's chin. 'Let's hope this whole thing blows over by the time they return.'

At about this time, summer took a ferocious leap into storm season. Shutters were fastened, outdoor furniture placed in storage and landscaping cut back, statuary clothed in protective mantles and mansions that had graced international magazine covers transformed into bunkers. Wiry Guatemalans armed with machetes scaled the tops of palm trees, lopping the heads of coconuts that could turn into flying projectiles during a storm.

The Alonsos were among the last to close up their home and leave. Carlotta's final decree was that Philip should move from the guest annexe into the main house and 'keep an eye on things' while the family was away. A few days before they decamped to the Hamptons in their private jet, Julietta's three older brothers swooped in from their various schools for a few riotous days of polo, sailing and late-night parties. To Philip's ears, all they did was argue, competing with each other on nearly every score except their unanimous disdain for Armando, the uneducated eldest brother with plebeian ideas. Not surprisingly, they also took an immediate dislike to the family's English houseguest, suspecting him of harbouring designs on their grandmother's fortune. No one they asked seemed to know much about him, raising the possibility that Philip Godolphin – if that was indeed his name – was one of a legion of con artists who frequented the Island during the season. The brothers would have liked to investigate this further but, at the moment, the family was in too much of an uproar over Armando's explosive announcement that he was leaving Consolidated Sugar.

Contention over the burning of sugar canes had led to the rupture, cemented by Armando's civil marriage to the waitress at the Dune Dog Dive Bar. They were expecting a baby in a few months – like his parents and grandparents in the run up to their own weddings – and planned to start an organic dairy farm near Lake Okeechobee. Overhearing a conversation on the subject between Malachi and the housemaid, it occurred to Philip, who rarely gave thought to such things, that in the Alonso family getting pregnant seemed to be the necessary first step to getting married.

Philip spent the day before the family took off transferring his belongings from the annexe into his new room in the main house. It required several trips up and down flights of stairs, and he ran a cold shower when the work was done. Letting the cool water spill over him, he fantasised about flying to New York to surprise

Hannah: about her husband being sentenced to jail, followed by their escape to the other side of the world. He imagined them on a plane, with Jesse seated between them, bound for the Great Barrier Reef and a new life together. Humming to himself, Philip parted the shower curtain and came face to face with Julietta.

He grabbed a towel to cover himself and tied it round his waist. I'll ignore her, he thought, hoping it would get the girl to leave. Turning to the mirror he soaped his face and prepared to shave. But when he looked up again Julietta was still hovering behind him, like the last awful time she had crept into his room, hurling recriminations and threatening to expose him and Hannah. In a moment of sudden illumination it occurred to him that Julietta was to blame for Hannah's silence.

'Grandmalita sent me,' she said with a determined toss of her hair, now straight and pulled fashionably like a curtain to one side of her face. 'To make sure you have everything you need.'

She'll offer to stay with me next, Philip thought, trying to swallow his fury.

'Actually,' Julietta continued. 'Grandmalita thinks I should spend the summer here to help you with the house.'

Philip stared in horror at the girl's face in the mirror. Her dark eyes were outlined with charcoal and black mascara, her cheeks and prominent Alonso nose powdered a shade lighter than her skin, bringing a ghoulish pallor to Julietta's long thin face in the bathroom light.

'I know you want me,' she said. 'You've always wanted me.'

She stood trembling before him, her painted lips parted and hands passively at her sides as Philip turned from the mirror and they faced each other. Reaching no higher than his chest, Julietta had never seemed more submissive, and Philip never more sure of his hold over her. With a feeling of revulsion he kissed her violently through clenched teeth, pushing her backwards into the bedroom.

'Get out,' he groaned, his chest heaving. 'And don't ever come near me again.'

GOD OF THE STORM

Left alone in the crushing silence of the shuttered hacienda, Philip spent the first few evenings prowling about the house. He was happiest nesting in Eduardo's home office, with his feet up on the oval desk and a cigar from the humidor in his mouth. Philip didn't light the cigars, nibbling the bitter ends while he perused Eduardo's collection of old maps and books on Spanish, Cuban and Florida history. What he learned from their pages was that over many centuries the territory that became known as Florida had once been everything from an ocean floor to a vast shoreline and grassy plain: a combination of wetlands and farmlands that for the past twelve thousand years the human race had been systematically adapting to its way of life. How much, Philip asked himself, did it really matter that Eduardo burned the sugar canes on acres of land that would soon be under water again? Would any of the things he had hoped to achieve at the institute make any difference? When he had suggested to Mrs Vine that the Island might one day become a lagoon, her old soul had been more charmed than upset by the prospect of fish swimming through the stony underwater palace of what had once been Villa des Vagues.

He hardly slept. Sometimes, feeling a desperate need for rest, he would curl up in Eduardo's leather armchair and lapse into a few hours of forgetting. When he awoke, looking about him in confusion, grief would well up inside him like silent laughter. To dispel the mood he turned to the books lining the walls of

Eduardo's study. Philip's favourite was a rare 1828 first edition on the subject of tropical storms, containing delicate pencil sketches and a few intriguing, little-known facts.

For instance, that the word hurricane was derived from the native Arawak *hurakan*, meaning 'god of the storm'.

Philip had first become interested in storms three years ago, when a sudden and totally unexpected night-time hurricane had struck England. It uprooted trees and gravestones in Highgate Cemetery and ripped a section of roof from his parents' home. A surprising number of people had slept through it, while mayhem tore through the streets and scores died. A quarter of a million trees fell in the nation's capital, and three days later, for reasons of its own, the London Stock Exchange had crashed.

Now, as storms on the Island grew more frequent, so did Philip's obsession with them. The first thing he did when he arrived at the institute each morning was to measure changes in the barometric pressure. He studied subtle shifts in the direction of the wind and rain, and the way the clouds lowered to just above the ocean, waves sputtering like lava as they rose to meet them. Purplish sargassum accumulated in slippery mounds along the shore, and by early afternoon it was usually either too hot or too wet to remain outdoors for very long.

Inside the Alonsos' boarded house the atmosphere became one of perpetual twilight. Philip no longer bothered to open the shutters – only to have to close them again – and rarely turned on the lights. When he did it was to read from the books that had become his friends, or to compose letters to Hannah that he still hadn't found the courage to post. Peering round the family's private rooms, late one evening he discovered a sliding panel that contained Eduardo's hidden liquor cabinet. On another occasion he made his greatest discovery – and Carlotta's best-kept secret: a private screening room built especially for her. The Alonsos had been among the first people on the Island to add a screening room to their home so that Grandmalita could watch her favourite

Hollywood and Latino films. For years, Malachi had served as the projectionist, devotedly threading old thirty-five-millimetre films through metal reels that had to be changed every fifteen minutes: watching, over and over again in the dimmed, blue-black light of his mistress's private room, the films of their youth.

Drinking straight from bottles of tequila and Bacardi rum, Philip became the sole spectator of this vast library of films. He taught himself to thread the reels and loved the ticking sound they made, with the last reel spinning until he got up to turn off the machine. His favourite were the films noirs of the 1940s that featured Robert Mitchum and Humphrey Bogart as tragic figures abandoned by the women they loved.

'No!' Philip shouted as the words *The End* faded from the screen. His love for Hannah wasn't a film noir, and it would never end. One of the reels had merely been paused while the next one was threaded: 'By the unseen presence on which our lives depend,' Philip whispered in the dark.

Late one night, tossing another empty bottle in the bin, he stumbled outdoors and carried the letters he had written to Hannah round the back of the house to the beach cottage. He remembered so well the first time he had seen it – like something from a fairy tale – and his first meeting with Jesse. He jiggled the lock, and, once he was inside, tried to bring back the sweet smell of Hannah the first time they had embraced: a moment for which he would now gladly exchange decades of life without her. Philip's eyes pooled with tears as he placed the letters he had written to her inside the desk, caressing with his thoughts every line of poetry she had secreted in that drawer. Lifting one of the poems, he thrust it inside his shirt and went down to the beach. Rambling here and there in a driving rain, he felt the paper dissolve on his chest.

The shore reeked of decay from the uprooted weeds. Brackish foam caught round his ankles, neuralgic clouds curdling on the horizon. I have ceased to exist, Philip laughed wildly, seeing his footprints fill with water. Like a reel of bad film replaying in his head, the world around him seemed cobwebbed with shadows. And the longest, darkest shadow was his own.

Time crawled with excruciating slowness as summer progressed. And still no word from Hannah.

Sunny was now Philip's only helper at the institute. The Sloans were year-round Island residents on account of Addison's legal practice, but this was the first summer that Sunny hadn't joined the party circuit to Newport and the Hamptons. When she wasn't doing odd jobs about the institute she took cookery lessons from Jerzy, studying Polish recipes that required converting grams to ounces and re-stocking her pantry with novel ingredients. It meant spending much more time at Villa des Vagues with her mother who, like Louisa, never left the Island during hurricane season. Unlike Carlotta, who lived only for her family and would have followed them to the ends of the earth, the two remaining chatelaines guarded their palazzos with competitive ferocity. (Mrs Vine would in any case have rather perished with her furry companions than survived a hurricane without them.)

Jerzy manoeuvred the Shadow as near the portal of Villa des Coquilles as he could to avoid the rain. Holding an immense blue-and-white striped golf umbrella over the heads of Mrs Vine and her daughter he helped them navigate an ankle-deep puddle that had formed outside the portico. Since the windows could no longer be left open, as Louisa preferred, the drone of air conditioning and rain pelting the balconies further dampened the mood. As the bridge players moved to their seats Mrs Vine, who had forgotten her parasol in the car, walked holding one hand to the furniture – pretending, when she noticed Louisa's hawkish gaze, that she was flecking at particles of dust.

Due to Carlotta's seasonal departure only two of the Big Three still participated in the weekly game of bridge. The number of alternates had also diminished, requiring Sunny and Dixie to become regulars. Sunny, having been taught to play expert bridge by her mother, was a far more advantageous addition to Mrs Vine's team than Dixie was to Louisa's – an inequality that inclined the latter to feel entitled to cheat whenever an opportunity presented itself.

Jerzy stood for a moment watching the little group before he withdrew to the kitchen for a late lunch genially provided by Louisa's cook. It was one of the unwritten codes on the Island that the help should feed each other generously and, in this regard, Jerzy regarded the cook almost as his equal. He was especially pleased, seeing Mrs Vine comfortably settled at the card table, that relations between her and Sunny had improved, hoping it would help soften the blow he was about to deal his beloved mistress.

Unwilling to contemplate the likely magnitude of Mrs Vine's reaction to his approaching departure, he had decided that her discovery should be made only after he was safely on his way home to Poland. It had been Jerzy's dream since the fall of Communism two years ago to use the money he had saved during his lucrative employment to open a pastry shop in Gdańsk. All in good time, Jaroslav Krzyzewski – as he would soon be known again – smiled to himself, accepting a plateful of cold poached salmon and asparagus tips from the cook.

Dixie dealt the cards. His horsey neck rose from the collar of a starched shirt that had become too big for him, his jaw moving in a rhythmic circular motion as he studied his cards. When he finished dealing he held his own suit far out in front of him so that he could see better, without considering that everyone else could see it too. For some reason the former banker could no longer recall he had brushed his hair forward in a Napoleonic style and put on his old gumshoes instead of the velvet loafers Louisa had left out for him that morning.

He is becoming a child again, Louisa thought – grinning at nothing and dozing off when I need him most. Dixie had no family left, only a great deal of money, and the disagreeable thought crossed her mind that she might bear a degree of legal responsibility for this man who had been living with her for the past fifteen years.

'I've got some interesting news,' she announced, glad to have a reason to drop the unpleasant subject from her mind. 'Thad called this morning, and it seems that Hannah is expecting another child.'

Well, well, thought Mrs Vine. 'So,' she said. 'You're going to be a grandmother.'

'I've been that before,' Louisa said, glancing at Sunny.

Dixie thought it a careless thing to say, remembering – in a rare moment of illumination – that Sunny had lost Paula. 'What I meant,' Louisa explained hastily, seeing the same expression on every face, 'is that I think of Jesse as my grandson – though, of course, strictly speaking, he isn't.'

'Congratulations,' said Mrs Vine. 'When is the baby due?'

'In early November – the same time as Thad's trial. Apparently Jesse hasn't been doing as well as they'd hoped, and Thad is bringing them all back to the Island. Not that they have anywhere else to go,' Louisa added in a not-so-subtle allusion to her largesse in having salvaged her son's home.

She stared at her cards with an almost unnatural pretence of studying them. But, as everyone could see, her mind wasn't on the game. 'I can't imagine how they will manage if the child turns out to be like Jesse,' she said.

Sunny, who was sitting on her mother's left, refrained from commenting on the matter. She and Addison had known about Hannah's pregnancy for several weeks, but had been sworn to secrecy until the test results were in.

'I didn't think Hannah Caulfield was supposed to have any more children,' Dixie said. 'On account of her genes – at any rate, something of the sort.'

There was another pause, during which the sound of rain hitting the windows grew louder. 'Bid,' Sunny said, placing a jack of diamonds on the table.

'Pass,' said Mrs Vine.

'I pass too,' said Louisa.

Dixie, still looking perplexed, repeated his question. 'But I thought Hannah Caulfield—'

'We heard you, Dixie,' Louisa snapped. 'And do, for God's sake, stop slouching.' Gathering their cards with one sweep, she nervously reshuffled the deck.

Sunny, harbouring the secret of her own pregnancy, could already envision the competition that would break out among the Big Three for who would be the first to produce a grandchild. Hannah's baby and hers would be cousins, with birthdays only a few weeks apart, followed a month later by the birth of Armando's child. For the love of Paula she had promised herself to do it all differently this time. And while the thought still sometimes crossed Sunny's mind that she might be better off dead, and the world better off without her, these days it was only a thought – something she could pick up or let go, without feeling that it had any power left over her.

But Sunny had another secret, something she had discovered at the healing Mass: that there were two kinds of light in the world – the seen and unseen – and that her Paula still lived in the unseen portion. Since then, she had appeared to Sunny several times – as she expected Paula would do a great deal more after the arrival of her little brother or sister.

Louisa made a face. 'Dixie is right, of course. Hannah had been warned not to have any more children because she carries the gene for that dreadful condition Jesse is cursed with – and which I've never been able to pronounce. It's hard to imagine why they would risk another pregnancy after what they've been through with Jesse.'

'Thaddeus always wanted another child,' Sunny said. 'He told Addison that he wouldn't mind what it was like.'

Louisa's nerves finally gave way. 'Thad imagines himself as some great scientific guru who can cure anything. And just look at him now.'

'Giving life to a child, even one who doesn't have long to live, is still life,' Sunny argued. 'It may be that they will have a perfectly healthy baby.'

'I suppose,' Louisa said, fanning her cards shut, 'it's not all that different from those fools who keep pets, even though they know the pathetic creatures only live for a few years.'

Mrs Vine, her eyes flashing, threw her cards at the table and reached for her knitting bag. Dixie, seeing war about to erupt, suggested they take a short break. Neither of the Big Two (as they were now) paid any attention to him, and Mrs Vine, slamming her arthritic fist on top of her cards, struggled to her feet. Until now, the most heartless thing she had heard Louisa say had been about a widowed friend they visited shortly after the woman's husband had died. Wearing a house coat and no make-up, the once glamorous Palm Beach hostess had burst into tears at the first mention of the deceased. The visit had ended abruptly, and on the way home Louisa had remarked caustically that it was a pity their friend 'has so completely let herself go'.

No doubt Louisa no longer remembered making the comment – or would deny it if she did. But Mrs Vine did remember it. Or rather, remembered the callousness with which it had been said, if not the exact words. Now, she was prepared to sever a decades-long bond of turbulent sisterhood rather than put up with any more of Louisa's affronts.

'You are a hard woman,' she said, shaking. 'I can bear insults to my person, Louisa, but not to innocent creatures who can't fight back.'

'Come, come, Vanessa, I didn't mean it like that.' Louisa, faced with the prospect of spending a rainy afternoon alone with Dixie, was determined to keep playing cards.

'We're leaving,' cried Mrs Vine, seizing Sunny's arm. 'And please don't invite us to any more of your silly bridge games.' Hobbling to the door she stopped halfway and, turning suddenly pale, peered helplessly this way and that. 'Jerzy,' she whispered hoarsely. 'Where are you?'

A woman in a loose-fitting frock stood waiting for the light to turn at the intersection of Sunrise Avenue and County Road. Her hands were resting on the handlebar of a a small, lightweight wheelchair in which a child lay sleeping, its face shadowed from the sun by the wide canvas hood.

Philip, who had been following the woman, called to her. He was out of breath, having covered a great deal of distance quickly. With only a few yards left between them, he couldn't understand why she didn't respond.

'Hannah,' he said. They were now so close that there was no need for him to shout.

The woman's back stiffened but she didn't turn.

Maybe it isn't Hannah, thought Philip. This woman was broader from behind and had a somewhat ungainly gait. Still, it was odd that even a stranger would ignore him at such close range.

As she waited for the light to turn green the woman leaned over the wheelchair to adjust the hood and Philip caught a glimpse of her profile. It was definitely Hannah. But a very different Hannah from the woman he remembered. Staring in shock at the baby bump protruding from her cotton shift and that brushed up against the handle of the wheelchair, he watched her cross the street.

'*Hannah!*' he screamed, his voice popping through the sultry air.

She didn't look back. Too stunned to pursue her further, Philip stood frozen at the curb, like an ice sculpture dissolving in the heat while the traffic light turned from green to yellow to red, and slowly back to green. He looked after her searchingly as she grew smaller with every step, taking their future with her. Hannah stopped when she reached the disabled ramp at the side of the church, tilted the wheelchair on to it and proceeded through the colonnade.

Philip knew who she was going to see; and that Fr Leo would wash her soul clean of their love. Feeling his fate already sealed, he ran to the beach.

The light along the shore had a peculiar opalescence, the ocean dreamy. A pack of turkey vultures swooped low, foraging for carrion among the seaweed. Philip ploughed through them, shrieking as he hurled himself into the turgid water. *Hannah is pregnant and doesn't want you, and Jesse is lifeless in the wheelchair,* he heard the ocean murmur. The words went round and round his head like the blades of a windmill. Swimming underwater among the loose weeds with his eyes open, he saw nothing. The road ahead was no road at all, but a jetty leading into the deepest water.

* * *

Something is scratching at his window. But each time Philip attempts to open it the force of the wind flings the shutters back in his face. He manages to unfasten them, only to find a palm branch making the noise. In a matter of seconds rain has drenched the entire room, wind gusting in his face and jet sprays bringing the storm indoors. The force of it excites him and he spreads his arms, holding on to the window jambs like a man fastened to the mast of a ship.

'I am god of the storm,' Philip laughs, the sound of his voice lost in the uproar.

A lull follows, during which the storm appears to pause, holding its breath. Then it reignites, howling as it forces everything in its path either to pull away or resist. There is sorcery in the wind, and the long shrill howl spreading like a mist over the Island. Even the royal palms that kneel to no one are bowed to the ground, their wearied fronds scraping the sand as the light dims. Another high-pitched wail rises from the sea, growing louder as rain lashes the shore. The tempest is unlike anything Philip imagined, stripping the arms off trees and depositing ruin.

Summoning his strength, he attempts to close the window. But the wind is too strong, and he shelters from it with his back to the wall, waiting for another lull. He tries the light switch, but nothing happens. Taking out a pocket flashlight, he checks the time on his wrist.

Nine o'clock.

Philip has no recollection of time passing since he came indoors. He also doesn't recall anything worse than the usual afternoon drenching in the weather forecast. Shining the flashlight over his room he sees a demolition site – the carpet soggy, furniture overturned. None of this concerns him.

More time passes, followed by a total secession of sound. The trees and shrubbery outside his window stand still. Radiantly full, the moon bursts through clouds, fleeing, like a curtain being drawn back, to one side of what has become a clear sky. Everything is illuminated with a shocking new brightness, showing the extent of the damage. Plant debris lies strewn over the pool deck and rear of the house where the garden statues and urns, wrapped in layers of white protective covering, stand like ghosts. Looking through the wreckage to the house next door, Philip is struck by how peaceful, silent and totally still it appears in the moonlight.

He changes into dry clothes and goes outside. He knows his way in the dark as he walks barefoot along the side of the house, squeezing between the wall and hedgerow. The fragrance of nightshade flowers, enhanced by the densely saturated air, brings back memories of the lost, happy times. Trying every door of Hannah's house, he finds them bolted from within.

Each new barrier impels him to find some other way. At last, a side door to the garage yields and he gains easy entry. He topples a broom and garden rake in the dark and sets them aright against the wall. Feeling his way, he comes to another door and turns the handle. Just as Philip hopes, it opens and admits him into the kitchen.

Without the purr of air circulating through the vents, the house is deathly still. No sound disturbs the eerie silence, the French doors shuttered and moonlight rippling through the slats on to the travertine floor. Philip climbs the back stairs, and when he reaches the top he pauses, listening for signs of activity. But the only noise is the shortness of his own breath as he stealthily continues his journey. Keeping close to the wall, he sidles in the opposite direction from which he had come the last time he was here: the remembrance of those few, never-to-return moments of happiness a terrifying reminder of what he has lost.

The moon is his friend, pointing the way to where Jesse lies sleeping – a pitifully small bundle covered lightly with a sheet. He seems already part corpse, and Philip's heart contracts with anguish as the cool rays of the moon shine a deathly pallor on the boy's cheeks. The wheelchair Philip had seen earlier is parked near the bed, bringing an invalid atmosphere to the old playroom.

But this is no time to linger, and he moves with fresh urgency into the connecting bathroom. Both sets of doors are ajar, allowing him to see into the master suite. The moon is there ahead of him, casting a bluish tint through the drapes. There is no mistaking the red-haired man, asleep on his side with his arm draped over Hannah, her heaviness cradled against him.

Philip knows that the tempest is merely paused and about to resume. Eventually it will pass, and the world go on as before. Jesse will die and Hannah will give birth to another child – and Philip will lose everything. For a few terrible moments he struggles to keep from hurling himself at the sleeping pair. Shaking with sobs, like someone laughing, he leans against the door frame, fighting the urge to destroy. He crouches on the floor, ready to spring, when he sees a feral-looking creature lunge towards him. But it's only Philip's reflection in the tall mirror, his hair shorn and tears streaming down his cheeks.

Turning away from it, he retraces his steps to Jesse's room, carefully shutting both connecting doors behind him.

This time the boy hears him. He attempts to raise himself on his elbow but doesn't have the strength. Jesse can barely make out someone bending over him, feels the touch of a kiss on his forehead as a pair of hands lifts his flaccid limbs from the bed. Looking intently at a face that is now only inches from his own, he recognises his old friend.

'Is it really you, Dolphin? They said you'd gone back to England.' A torrent of questions wants to rise to his lips.

'It was you who went away.'

'We were in New York. I didn't like it there.' Jesse's breathing is laboured, his voice strained. 'Have any more turtles washed up on the beach?'

'Just one. It's doing fine. But I want to hear about you. What has the outlaw Jesse James been up to?'

The boy says nothing. Without his glasses, Jesse's eyes have a strange lustre in the moonlight, his skin pasty.

'I'm not so well,' he says at last. 'But I don't like to say so because it makes Ma sad.' He tries to embrace Philip but can't lift his arms. 'Has the storm passed?'

'No. It's only a pause. The eye.'

Philip lifts the goggles from the nightstand and fits them over Jesse's face. 'I have something to show you,' he says.

'What?'

'Ssssh.' Philip places a hand over the boy's mouth. 'They mustn't hear us.'

'What are you going to show me?' Jesse whispers.

'The Belt of Venus. It sometimes appears during a lull in the storm, and I have a feeling we're going to see it tonight.'

'Should we tell the others?'

'No. Your ma needs her sleep.'

'Oh yes, for the baby.' Jesse smiles weakly. 'I'm going to have a little brother. The hospital took a picture of him and Pa says he's going to be just like me. Ma was so happy, she cried for days.'

Jesse is bone-thin, his body ravaged by the disease, and Philip's eyes fill with tears. 'What would you say if I told you that you and I are brothers?' he asks.

'I wish.'

'With God everything is possible.'

'Do you believe that?'

'Fr Leo does.'

Philip's heart pounds like a hammer in his chest.

'Why did you cut off your hair?' Jesse asks, touching his face.

'Because I missed you.'

'I won't leave again.'

'Promise?'

'The outlaw Jesse James always keeps his promise.' Finding it hard to hold himself up, he rests his head on Philip's shoulder.

'Are you ready?'

'I am,' Jesse says quietly.

Philip carries the boy down the back stairs and they leave through the garage, past the jasmine-scented pergola and cottage to the beach, moving swiftly over the rain-hardened sand. The ocean spread before them has an oily texture that makes it seem to percolate as the moon dips behind a frontier of clouds in one half of the sky, the other half still clear. The air feels unctuous and caressing, and for Jesse, who sees only shadows, the scene is transformed into something magical.

In the moon's afterglow a black cone shows faintly in the distance. Philip observes attentively the tower of air writhing snakelike between earth and sky, twisting like a top and advancing with astonishing speed. He presses towards it, fighting the wind that is trying to stop him and his blood on fire.

'Are we going the right way?' the boy asks.

'It's the only way. Are you afraid?'

'Not if you're with me.'

Philip clasps him in a protective embrace, never taking his eyes off the dark shape drawing nearer. 'Let's go then. Quick, or we'll miss it.'

* * *

Hannah was in a deep slumber when the trunk of the coconut palm crashed over the balcony. The tornado that had swept the beach roared past her house, ripping everything out by the roots and hurling the white picket fence and pergola into the swimming pool. Becoming distantly aware of the mounting noise, Hannah continued to sleep, the edges of her lips curled into a smile over a dream she had been having.

In it, all were reconciled, and she had already given birth to the little boy stirring inside her. The lasting impression of this dream, from which Hannah was so loath to wake, would become her refuge in the coming years. Filling her with hope for the future it had foretold, and the absolute certainty that, of all the mistakes she had made, giving Thaddeus the child he had always wanted would never be among them.

ABOUT THE AUTHOR

GINA GOLDHAMMER studied English and Creative Writing at Syracuse University, has a master's degree in literature from Harvard, and after graduation worked briefly on Wall Street and at *US News & World Report* magazine. For the next twenty years, she was the personal editor of the former US Secretary of State, Henry A. Kissinger, and worked with him closely on all his books, speeches and news columns, including his 1994 seminal work, *Diplomacy*. Gina's father was involved in geopolitics during the Cold War, attaining prominence in 1961 as the highest-ranking defector from a communist country – a story she is working into a novel. Gina is a Florida snowbird who spends time in London and Venice.

WWW.GINAGOLDHAMMER.COM